CARUSO

Also by Howard Greenfeld

BOOKS: FROM WRITER TO READER
PUCCINI

CARUSO

Howard Greenfeld

A DA CAPO PAPERBACK

For Daniel, with love

Library of Congress Cataloging in Publication Data

Greenfeld, Howard.
    Caruso.

    (A Da Capo paperback).
    Reprint. Originally published: New York: Putnam's, 1983.
    Bibliography: p.
    Includes index.
    1. Caruso, Enrico, 1873–1921. 2. Singers—Biography. I. Title.
ML420.C259G7 1984   782.1′092′4 [B]   83-26165
ISBN 0-306-80215-5 (pbk.)

This Da Capo Press paperback edition of *Caruso* is an unabridged
republication of the first edition published in New York in 1983.
It is reprinted by arrangement with Putnam Publishing Group, Inc.

Published by Da Capo Press, Inc.
A Subsidiary of Plenum Publishing Corporation
233 Spring Street, New York, N.Y. 10013

Acknowledgments

This book is the result of many years of research. I could not have written it without the help and cooperation of a number of persons, most of whom were strangers when I began and some of whom became good friends in the course of my work. I am grateful to all of them and apologize to those I have inadvertently forgotten to mention in this brief note of thanks.

Enrico Caruso, Jr., has been extraordinarily generous in sharing with me some of his memories of his father. His intelligence, charm, and humor have also provided me with invaluable insights into the unique Caruso magnetism, which the great tenor passed on to his son. James Camner and Lim M. Lai, too, deserve my special thanks; giving unselfishly of their time and knowledge, they made a difficult task a pleasant one.

I would also like to express my gratitude to the following individuals and institutions: Edwin A. Quist of the Peabody Institute, Baltimore; Robert Tuggle and Heloise Pressey of the Metropolitan Opera Archives; Monty Arnold of the Theatre Collection of the Library for the Performing Arts, New York; Mary Ann Jensen of the William Seymour Theatre Collection of the Princeton University Library; Reina Hernandez of the Library and Museum of the Teatro Colon, Buenos Aires; V. A. Glotov, of the Theatre Museum of the Kirov Theatre, Leningrad; and Luciano Pituello and Michele Forges Davanzati of the Centro Studi Carusiani, Milan; as well as the staffs of the Biblioteca Nazionale, Florence; Museo Teatrale alla Scala,

Milan; the Music Division of the Library for the Performing Arts, New York; and the Library of Congress, Washington.

Among the individuals who assisted me were: Ida Angelucci, Piero Angelucci, and Ruffo Titta in Rome; Professor Giovanni Nardone in Naples; Margot Leigh Milner in London; Patricia Levieux in Paris; and Claire M. Smith in New York.

I am most grateful to George Nyklicek for his translations from the German, Russian, and Polish.

The books used as sources for this biography are listed in the bibliography. Of them, memoirs by Caruso's associates Richard Barthélemy, Emil Ledner, Nicola Daspuro, and Adolfo Bracale have been especially useful. *Enrico Caruso*, written by Pierre V. R. Key in collaboration with Bruno Zirato and published in 1922, has been a valuable source, though the authors chose to ignore many "negative" aspects of their subject's personal and professional life and were unable to document accurately his career from beginning to end.

Other sources include Caruso's own scrapbooks, which are in the library of the Peabody Institute in Baltimore, and the Robinson Locke scrapbooks, which are part of the Theatre Collection of the Library for the Performing Arts in New York. I have also made use of contemporary newspaper accounts of the tenor's career. Never having personally witnessed a Caruso performance, I have depended upon the opinions of critics and of the tenor's colleagues for any evaluations of his appearances. His recordings, of course, have been an enormous source of both knowledge and pleasure. I have not included a discography, but many excellent recordings, issued in this country by RCA, are still available, as are a few recordings issued by Rubini in England. The finest comprehensive collection, of twelve records, issued by RCA in Italy in 1973, is unfortunately out of print.

Finally, and above all, I am deeply indebted to my wife, Paola, whose assistance in every way and at every stage in the preparation of this biography has been invaluable. I would not have undertaken it, nor could I have completed it, without her unfailing support.

Contents

"I believe that to speak of this [a successor to Caruso] is a sacrilege and a profanity to his memory; it means violating a tomb which is sacred to Italy and the entire world. The efforts of every artist today aim to gather and to conserve the artistic heritage received from the great singer, and everyone must strive to do this, not with vain self-advertisement, but with tenacious study for the triumph of the pure and the beautiful. He struggled for this, and we for the glory of his art must follow his example with dignity."

BENIAMINO GIGLI in a letter to the New York *Times* following the death of Caruso

"I know, of course, that distance lends enchantment to the view; and years, to the ears. All the same, I'm convinced that in singing we have gone off the gold standard. It's not to be wondered at. The attitude of the modern student towards the art of singing is completely different from that of the student in my days. We have fine singers to-day; Flagstad the magnificent, Rethberg, Melchior, Tauber, Pinza, John Charles Thomas, and Lawrence Tibbett — but where are the Melbas, the Terninas, the Schumann-Heinks? Where is there anyone to set beside Caruso, or Plançon, or Battistini, or Jean de Reszke? Damn it, man, there's no comparison. . . . He [Caruso] was unique and glorious,"

JOHN McCORMACK, quoted in *John McCormack* by L. A. G. Strong, London, 1941

"The artistic career of Caruso is as well known as that of any great general or statesman. He is a national figure. The fairy-godmother who at his cradle wished him a golden voice also dowered him with a golden heart. . . . He is a great artist, and he is something rarer, a genuine man."

JAMES GIBBONS HUNEKER, following the Caruso jubilee in 1919

I. Naples: The Beginning

If the modest apartment on the second floor of 7, via San Giovanello agli Otto Calli, a cheerless street in one of Naples' thickly populated working-class neighborhoods, might seem inappropriate as the birthplace of a man who would one day be called the King of Tenors, the city itself, with its important role in the history of opera, is an altogether suitable setting for such an auspicious occasion.

The birth on February 27, 1873, of the infant Enrico Caruso and his survival at the time of a cholera epidemic were as miraculous as the gift he would one day offer to the world, for he was the first of eighteen Caruso children to live beyond infancy. Even under normal conditions, the rate of infant mortality was high in the disease-ridden city, and the child's survival in the midst of an epidemic was largely credited to the aid of a strong woman of high birth who nursed him in place of his own mother, who was too weak to do so. Later he would claim that it was the milk of this woman that had made him different from those members of his family born after him — a brother, Giovanni, born in 1876, and a sister, Assunta, born in 1882.

Caruso's parents, who had come to Naples from the small village of Piedimonte d'Alife to the north, were far from wealthy; nor were they as poor as some legends would have it. Marcellino Caruso was known for his heavy drinking, but he was steadily employed as a mechanic at the Meuricoffre factory — a combination factory and importing concern — and his family lacked neither food nor housing. His wife, Anna Baldini, was a kind and gentle woman, whose health had steadily deteriorated with each of her many pregnancies, but who lavished her first healthy child with her quiet strength and profound affection.

By the time the child was eight years old, the family had moved twice, finally settling into a home in Sant'Anna alle Paludi, which belonged to the factory — by that time, Marcellino had been promoted to superintendent. Enrico, a good-natured boy, was intensely devoted to his mother. In the absence of his father, who preferred to spend many of his evenings drinking at local cafés, he undertook even before his eighth birthday many household responsibilities that were far more suited to a boy twice his age. Although he was a lively, noisy child, he showed an unfailing sense of responsibility, as well as an unusual preoccupation with personal neatness and cleanliness that would characterize him throughout his life.

His playground was the colorful Neapolitan waterfront, where the teeming city came to life. There he learned to swim and to dive, and there, like so many other boys who lived near the harbor, he dreamed of being a sailor. His parents had other plans for him. His mother, who had taught him to read, wanted him to have an education, while his father was intent on apprenticing him to a mechanical engineer. A compromise was reached; the boy was sent to work at the age of ten, but he was also allowed to attend classes at a school run by Father Giuseppe Bronzetti at 33, via Postica Maddalena.

His job at the De Luca mechanical laboratory interested him little, but he worked at it diligently. When only eleven years old he asked his employer for a raise, and when he was refused he moved on to the factory of Giuseppe Palmieri, where he was involved in the manufacturing of public drinking fountains.

His studies at the school proved more rewarding. The regular classes bored him, but the Bronzetti Institute specialized in training young boys to sing in local church choirs, and one of the school's teachers, Alessandro Fasanaro, discovered that the new student had an extraordinarily rich contralto voice. More than that, he loved to sing, and in time he became the principal soloist of the school's choir, a choir known throughout the city for its excellence and much sought-after by churches for use in their services and religious processions. Bronzetti's choir was also hired for weddings, informal concerts and social occasions, and though young Caruso earned no money for these, he could stuff his pockets and stomach with candies and cakes.

Though his father showed nothing but contempt for his young son's talent, his mother encouraged him and came to hear him sing whenever possible, filled with pride as the young child's voice was singled out for admiring attention. "It was as natural for me to sing as to play," Caruso told an interviewer many years later. "I came of a singing family. My mother had a beautiful soprano voice — very high and clear, like a flute; my father had a deep bass." There is no indication, however, that any of the tenor's ancestors ever developed professionally whatever native talents they might have had.

The young boy's extraordinary voice came to the attention of others, apart from his teachers at the school, and when he was only ten years old a pianist, Ernesto Schirardi, and Maestro Raffaele de Lutio undertook to help him in the proper use of his voice and teach him his first operatic arias.

Inevitably, for he showed little interest in them, his other studies at school were abandoned. He had shown an aptitude for drawing and for penmanship, which would prove to be useful later in life — the former served him as he developed his skills as a caricaturist, the latter enabled him to copy scores, which would be his method for learning them — but the school's routine courses bored him. He did, at the insistence of his mother, agree to be tutored in the pure Italian language — as opposed to the colorful Neapolitan dialect — by Amelia Tebaldi Niola, the sister of the doctor who was taking care of Anna Caruso. Though this tutoring was to be of invaluable help to him later in his life, he resisted it at the time. After a few months of study, he devised a ruse whereby he would leave his home at the scheduled hour, go to the railroad yards to play with friends, and return home, without ever having seen Signorina Niola. The deception did not last long, for one day the doctor asked Enrico's father why the boy had stopped coming to the teacher's home for his lessons. Marcellino was enraged. His disdain for his son's education vindicated, he demanded that the boy give up his "studies" and start work at the Meuricoffre factory — where his activities would be strictly supervised. He could sing all he wanted, or all that his mother wanted, but only after having done a full day's work which might prepare him for a serious future.

Enrico had no choice but to give in to his father's wishes, but neither could he give up singing. He was frequently called upon to offer a serenade to young ladies on behalf of their unmusical fiancés, and he offered his services at occasional social functions. Before long, he made his theatrical "debut" in a little opera written by his teachers at the Bronzetti school. It was called *I briganti nel giardino di Don Raffaele,* and young Caruso sang, with considerable success, the role of Don Tommaso, the janitor.

He also sang whenever possible at church services. Before one such appearance, on June 1, 1888, he hesitated before leaving home, torn between his obligation to sing at the Church of San Severino and a wish to stay at the side of his mother, who was seriously ill. At his mother's urging, however, he kept his word and set off for the church. In the midst of the service there was an interruption. Neighbors had come for Enrico, to tell him that Anna Caruso was dead.

It was a terrible moment for the fifteen-year-old boy. His attachment to his mother had been profound, and it was her faith in him that gave him the courage to continue his singing. It was also a decisive and liberating moment. He had worked at the factory largely because he felt a responsibility to his mother, never having considered seriously the possibility of helping support her through his music. Now he was free to do what he wanted, and to fail at music seemed to him more worthy than to succeed in his work at the factory.

He needed to be patient, however. His strong contralto voice was changing, and during the period of change he feared that his singing voice might never return. He knew that this was the fate of many promising boy sopranos. In addition, his responsibilities toward his younger brother and sister were, for a while, greater than ever; he had to be a mother to them in as many ways as he could. Happily, this latter responsibility was of short duration. Only five and a half months after the death of Anna Caruso, Marcellino remarried. His second wife, a widow named Maria Castaldi, took charge of the home with intelligence and kindness; she was especially drawn to young Enrico, and her devotion to him was reciprocated by the warm and affectionate adolescent, who, while always revering the memory of his own mother, came to think of Maria Castaldi as a worthy successor.

For two years Enrico continued to mark time at his job, though he showed little interest in it. His musical activities were necessarily curtailed as his voice changed and developed, but he managed to sing whenever the opportunity was presented to him — the boy with the sweet contralto was being transformed into a man, with a voice somewhere between tenor and baritone. Even his father had reluctantly come to realize that his son's future lay beyond the confines of the factory and that he would, no matter how foolishly, pursue with growing determination his career as a singer.

❇

The first concrete steps in this direction were taken in the summer of 1890, when Enrico was seventeen years old. Naples at the end of the nineteenth century was one of the liveliest and most picturesque cities in all Europe. Rising above and enclosing a magnificent bay, dominated by the imposing sight of the ever-threatening Mount Vesuvius, distinguished by its labyrinths of narrow, winding streets and animated by its vigorous, high-spirited people, it drew visitors from every part of the world. The rebirth in the early 1880s of the Neapolitan song — that unique, popular, hauntingly melodious expression of the population's joys and sorrows — added immeasurably to the city's charms; and these songs, derived from the soul of the people of Naples, gave rise to a new and immensely popular form of entertainment known as the *café-chantant* — the singing café. Neapolitan songs were sung throughout the city — in the theaters, restaurants, and on the streets — but nowhere more effectively than in the cafés that lined the city's colorful harbor, and that featured these heart-rending songs as part of their variety shows. It was these cafés that young Caruso visited after a day's work at the factory — to learn from the singers of Neapolitan melodies, and whenever possible to become part of the entertainment himself. His sweet voice began to attract attention, and one evening he was approached by a man who suggested that he could profit from professional training, that a voice as good as his could be greatly improved with the aid of a teacher. Caruso agreed, but protested that he had no money for lessons; his admirer said it didn't matter, that his brother was a singing teacher who would work with Caruso without pay. Caruso was delighted; he accepted the offer and gratefully began his studies. Before long, however, he instinctively realized that his teacher was doing him more harm than good. It was, he felt, best to give up the lessons and wait for something better.

In spite of this disappointment, Caruso was not discouraged. In the course of the summer, he had been singled out as a young man of promise, so much so that by the next summer the owner of a well-known seaside café, the Risorgimento at the rotunda of the via Caracciolo, suggested that Caruso join the entertainers at his café and agreed that he could keep whatever money the customers cared to give him. Each evening after work, Caruso would go to the Risorgimento, often receiving nothing for his troubles, but occasionally earning a few lire. Toward the end of the summer, though he had earned little, he was rewarded by the friendship of Eduardo Missiano, a young baritone whose interest in his talent radically changed Caruso's life. Missiano, the son of a well-to-do Neapolitan family and a few years older than Caruso, had never sung in public, but he was studying with one of the city's most distinguished teachers, Guglielmo Vergine. He offered to take Caruso to Vergine, in spite of the young man's protests that it would be impossible for him to pay for lessons even if the maestro agreed to accept him. One evening after work, the two young men climbed to the upper floors of the modest building on the Vico Sargento where the classes were held. The first meeting between the teacher and his prospective pupil was not a successful one. Caruso sang, and the stern and severe Vergine was unenthusiastic. He found that the young man's

voice sounded "like the wind whistling through a window," that his
future was close to hopeless. Missiano was not daunted. He took Caruso
home and taught him two arias—one from *Les Pêcheurs de Perles* and one
from *Cavalleria Rusticana*. A week later, they returned to Vergine, who
this time agreed reluctantly to take Caruso on as a pupil. There was one
condition: if the young man was unable to pay for his lessons, he would
have to sign a contract stipulating that Vergine would receive 25 percent
of his total earnings for five years of singing in return for four years of
lessons. It was an enormous price to exact from a young artist, for it meant
not a percentage of his earnings over a period of five years, but five solid
years—or almost two thousand performances—of actual singing. Caruso,
grateful for any opportunity to study, paid little attention to these unfair
terms. He could not yet take his career that seriously. However, this
bizarre contract was annulled by an Italian court several years later at great
expense to the tenor.

Caruso had had no formal musical education, and he did not receive one
from Vergine, yet he had an innate musical sense, had been gifted with
perfect pitch, and was able to absorb quickly and with intelligence the
lessons of his unsmiling, demanding teacher. Vergine was the first to train
him in the art of singing and show him how to use his voice, turning him
into a true tenor—but he never encouraged him or hinted that he had a
voice of more than mediocre quality. On the contrary, he seemed pointed-
ly to offer more encouragement and pay more attention to other members
of his class than he did to his new pupil. In spite of this, Caruso refused to
be discouraged and continued to attend the classes, learning what he could
from observing the maestro's criticisms of other singers. In retrospect, and
despite his later disagreements with Vergine, Caruso always gave him a
share of the credit for his success. "It was Vergine," he would say, "who
emphasized the necessity of singing as nature intended" by refusing to
allow him to add volume to his voice prematurely.

Forced to continue his work as a mechanic in order to help his family,
Caruso was unable to devote full time to his musical training during those
years with Vergine. He did, however, gain further practical experience by
singing, whenever possible, at the popular waterfront cafés. He was a slim,
good-looking young man with an engaging smile, and his voice, though
still small, had an uncommonly appealing warmth and sweetness which
aroused considerable admiration. Adolfo Narciso, a well-known Neapolitan comedian, recalled listening to an outdoor concert at the Café dei Man-
nesi and being moved by the unknown tenor's interpretation of a popular
song, "*Se*," by Luigi Denza. Equally impressed by Caruso, according to
Narciso, was the leader of the small orchestra, who informed the young

singer that he had a "golden treasure" in his throat. Even at this very early stage of his career, it seems, he was showing signs of the unique talent that would set him apart from his colleagues later in his career.

In addition to his participation in the *café-chantant*, Caruso joined friends in singing at public baths, baptisms, weddings, and birthday celebrations, and continued to take part in church festivities. One such occasion took him to the village of Majori, on the Amalfi coast fifteen miles from Naples. Having finished his performance at the church, he prepared for his return to Naples, but before he could leave he was informed that his night's work had not yet ended: he had been commanded to sing at the home of the mayor, Baron Zezza. Though they had assured him that he would have to sing no more than a few songs, the mayor and his friends, delighted with the young man's voice, insisted that he continue to entertain them until six in the morning. Though no extra pay was forthcoming, the mayor did give the weary tenor an old hunting jacket, to protect his throat from the cold morning air during his trip home. Caruso promised to send the jacket back the next day, but the mayor insisted that he accept it as a gift.

The episode was not forgotten. More than twenty years later, Caruso, then a major star and engaged at London's Covent Garden, received a letter from the same Baron Zezza. The baron wondered if the famous Caruso was the same man who had once entertained his guests in Majori, and if so why he had not yet returned the hunting jacket or, at least, the price of it. The tenor answered that he was indeed the same man, but that he no longer had the jacket, which, he reminded him, had been a gift and not a loan. However, since the baron had brought up the matter, Caruso suggested that he might finally pay him for that long night's work — a fee appropriate to his current position in the world of opera plus twenty years' interest. Zezza answered at once. Of course, he wrote, he was no longer interested in the coat; he merely wanted to make certain that the young man who had sung at his home many years before was the now-famous Enrico Caruso. In place of the coat he was more than satisfied to settle for the autograph letter from the famous man. Caruso was amused; by return mail he sent the baron an autographed photo as well as a silver hunting flask.

❊

In February 1894, Caruso celebrated his twenty-first birthday. His years of study had served him well; even Vergine agreed that he was ready to make his operatic debut in one of the lesser Neapolitan theaters or in a nearby provincial opera house. A twenty-first birthday, however, meant more than a coming of age for a young Italian male; it meant that the time had come for his three years of military service.

Caruso had hoped that he might be rejected because of his far from sturdy physique, but shortly after his birthday he was called up and ordered to join the Thirteenth Artillery at Rieti. During the trip to the army camp some fifty miles from Rome, he was disconsolate. He knew that at this crucial stage three years without singing could mean the end of his career. All of his study — his years of dedication — seemed to have been wasted. There was no way then that he could foresee his meeting with an army major who would turn the potentially disastrous three years into nothing more than a forty-five-day interruption of a promising career.

The story of the young tenor's military service is one that could only have as its background the Italian army. Caruso the soldier was inept; he performed his duties perfunctorily, and in his free time he sang. He sang in an effort to improve his voice — in spite of his despair at the prospect of three years in the army, he did his best to ensure that all was not lost. He sang, too, for the joy of it, and his songs gave pleasure to his fellow soldiers, though his vocalizing and impromptu recitals soon came to the attention of the commanding officer, Major Nagliati. Nagliati, known as a gruff disciplinarian, protested that the young man's sounds were disturbing his own work as well as the camp's routine. He angrily summoned Caruso to his office, where he questioned him sharply, revealing himself to be not only an exemplary soldier but also a knowledgeable music-lover. When the major learned that the young tenor had studied long and hard to perfect his voice, he realized that he might be of more use to his country as a singer than as a soldier. The two men talked of music, and to confirm his own feelings the major introduced Caruso to one of Rieti's noblemen, the Baron Costa, who was both an accomplished student of music and a pianist. The baron agreed that the young man was gifted — in his opinion, he was extraordinarily so. He took Caruso in hand, offered his own home as a practice studio, and accompanied Caruso on the piano, coaching him and correcting his mistakes. In only five days he managed to teach him the demanding role of Turiddu in Mascagni's *Cavalleria Rusticana* — the first complete role Caruso had learned.

Deeply impressed by the young soldier's talent, the baron and the major quickly agreed that it would be a waste to keep him in the service — and they reached a solution. After less than two months of military service, Enrico Caruso was dismissed from the army. He was, it was claimed, needed at home to support his family, and his younger brother Giovanni was called up to replace him, a not too uncommon practice at the time.

II. From Naples to Palermo: The First Steps

Caruso, again a civilian, arrived in Naples on Easter Sunday, 1894. Thanks to the almost miraculous intervention of the major and the baron, his experience in the army had encouraged rather than discouraged him. He was more determined than ever to make a place for himself in the world of the opera — no matter how great the sacrifice. As a first step, he gave up his job at the factory; the money he made there could not compensate for the time lost in the pursuit of his career, though he realized that by giving up his steady employment he would have to content himself with the meager earnings from his occasional appearances at church festivities and at the city's waterfront cafés.

He resumed his studies with Vergine with increased energy, able to devote far more time to them than he had in the past. His teacher's attitude had changed. He openly displayed enthusiasm for Caruso's abilities and actively took an interest in trying to further his professional career — he did, of course, have a considerable financial stake in the latter. He encouraged Caruso to persevere in his studies and to accept any opportunities that might be offered him — among these a chance to appear in an amateur production of *Cavalleria Rusticana*, which he was able to accept because of the coaching of Baron Costa — and he arranged auditions for the young tenor whenever possible.

The most promising of these took place in the early fall of 1894. Among

Vergine's contacts was Nicola Daspuro, who had recently been asked by the Milanese music publishing firm of Sonzogno (which he represented in the South) to organize an operatic season at the newly remodeled Teatro Mercadante in Naples. The firm's director, Edoardo Sonzogno, who had organized similar seasons in other Italian theaters, was too busy at the time with the construction of his own Teatro Lirico in Milan to do so. Daspuro was a man of many talents: a distinguished journalist, he was also a knowledgeable musician and had written the librettos for two verismo, or naturalistic, operas, Mascagni's *L'Amico Fritz* and Giordano's *Mala Vita*. In his new role as impresario he had managed, in a short time, to bring together some of Italy's finest singers for the Mercadante, and by the time Vergine approached him with the request that he hear this extraordinary pupil, the season's roster of singers was already full. The teacher persisted, however, assuring Daspuro that Caruso had "a voice of exceptional beauty, with warm and velvety tones," and finally Daspuro agreed to the audition.

The following morning Caruso and Vergine came to the theater. The young tenor was nervous—he admitted that he had never before sung professionally—but Daspuro was sufficiently impressed by his audition to promise to try to give him a part in a matinee performance of the forthcoming Carnevale season. "I found the quality of his voice, round and soothing, very beautiful, and I also thought he showed an uncommon artistic sensitivity," he wrote later.

When the company's conductor, Giovanni Zuccani, arrived in Naples, Vergine and Caruso were summoned to the Mercadante for another audition. Zuccani, too, was enthusiastic, and it was agreed that Caruso should study the role of Wilhelm Meister in Ambroise Thomas's *Mignon*, which would serve as his debut.

That debut never took place. "After having studied his role, poor Caruso, when called, together with the other singers, to the piano rehearsal, seemed to us a changed man," Daspuro remembered—

> His great sensitivity and the nervous excitement of finding himself in the company of so many experienced singers had almost completely paralyzed both his mental faculties and his throat. He did everything wrong: he forgot his lines, he missed his cues, he sang out of tune, and he stared at Zuccani as if stupefied. It was, in short, a real disaster. Vergine was pale as a sheet, and his eyes were filled with tears. The kindly Maestro Zuccani, instead, was patient and for a long time did his best to calm the tenor. But it was useless. Caruso was in a complete state of amnesia, and finally Zuccani, no longer able to continue, arose from the piano, turned to Vergine, and said, "Tell him yourself, Mae-

stro, that it is impossible to present him on the stage in such a state." Vergine lowered his head and, without comment, he and his pupil left. . . .

It was an inauspicious beginning, but it represented merely a temporary setback. Within a few months, another opportunity presented itself to Caruso, one of far less importance but which nonetheless enabled him to make his first professional appearance as an opera singer. The occasion of the debut was the première of Domenico Morelli's *L'Amico Francesco*. Morelli, a wealthy young composer, had hired a theater and was putting together a company so that his new opera might have a hearing. At the suggestion of a musician who had performed with Caruso at a number of church festivities, he offered the young tenor the role of the protagonist. The pay was poor, chances for the new work's success minimal, but Vergine and Caruso agreed that no opportunity to sing in public should be passed up. They proved to be right. The date of March 15, 1895, will remain an important one in the history of opera not for the first performance of *L'Amico Francesco*, but because it marked the professional debut of Enrico Caruso. The opera itself was a dismal failure (only two of four scheduled performances were given), but Caruso's appearances in this now-forgotten work enabled him to be heard by two men who would be of great help to him at this early stage of his career. One was Francesco Zucchi, an elderly Sicilian theatrical agent, whose office was a table at a local café from which he supplied singers to provincial opera houses. The other was Carlo Ferrara, the impresario of the Teatro Cimarosa in the nearby town of Caserta. Zucchi, one of the first to recognize the young tenor's potential, took him under his wing and promised to find engagements for him, while Ferrara hired him at once for his next season at the Cimarosa.

That season began less than two weeks after Caruso's last performance in *L'Amico Francesco*. His appearances in Caserta brought him as little acclaim as had his performances in Morelli's opera, but they did offer him the chance to sing for the first time in two works of the standard repertory — *Faust*, in which he made his debut on March 28, and *Cavalleria Rusticana* — and in a new work of little distinction, *Camoens* by Musone. Though Caruso was criticized for both his singing and his acting (which he later admitted had been awful), the short Caserta season added to the tenor's experience and proved that he could master new roles with surprising speed.

The four-week season ended badly — business at the box office had been as poor as the company's reviews — and Caruso went home penniless. (He returned to Caserta only one more time, less than a year later, with even more disastrous results—a special performance of *Faust* was so badly received that the audience was dismissed after the second act.)

His first season at Caserta, however, did lead to another engagement, this time in Naples itself. Shortly after Caruso's return to Naples, the leading tenor at the Teatro Bellini took sick and a substitute was urgently needed. Enrico Pignataro, a baritone who had sung with Caruso at Caserta, suggested that he would be the ideal replacement, and the theater's impresario immediately went out in search of Caruso. He found him at a small restaurant, playing cards, and asked him to sing *Faust* a few days later. The Bellini, along with the somewhat more distinguished San Carlo and Mercadante, was one of the city's important opera houses and Caruso accepted the assignment with enthusiasm. His first performance there, in early June, was a successful one. He was by no means a sensation—he did not become a star overnight—but for the first time in his very short career he was singled out for praise by the press, the critic for *Il Mattino* commenting that "Caruso has a beautiful voice, and if he is willing to develop it with perseverance, it will bring him great profit."

He continued to sing at the Bellini for the rest of the season, appearing again in *Faust* and singing, for the first time, in *Rigoletto* and *La Traviata*. His reviews were not always good—Ettore Jovinelli in the *Cosmorama di Napoli* of August 27 complained of his lack of artistic intelligence and his awkwardness on the stage, noting that though he didn't ruin the performance of *La Traviata*, he didn't contribute to its success—but his fresh, sweet voice pleased the public and in the course of the season he was offered a contract to sing at the Bellini again the following fall. This promise of a fall engagement was the tenor's first assurance that he could earn a steady, if modest, income from his singing. Equally encouraging was still another offer, to perform for the first time outside of Italy.

✳

Word of Caruso's achievements at the Bellini had reached Adolfo Bracale, a young Italian musician working in Egypt. Bracale, whose path would cross with that of Caruso throughout the tenor's career, had been engaged as a cellist with the orchestra of the Khedival Theatre—the country's leading opera house—but his ambition was to become the impresario of his own company of Italian singers whom he would present to audiences in Egypt's important cities. Bracale had learned of Caruso through a violinist friend in Naples, and on the basis of his friend's enthusiastic reports was led to believe that the promising tenor might well become the star of his new company. It was, of course, a gamble, but one that the young man was willing to take. He was so certain of success that he obtained the necessary backing for his new venture on the promise that his company would include this extraordinarily talented Neapolitan, whom he would put under contract on his forthcoming trip to Italy.

Bracale was not disappointed when, after arriving in Naples, he met and listened to Caruso for the first time. Though he noted, as had others, that the tenor's range was somewhat short, he was profoundly impressed with his phrasing, his tone color, and the timbre of his voice. In a short time, contractual arrangements were made: Caruso was to sing in Egypt for a period of one month and would be paid six hundred lire for the engagement, more than he had ever earned before. Bracale was enthusiastic: he had found the star he wanted and within a few days he brought together the rest of his company. His judgment was sound, for among his singers he engaged Elena Bianchini-Cappelli, who had sung with Caruso in Caserta, and Emma Carelli, an eighteen-year-old Neapolitan soprano—both of whom would later establish international reputations.

The company of young singers sailed for Egypt at the end of August, and it was a voyage Caruso never forgot. For many years, he took special pleasure in recounting one episode that took place during the crossing. It involved a group of young Englishmen who had so greatly appreciated a concert he had given for the ship's passengers that they had accosted him in the bar one night and demanded good-naturedly that he sing for them again. He refused, saying he was too tired, but after they threatened him with a swim in the Suez Canal if he continued to refuse, he agreed. After this impromptu recital, the hat was passed and Caruso presented with one hundred pounds—the largest compensation he had yet received for his talents. More than twenty-five years later, one of these "Englishmen" (actually a Scotsman) confirmed the episode to a reporter from the New York *Times*. "To this day I can picture the Caruso laugh as he measured the situation to which he literally had been dragged, and the scene of enthusiasm when he had finished his first song." He added: "We recognized at once that he was a singer of no mean order and the feeling was that he would immediately secure in Cairo the appreciation that lays the foundation of a great career. . . . We had many gratuitous performances before we reached Port Said, and at such close quarters it was easy to see that he was a man of grit and personality. . . . Even then one could imagine him swaying large audiences at will and thrilling them through and through with some of his master strokes. . . ."

Caruso was, as predicted, a great success in Egypt. Indeed, the entire company was enthusiastically acclaimed by the large Italian colony which populated both Alexandria and Cairo. The tenor made his debut in Alexandria in *La Traviata* and immediately won favor with the public, at the same time helping fulfill Bracale's dream of becoming an established impresario. By the time the company moved on to Cairo for a series of performances at the Eskebian Gardens, the young Neapolitan's reputation seemed secure—though it proved to be not quite secure enough to withstand a near disaster that occurred in the middle of the season, a proof that the young man could not yet accurately measure his own strength, or weakness. The occasion was a performance of *Cavalleria Rusticana*. Caruso, basking in the glory of his triumphs, had agreed, against the advice of Bracale, to attend a lavish luncheon in his honor before the performance. There were women, and there was wine, both irresistible to the spirited young man, and it took a great effort on the part of the impresario to drag his leading tenor away, hoping that a few hours' rest before the performance might sober him up. A few hours, however, were not enough. At the very beginning of the opera, while singing the introductory "Siciliana," the tenor's voice cracked, causing the audience to break out in a chorus of boos and hisses. Caruso's performance did not improve, and when his voice cracked again during another important aria, pandemonium broke out. As they left the theater, many members of the audience angrily ripped off posters announcing the tenor's next performance, his first in *La Gioconda*. In spite of Bracale's fears—Caruso's failure could mean the failure of his own venture—the tenor completely vindicated himself at his next appearance in Ponchielli's opera. His singing so moved the audience that the same persons who had booed him a few nights before cheered him insistently, called for encores, and, at the conclusion, rushed up to the stage and carried him to his hotel on their shoulders. He was a hero once again.

The successful Egyptian season had afforded Caruso the opportunity to sing two new roles. One was that of Enzo in *La Gioconda* in the performance which had restored his honor; and the other was that of Des Grieux in Puccini's newest opera, *Manon Lescaut*, in a performance that might have been disastrous had it not been for the fact that the opera was being sung for the first time in Egypt, before an audience that was completely unfamiliar with its score.

The Egyptian première had been hastily arranged and the principals, Caruso and Bianchini-Cappelli, were given only five days to learn their roles. The result of their hurried study of the opera was, all too often, quite different from what the composer had in mind. All went surprisingly well, with few non-Puccini aberrations, until the last act when the grief-stricken tenor leaves the heroine, near death on the plains of Louisiana, to go in search of help.

Bianchini-Cappelli later recounted:

> Enrico had gone off the stage. I was suddenly startled to hear him
> call to me from the wings, "Don't move; I am going to put the

> score against your back—otherwise I cannot go on." Then he returned to where I was lying, the score of the opera concealed from the audience's view. Never have I felt such embarrassment before the public. I was supposed to be dying and had gestures to make and movements of my body. But with that score propped against my shoulders, and realizing what it meant to Enrico, I was helpless to do more than hold as still as possible, serving as a human music rack for my comrade. And what did the rascal do? He was bursting to laugh! I could feel that he was, and the thought made me furious; for I had to die lying quite still, and with no chance to make any effect. When the curtain fell I rose and chased Enrico, and threw the score at him, which he had dropped in his flight. Later we made up. Of course, there came a good laugh—not only over that situation but over the mistakes we had made with the words and the new music we had sung instead of what Puccini had written—which had quite gone from our heads.

Egyptian audiences never knew that they had heard an unauthorized version of Puccini's opera, and the work's première was a great success, which served to confirm Caruso's popularity. When he embarked on his voyage home, he did so certain of his complete triumph before a foreign public. He had thoroughly enjoyed his first taste of international acclaim.

*

The significance of Caruso's success in Egypt should not be overestimated. The public which cheered him in Cairo and Alexandria was relatively unsophisticated, much like the public that filled any provincial Italian opera house—it was, in fact, made up of a large number of Italian immigrants. Though the young tenor had demonstrated his ability to bring an audience to its feet, he was still a far from polished artist. At the very beginning of his career, and without the advantage of formal musical education, he could only develop his considerable gifts through actual experience on the stage.

For this reason, it was especially heartening for Caruso to learn upon his return to Naples that he had been offered a contract to sing at the Teatro Mercadante in late November—following the few appearances at the Bellini which had already been scheduled. The Mercadante was an important opera house; though its company was not as distinguished as it had been when under the direction of Daspuro the previous year, it drew intelligent, knowledgeable audiences and received careful attention from the press, not only in Naples but throughout Italy. The decision to hire the young tenor had evidently been made at the last moment, for there was no advance announcement of his engagement and he joined the company without even a minimum of pre-season publicity. In spite of this, his season — which lasted almost three months — was an extraordinarily active one during which he appeared in fifty performances: fifteen each of *La Traviata* and Bellini's *Romeo e Giulietta*, and ten each of *Rigoletto* and *Faust*. At times, his youthful energy was put to a severe test as he was called upon to sing twice a day, both matinee and evening, and over a period of eight days (between Christmas and New Year's Day) he sang nine times; but he never failed to acquit himself with honor throughout the season. Critics took note of his unusual gifts. Following his first performance in *La Traviata* on November 29 (he sang with an American soprano, Kate Bensberg, who had not long before made her debut in Germany), the reviewer for *La Gazzetta dei Teatri* made the astonishingly accurate prediction that "the most brilliant and glorious success awaits the young tenor." After his performance in the rather small role of Tebaldo in Bellini's opera, the critic for *Il Mattino* wrote: "Caruso is constantly improving, and we can foresee a wonderful future for him, especially at this time when so very few tenors are available," but also warned that the young man would have to continue to work with dedication in order to gain fuller control over his voice.

The critics were not alone in recognizing Caruso's natural gifts. The great French soprano Emma Calvé, many years later, wrote in her autobiography of having been invited by a friend to hear him sing at the Mercadante that season. "I was overcome with astonishment," she recalled. " 'What a marvellous — what an extraordinary voice!' I exclaimed. 'I have rarely heard anything so beautiful. It is a miracle!' At the end of the opera, I turned to my friend. 'Tell me again,' I asked, 'the name of this remarkable artist!' CARUSO!''

The tenor's progress had been remarkable — he had made his first appearance on any stage less than a year before — and his popularity was such that at the end of January 1896 a special performance of *Faust* was given in his honor at the Mercadante. Such *serate d'onore* were not uncommon in Italian theaters at the time, but they did signify the recognition of a singer's achievements in the course of a season. An elegant crowd filled the theater, and Caruso was presented with gifts and flowers. The reporter from *La Gazzetta dei Teatri* wrote that Caruso "was given ample opportunity to display his magnificent vocal riches and all the grace and charm of his sweet voice, the equal of which I have rarely heard."

Caruso sang his last performance of the season on the night of February 18, 1896. His achievements during that season had been more than merely encouraging, for they had guaranteed him contracts for future engagements and subsequently the chance to develop his art more fully.

One of these engagements, shortly after the close of the Mercadante season, almost marked the end of his promising career. The setting of the near disaster was Trapani, where Caruso was to appear for the first time in *Lucia di Lammermoor*, as part of a tour of Sicily arranged by Zucchi. The story of his misadventures in the Sicilian seaport, while a guest in the home of his friend, the baritone Pignataro, has become part of the Caruso legend, and the tenor told his own version of it many years later to Grenville Vernon of the New York *Tribune*.

All had gone smoothly until the day of the public dress rehearsal, a special performance attended by an invited audience including members of the municipal board, who had a right, if dissatisfied with a performer, to "protest" him or her and end the engagement. Caruso, by his own account, was unafraid of this test. "I knew my voice and I knew what I could do," he said. The only problem was that he did not know what to do with the wine of Trapani. The rest of the story follows in his own words, as told to Vernon.

I was never a drinker, though, like every Neapolitan, I always had my glass at dinner. The wine of Naples, is, however, light, and though I did not know it the wine of Trapani heavy. With my host, the baritone, I sat down to dinner, and on the table were two bottles of wine, one red and one white. I chose the white, and of it I drank two large tumblers, as I would of the wine of my native city. When I attempted to rise, I found that I could hardly stand. My host realized the situation and, thinking that the air would do me good, he led me onto the quay. But the salt air only made me worse and I stumbled from one side to the other in truly glorious fashion. Suddenly a man passed us — it was our impresario!

My host now lost his head completely. My impresario had seen me drunk and he would blame my host for it. I was dragged into a café and then my host insisted on pouring down my throat a stiff glass of hot grog. He had gone crazy with fear and had taken this method of sobering me up. The result was, of course, that I became dead to the world and had to be carried home and put to bed. This was at two o'clock — the dress rehearsal was at eight. Meanwhile I slumbered on. Eight o'clock arrived and the public with it, but I arrived not. Eight-fifteen, eight-thirty — still no Caruso. Despair, tears, the impresario making explanations, the baritone questioned, confessing. Five minutes later I was

pulled out of bed, dressed and hurried to the theater—but, alas
the wine was still with me.

The performance nearly an hour late, the audience angry, I
was hustled onto the stage. I knew my music, but I could not
pronounce my words. Suddenly I came to the words "*Sorti della
Scozia,*" and what I sang was "*Volpe della Scozia*"; instead of
singing "Future of Scotland," I sang "Fox of Scotland." Then pandemonium broke. "He's drunk, this fox of Scotland!" roared the
audience. I stumbled off the stage. The impresario tried to
explain that "Signor Caruso is suffering from a sea voyage."
(Yells of derision) I went home and to bed, and the dress rehearsal continued without a tenor. The newspapers the next morning
referred to my indisposition and remarked sarcastically that "it is
to be hoped that Signor Caruso will take no more sea voyages."

At the first performance I was sober, but the audience had not
forgotten. On my entrance I was greeted with yells of "Volpe
della Scozia!" Then there were counter yells of encouragement. I
battled through the tumult, but couldn't finish the last act. My
nerve was gone.

I was awakened early the next day by a pounding on my door.
I opened it. It was the dramatic tenor of the company. He was
very excited and explained that he had been told that he would
have to sing Edgardo that night. Why was I not singing it? If he
sang it he would make a terrible fiasco. He was desperate and
begged me on his knees to sing. I explained that I was only too
willing to sing and that I didn't understand. But later in the day I
did. The impresario's secretary met me in the street and handed
me a letter. It was from the Municipal Council. I was "protested."

I was penniless and my career was ended. I was truly in despair. But how should I get back to Naples? I hadn't enough money to take the train or the regular steamer, and so I searched the
docks. At length I found a sailing vessel which was leaving and
which agreed to take me for fifty lire. But as it was against the
law to take passengers on a sailing vessel, the boat would have to
leave at night. This was what saved me.

At nine o'clock that night I was sitting down to dinner in the
cabin, when I heard someone shouting my name on the quay
above. I ran up on deck and met the impresario's secretary, and
from him I heard some extraordinary news. The new tenor had,
as he feared, made a disastrous appearance and the audience was
in revolt and was yelling madly for the "Fox of Scotland." I was

tumbled into a cab, to the theater and onto the stage. By the time I arrived I had grown immensely popular. I was a triumph.

But my troubles were not yet ended. The impresario had already sent for another tenor, one Udo, to whom he paid in advance seven hundred and fifty lire. Udo arrived, appeared two nights later and was met by an audience yelling for the "Fox of Scotland." Again I was summoned and again I was a triumph. To this day Trapani remembers me as the "Fox of Scotland." I don't really know whether it was my voice or my drunkenness which appealed to them. Sicilian audiences have a sense of humor.

✻

Caruso returned to Sicily one year later, not to sing at one of the island's provincial theaters but at the important Teatro Massimo in Palermo. Before then, he continued to gain experience in Naples, both at the Bellini and the Mercadante, winning praise for his performances in operas that were already part of his repertory and adding to that repertory by singing new roles—in Meyerbeer's *Les Huguenots* and in two works which have since been forgotten, Gianni Bucceri's *Mariedda* (on June 24, 1896) and *Un Dramma di Vendemmia,* by the conductor Vincenzo Fornari, which he sang in early 1897. His steady progress was duly noted whenever he sang, but even more important to his future were his appearances in nearby Salerno, where he found a wise and experienced teacher who could help him expand his vocal capacities, and where he again met—this time with positive results—Nicola Daspuro.

Caruso's first appearances in Salerno, arranged by Zucchi at the request of the mayor, took place in early June, when he sang two performances of *Rigoletto* to mark Constitution Day. According to *La Gazzetta Musicale di Milano,* he "earned the whole-hearted admiration of the public with his firm and beautiful voice." More than that, he established extraordinary personal rapport with that public. They cheered his performances and they delighted in his behavior away from the theater. Witty, gay, and lighthearted, he was offered invitations which he willingly accepted from the town's leading citizens, sharing their meals and ingratiating himself by generously singing arias and songs whenever requested. Salerno's opera-goers wanted him back as soon as possible—he had become a local hero—and so did the conductor Vincenzo Lombardi. Lombardi was not merely a conductor—he was also a distinguished vocal coach, who had worked with Calvé as well as the reigning favorite of the Neapolitans, the tenor Fernando De Lucia—and he summoned Caruso to his studio and asked him to sing the role of Arturo in Bellini's *I Puritani* in a series of performances to be given in August and September of 1896. Caruso reluctantly declined, explaining to Lombardi that he could not face the tessitura, or range, of Bellini's opera. The maestro, though impressed with the young tenor's voice, was aware of his difficulties in the upper register. Nonetheless, he felt that he could help him with his problems and enable him to sing the extremely demanding role in Bellini's opera. With the promise of Lombardi's help, Caruso agreed to return to Salerno, to sing both *I Puritani* and *Cavalleria Rusticana*.

Lombardi's training was invaluable. "He got me to put more power behind my tones," the tenor explained to his early biographer, Pierre Key, "and although I did not, until much later, get the top notes as I should, I was finally able, through his instruction, to give all those in the *Puritani* music which the tenor must sing." As a result, Caruso's performances in the Bellini opera were even more successful than his appearances in the less spectacular *Cavalleria Rusticana*. He was praised by De Lucia himself, who came from his home at Cava dei Tirreni to hear the young singer, already mentioned as his potential successor. Caruso was also flattered by an offer from Milan to sing in the world première of Alberto Franchetti's *Il Signor di Pourceaugnac* at Italy's most distinguished opera house, La Scala, an offer which he had to decline because of his commitments in Salerno. More important to his career at this point — it is doubtful that he was ready for La Scala — was the special interest shown him by one of the most influential citizens of Salerno, Giuseppe Grassi. Don Peppe, as he was known, was a journalist and owner of *La Frusta* (The Whip), a powerful weekly newspaper which kept local politicians on their toes by threatening to expose their wrongdoings. He was also official impresario of Salerno's Teatro Comunale and his enthusiasm for Caruso, as well as his awareness of the tenor's popularity at the box office, was such that he decided with the help of Lombardi and Vergine (who was keeping a close eye on his pupil-investment) to organize a special Caruso season for the following October and November.

Caruso eagerly accepted Don Peppe's offer; it was a chance to gain further experience before friendly audiences and it would permit him more time to study with Lombardi, who was making steady, if slow, progress in extending the tenor's range. The season's program was a challenging one. In addition to appearing again in *La Traviata*, Caruso was scheduled to sing three new roles: in Donizetti's *La Favorita*, Bizet's *Carmen*, and in a new one-act opera, *A San Francisco*, by the popular Neapolitan team of Salvatore di Giacomo and Carlo Sebastiani. Caruso was once again a huge success; he caused Don Peppe to wince each time he attempted and failed to reach — despite Lombardi's training — the high note at the end of the

"Flower Song" in Bizet's opera, but for the public he could do no wrong.

The highlight of the season, however, was his unscheduled debut as Canio—a role he had recently studied—in Leoncavallo's *Pagliacci*, which took place in November 1896, the same night he sang the first performance of *A San Francisco*. The short Neapolitan opera had been a triumph for all concerned, and Grassi and Lombardi were overjoyed—but they worried about the performance of *Pagliacci* which was to follow, since they doubted that Pagani, the tenor who was to sing, could satisfy the public—he had complained to them that he was not in good voice. Following *A San Francisco*, the two men went to Caruso's dressing room and asked him not to leave the theater, but to stand by in case he was needed to substitute for Pagani. Caruso was angry; he had already fulfilled his obligation and done an evening's work, and he was hungry. . . . The two men were sympathetic—they had a huge dinner brought to his dressing room—but they prevailed upon him to remain in case of trouble. Trouble came, and Pagani was barely able to finish the first act of *Pagliacci* in the face of the catcalls of the irate public. After the first act, Caruso put on the clown's costume, painted his face, and went onstage to sing the last act. His first performance in a role he would make his own earned him the most thunderous ovation of the season.

Caruso left Salerno in triumph, promising to return, after fulfilling a few engagements in Naples, for a longer season beginning in March 1897. His place in the hearts of the citizens of Salerno was secure, and he had also won the heart of Giuseppina Grassi, the impresario's daughter, whom he had rather impetuously promised to marry. Salerno had brought him every honor—both professional and personal—to which he had aspired.

His progress as a singer and as a musician had been such that Vergine felt that he could again approach Nicola Daspuro to enlist his aid in furthering the tenor's career. Not without difficulty, he convinced him to travel to Salerno to give the young man another chance. Caruso's season there was to include performances in *La Traviata*, *Manon Lescaut*, a now-forgotten work by Daniele Napolitano, *Il Profeta velato di Korasan*, and *La Gioconda*. It was in the last opera that Sonzogno's representative again heard Caruso sing. "When I arrived in Salerno, I was met at the station by Vergine and Don Peppe Grassi," Daspuro remembered. "Vergine asked me if I could possibly try not to be seen by Caruso until after the performance as he feared that my presence might make Caruso nervous. Accordingly, I went to lunch with Don Peppe, and when the time came I went to the theater and sat in a box from which I could not be seen by Caruso.

"He sang the entire opera with great ease, and his voice was full, warm, and vibrant with passion. . . . I almost couldn't believe my eyes and ears. When the performance came to an end, I went backstage. I congratulated Caruso and Vergine and Maestro Lombardi. I promised to do what I could to have him engaged for a series of performances at the Teatro Lirico of Milan. He was very happy. . . ."

Daspuro kept his promise. After a meeting with Sonzogno in Rome, he arranged for Caruso's debut in Milan the following fall. Furthermore, at his suggestion, Carlo di Giorgio, impresario of Palermo's Teatro Massimo, came to hear the tenor sing in Salerno and signed him for an engagement at the Massimo immediately following his last performance at the Comunale. On the night of April 30, 1897, Caruso sang his farewell performance as Enzo in *La Gioconda*. Shortly afterward, he left Salerno, no longer engaged to Signorina Grassi (whose father had already made plans for their wedding), but in the company of a new love, one of the twelve ballerinas who had performed the "Dance of the Hours" in Ponchielli's opera.

✳

When Caruso arrived in Palermo in May 1897, he was in high spirits. With little more than two years of professional experience behind him, he was about to make his debut at one of Europe's most important theaters — at the time, the stage of the Massimo was the second largest in Europe, surpassed only by that of the Paris Opéra — and a debut in Milan had been arranged for the fall. He was carefree and again apparently in love — and he approached this new professional challenge with a youthful self-confidence, the inevitable result of his triumphs in Salerno.

That self-confidence, however, was soon shattered. At the very first rehearsal of *La Gioconda*, it became apparent that it would be difficult, if not impossible, for the young tenor to win the approval of the Massimo's conductor, Leopoldo Mugnone. Mugnone, a fellow Neapolitan, was one of Italy's leading musicians: he was already established as a favorite in Rome, Venice, and at La Scala; and he had conducted the world première of *Cavalleria Rusticana*. He was a far more important figure in the world of opera than Vergine, Lombardi, or even Daspuro, and he greeted Caruso coldly upon his arrival and throughout the first rehearsal. There were rumors that the conductor was in love with the same young ballerina who had demonstrated her preference for the young singer; there was also more serious talk that Mugnone was dismayed by Caruso's inability to reach the high notes of Ponchielli's score. Whatever the reason, he drove Caruso mercilessly from the start, constantly reiterating his dissatisfaction and wondering if the tenor could ever master the role. On the night of the public dress rehearsal, however, Mugnone succumbed to Caruso's natural gifts, which had become increasingly evident, spontaneously shouting "bravo" in response to the tenor's performance. From that time on, the two men became friends—and the ballerina was apparently forgotten by both of them.

Caruso also experienced initial difficulties in winning over the public at the Massimo. At his first appearance there—it was an historic event, part of the twenty-five-hundred-seat theater's inaugural program—he was greeted coldly by an audience which believed that the honor of singing on such a gala occasion should have gone to a Sicilian tenor. Knowledgeable musicians noticed with disappointment that the aria *"Cielo e mar"* had to be lowered a half tone to suit the tenor's limited range. Caruso was unnerved by his reception, but he soon regained his confidence and won the affection of the reticent public. According to *La Gazzetta dei Teatri*, in subsequent performances he proved himself to be "an enchanting lyric tenor." The local *Giornale di Sicilia* agreed, noting that he was applauded for *"Cielo e mar,"* which he sang with feeling, "in spite of the fact that the tessitura seemed to be too high for him," and concluding that "a splendid future undoubtedly awaits the young artist."

III. Ada and *Fedora*

Many years later, Caruso declared that his performances in Palermo in June 1897 signaled the end of one period of his career, and that a new period began with his appearances in Livorno later that same summer. Without a doubt, the Palermo engagement had been important for a number of reasons. The promising tenor had never before faced—or been accepted by—as discriminating an audience as that which filled the Teatro Massimo for each of his thirteen performances of *La Gioconda*. By the end of the season, he was no longer merely "promising." He was never again without work, and if he wasn't exactly deluged with offers yet, he was certain that offers, based on his successes and his contacts, would be forthcoming. Also, his appearances in the Sicilian capital marked—with one notable exception—his last performances in any Italian city south of Rome. Though unaware of it at the time, his horizons were expanding and before long he would be acclaimed by the world and not merely by the opera-goers of a small corner of his native country.

As for his short engagement in Livorno, it marked not only an important turning point in his career—he was unofficially endorsed by Giacomo Puccini—but also in his personal life, for there he met the woman who would be his companion for more than ten years.

The month-long season in the Tuscan city was unexpected. Following Palermo, he planned to mark time before his eagerly anticipated debut in Milan, but, at the recommendation of Mugnone, he was hired by impre-

sario Arturo Lisciarelli to take part in a number of performances at Livorno's Teatro Goldoni. The operas assigned him were *La Traviata* and Puccini's *La Bohème*. The former presented no problems; he had already sung
the role of Alfredo with considerable success. Before he could sing the
latter, however, there was a formidable obstacle to overcome. Puccini's
newest opera, though only moderately successful at its première in February 1896, had in a short time achieved enormous popularity wherever it
was performed. *La Bohème*'s publisher, the Milanese house of Ricordi,
carefully guarded its property and jealously watched over each production
of the new work. The first production in Livorno was of special concern
because the city was so close to the composer's home at Torre del Lago, and
the casting of each and every role had to be approved by the Milanese
publisher. Lisciarelli's choice for the leading soprano role of Mimi — a competent singer named Ada Giachetti — had been approved, as had his choice
for the baritone role of Marcello — Antonio Pini-Corsi, who had created
the part of Ford in Verdi's *Falstaff*. Ricordi expressed unhappiness only over
the choice of Caruso for the tenor role of Rodolfo. Word of Caruso's talent
had reached Milan, but as far as the Milanese publisher was concerned,
there was still no proof that he could master the leading role in the Puccini
opera.

There was only one possible solution: if Caruso could audition before
and satisfy the composer, Ricordi would allow him to sing the role of
Rodolfo in Livorno. With this in mind, Caruso traveled the short distance
to Puccini's lakeside villa, only an hour from Livorno. He had studied the
role and knew every note, and he approached the composer confidently, if
cautiously. Puccini had heard of the young singer and listened carefully as
Caruso sang Rodolfo's first-act aria, *"Che gelida manina."* At the end, he
was moved; he turned to Caruso and asked, "Who sent you to me — God?"
Inviting Caruso to spend a few hours with him, Puccini assured the young
man that he would transmit his approval to Ricordi the next day.

Impressed by Caruso's voice, he was equally impressed by his honesty in
expressing misgivings over his ability to sing the high C in Rodolfo's first-
act narrative. There was, as far as Puccini was concerned, no need to worry: the note was optional. And he completely disapproved of those singers
who would save themselves for one high note. He much preferred that the
entire aria be well sung, with or without the high C.

✳

In the presence of the composer — who had personally coached him in
the role — Caruso sang his first *La Bohème* at the Teatro Goldoni in
August. The entire performance was a great success, and *La Gazzetta*

Musicale di Milano reported that Caruso "was an excellent Rodolfo, sur-
passing all expectations," also commenting that "Signora Giachetti-Botti
was an attractive Mimi, full of charm and passion." In spite of the warm
reception accorded this production, the Livorno season was, in some ways,
a failure for the tenor. Through a series of contractual misunderstandings,
he was paid far less than even his usual modest fee; in addition, he was
subjected to the constant badgering of a rival tenor who insisted that he
was better qualified to sing the role. Though urged by Vergine to return to
Naples, where he might arrange to earn some more money, Caruso finished the season. His meetings with Puccini, who often invited him to his
home, were, he felt, invaluable, and he assured Vergine that the composer's coaching had advanced his career by at least two years. There was one
more reason for Caruso's refusal to leave Livorno, one he did not explain to
Vergine; in the course of the season, he and his Mimi, Ada Giachetti-Botti,
had fallen in love.

Caruso had fallen in love before, but this time his involvement was a
serious one. Though several years older than he was, and married (she was
separated from Botti, her husband), Giachetti was an ideal partner. An
attractive, strong-willed woman of unusual intelligence, she was a soprano
of no special distinction, but she was a trained musician and an energetic
teacher. Her wisdom and experience were of great help to the young,
unschooled tenor. Ada studied roles with him, helped develop his voice,
and taught him the elements of acting, which made his onstage portrayals
more effective. She, too, was in love, and her devotion to Caruso during
their early years together gave him courage during his difficult times and
gave him the strength necessary to cope maturely with the fame that came
to him so quickly and might have turned his head.

Following his last performance in Livorno, Caruso was concerned not
with fame but with the need to sustain himself until the time of his
autumn engagement in Milan. In one month, he had won the admiration
of Puccini and the love of Giachetti, but he was penniless. His contract to
sing at the Teatro Lirico, though a firm one, was vague in that it stipulated
that he had been engaged to sing there sometime during the fall season,
without specifying a date. In order to reach Milan, he was forced to borrow
money from Florentine friends; in order to stay in the thriving metropolis,
so far from his Neapolitan home and family, he had to approach Sonzogno
and ask for an advance against his salary at the Lirico.

The publisher-impresario agreed to help, generously giving Caruso even
more money than he had requested, but he failed to tell him exactly what
he would be singing or when. He was in no hurry; unknown to Caruso at
the time, Sonzogno had received discouraging reports claiming the singer
was more a baritone than a tenor. Sonzogno had reacted by writing sarcas-

tically to Daspuro to thank him for presenting him with a baritone rather than a tenor. Daspuro confidently replied that Sonzogno should listen to Caruso before judging him, and added that if the young man was a baritone, De Lucia was a basso profondo.

While he nervously awaited a call from Sonzogno, Caruso managed to fill one engagement — for a single performance of *La Bohème* at Fiume; he spent the rest of his time preparing for his debut at the Lirico. When he had signed his contract, he had been asked to study three new roles which he might be called upon to sing: in Umberto Giordano's *Il Voto* (a revised version of *Mala Vita*), *L'Arlesiana*, a new opera by Francesco Cilea, and Leoncavallo's *La Bohème* — the composer of *Pagliacci* had used the same source for his latest work as had his rival Puccini. The tenor had diligently studied the first two, but on the advice of Vergine, who felt the role was not suitable for his voice, he had not attempted to master Leoncavallo's score.

Caruso waited patiently — he had no choice — and in October, after the Lirico season had already begun, he finally received the summons to Sonzogno's office. Hoping that he would at last be given a specific assignment, he was disappointed to find that the impresario merely wanted to know if he had prepared the three new roles; upon learning that he had studied only two of them, he urged Caruso to ignore his teacher's advice and start work on the third.

Because of this, Caruso was stunned a few weeks later when he was again called to the Lirico and informed that his debut was to take place five days later — not in any of the roles he had studied so arduously, but in Jules Massenet's *La Navarraise,* an opera he had never even heard. His protests that he could not possibly learn the role (though admittedly a short one) in so little time were ignored, and he was ordered to begin work at once with the help of the conductor Rodolfo Ferrari.

It was an unpromising beginning for what Caruso hoped would be the most important opportunity of his life. Ferrari was hardly encouraging; convinced that the new tenor would ruin the Milan première of the Massenet opera, he continued to work with him only to satisfy Sonzogno, who urged patience.

The conductor's forebodings seemed justified at the first general rehearsal. Caruso was visibly nervous; before he even sang a note he angered the prima donna, a Madame De Nuovina, recently arrived from Paris, by forgetting to take off his hat in her presence. Unsure of himself and shaken by the soprano's undisguised hostility, he sang badly. The situation seemed hopeless and there was practically no time to remedy it; the only consolation for Sonzogno and Ferrari was the belief that the heralded soprano's triumph would be so overwhelming that Caruso's shortcomings would be overlooked. Gone, apparently, were all hopes that the new singer could possibly repeat in Milan the successes which had marked his appearances in the South.

Both the impresario and the conductor had overestimated the opera and the soprano, just as they had shown too little faith in Caruso. *La Navarraise*, at its Italian première on the night of November 3, 1897, and Madame De Nuovina, were received with cool indifference; the only applause was reserved for the Lirico's new tenor. Caruso had not salvaged the evening, but his performance had made an impression. One critic, the influential Gianbattista Nappi of *Perseveranza*, noting "the beauty of his homogeneous voice and its rousing, full, spontaneous timbre," felt he was already "on the path to a brilliant career."

These were heartening words, encouraging to Sonzogno, who had been counting on him, as well as to Caruso; but the role had been a small one and the tenor's success could not be classified as a real triumph. The same could be said of his performance in *Il Voto* one week later, on the night of November 10. Once again the opera did not meet with the public's approval, but Caruso's duet with the beautiful Rosina Storchio (who was later to create the role of Madama Butterfly) had to be repeated, and he was singled out for praise by the reviewer for *La Frusta Teatrale*, who wrote that he confirmed the good impression he had made earlier and had "a truly appealing natural voice and knows how to sing with great feeling."

Caruso gave further proof of his artistry in subsequent performances of these two minor operas, as well as in his first Milan performance of *Cavalleria Rusticana*, which he sang on November 23 (he sang *La Navarraise* the same evening). His greatest success of the season, however, did not come until the night of November 27, when he took part in the world première of Cilea's *L'Arlesiana*. The first performance of a new work by Cilea was an important occasion for the publishing house of Sonzogno: the thirty-one-year-old composer was—along with Giordano, Mascagni, and Leoncavallo—one of its greatest assets in the battle with the house of Ricordi (who had backed Puccini) to find a successor to the aging Giuseppe Verdi.

Cilea had personally chosen Caruso for his new opera. A distinguished teacher, he spent long hours coaching him in the new role, patiently helping the somewhat over-energetic tenor realize the importance of achieving more delicate vocal subtleties by means of pianissimo and mezza voce, and helping him overcome his all too frequent difficulties with high notes.

Cilea's accomplishments as a teacher proved to be more successful than his achievements as a composer on the night of the première of *L'Arlesiana*. The opera was greeted without enthusiasm from the very beginning, as was the singing of Minnie Tracey, an American soprano who undertook the title role. The public remained unmoved until Caruso, in the role of the young farmer Federico, concluded his aria lamenting his lover's unfaithfulness—"*É la solita storia.*" Suddenly the new opera came to life. Cheers rang throughout the house, and the tenor was forced to repeat the aria twice; at the end of the evening a grateful public called him before the curtain twenty times.

It had been Caruso's night, and even the composer admitted that whatever small success his new work had achieved was due to the tenor's performance. The critics the following day showed their appreciation in glowing terms. Achille Tedeschi, writing in *L'Illustrazione Italiana* under the name "Leporello," proclaimed that Caruso's singing was the highlight of the evening. Annibale Ponchielli, writing in *La Sera*, agreed, commenting that "Caruso distinguished himself above all the others; he had a splendid voice and is most effective on the stage," while Nappi of *Perseveranza* again noted the tenor's "full, warm, and impassioned singing."

Each succeeding Caruso appearance was enthusiastically acclaimed, and by the time his season ended on January 2, 1898—with a performance of *Pagliacci*—his popularity had exceeded all expectations. He had even won the admiration of the brilliant dramatic tenor Francesco Tamagno, creator of Verdi's Otello, who, upon meeting the editor of *Il Secolo* after one of the young tenor's performances, commented: "He will be greater than all of us."

✳

In spite of Tamagno's perceptive enthusiasm, it was only a beginning: with the exception of *Pagliacci*, Caruso's successes in Milan had been attained in operas unfamiliar to the public. He had not yet been judged in the more demanding works of the standard repertory, where comparisons might be made more easily.

By the terms of Sonzogno's contract, the Lirico had an option on Caruso's services for the following season, beginning in March—an option which was eagerly exercised. Before then, Caruso agreed to sing for the first time in Genoa, at the Teatro Carlo Felice, one of the most beautiful in Italy. It was there in January 1898 that he made his debut in Leoncavallo's *La Bohème*. This was another important occasion for Sonzogno—a chance to redeem Leoncavallo's newest opera which, though it had been accorded a somewhat more enthusiastic reception at its première than had Puccini's work on the same subject, had failed to take hold with the public. Caruso's presence in the cast—which also included the soprano Storchio and a young Roman baritone Giuseppe De Luca—helped, and the work was performed thirteen times in the course of the season. More important for

Caruso was his first appearance, on February 3, as Nadir in Bizet's *Les Pêcheurs de Perles*, which he sang with De Luca and a promising Polish soprano, Regina Pinkert. On the opening night, Pinkert brought the house to its feet, and Caruso's singing of his first-act aria so pleased the crowd that he had to sing an encore.

The short Genoa season confirmed Caruso's Milanese successes; it was also notable as the beginning of a long professional and personal relationship between Caruso and the hardworking De Luca—they remained friends and colleagues until the time of the tenor's death. While in Genoa, the two young men lived in the same *pensione*, the Mancinelli on via Assarotti—Caruso's accommodations, since he was earning five thousand lire for the Genoa season, were far more luxurious than those of the younger baritone, whose pay was a mere seven hundred and fifty lire. The friendship between the two developed easily. Not finding the food at the *pensione* to their liking, they would often dine together at the Righi restaurant in the hills overlooking the port; following a performance, they would usually join other colleagues for a meal at Peppo's, a restaurant in the fashionable Galleria. Almost always the meal would be followed by a race, with the singer who finished last paying for the after-dinner coffee. The one who paid most often was Caruso—he was no longer slim and had shown no interest in developing his athletic prowess.

The exuberant Neapolitan, so recently arrived from the South, was enjoying his successes. At ease among his colleagues, he had gained self-confidence over the past months. He was not yet near the top of his profession—there were far greater and more popular tenors, among them Tamagno, De Lucia, and the elegant Pole, Jean de Reszke—but he was already established in the world of opera, and a bright future seemed certain. His personal life, too, brought him much pleasure. Giachetti had encouraged him and given him a sense of security; she stood loyally by his side whenever her own commitments permitted. Their relationship had matured, and they joyfully shared the news that they would become parents early in the summer.

Caruso began his second season at the Lirico on March 8 with the first of eight performances of Leoncavallo's *La Bohème*. Sonzogno was persisting in his efforts to promote the new opera, but he was clearly fighting a losing battle against Puccini's version, which was steadily growing in popularity. Caruso, again, drew more praise than did the opera in which he was appearing. Nappi of *Perseveranza* was even more impressed. "If Caruso will study," he wrote, "he can in a short time be an outstanding tenor, with his most beautiful voice, so full of freshness and color, and with his impassioned singing."

On March 16, Caruso sang his first of five performances of *Carmen*, an opera more worthy of his talents, and his success was such that he had to encore the "Flower Song." On April 2, he again appeared in the world première of a lesser opera, *Hedda* by Fernand Leborne, a Belgian composer and student of Massenet. Another of many attempts by Sonzogno to introduce the French repertory to Italy, the work was a failure. Caruso, in a role unsuited to his voice, made as little impression as did the opera.

The tenor's last performance of what had been an unexciting season took place on the night of April 10, 1898. In the months following it he appeared in Fiume and in Trent, adding to his expanding repertory by singing for the first time in Boito's *Mefistofele* and Massenet's *Sapho*. The highlight of the summer, however, was nonprofessional: on July 2, Ada Giachetti gave birth to their first child, whom they named Rodolfo in honor of their meeting during the Livorno performances of Puccini's *La Bohème*.

Coincidentally, Caruso's first appearances after the birth of his son took place in Livorno, where in the early fall he sang *Pagliacci* and *Cavalleria Rusticana*. Following these, he traveled to Milan and a season at the Lirico which marked a significant turning point in his career.

The season began on the night of October 22 with the first of seven performances of a revised and expanded version of *L'Arlesiana*. Caruso acquitted himself with honor, as he did in additional performances of Leoncavallo's *La Bohème*. On the night of November 17, however, he came fully into his own.

The occasion was the world première of Umberto Giordano's *Fedora*. Giordano had won fame with his rousing *Andrea Chénier*, first presented in 1896, a masterpiece of verismo opera. Following it, he had set out to write a new work for Gemma Bellincioni and Roberto Stagno, a popular couple (onstage and off) who had gained success in the first performance of *Cavalleria Rusticana* in 1890. Giordano had won the couple's admiration early in his career, and he wrote much of his new opera in their Florentine villa. Their relationship was so close that the elder Stagno—he was sixty while Giordano was barely thirty—would often good-naturedly close the composer in his room to force him to write.

In April of 1898, when the opera was almost completed, tragedy struck the Stagno-Bellincioni home: the tenor died suddenly of a heart attack. A frantic search began for his replacement—the new work was scheduled for the Lirico's fall season. Sonzogno and Giordano immediately thought of De Lucia, but the noted tenor had commitments elsewhere. Sonzogno's second choice was Caruso, who, though still inexperienced, had been a mainstay of the Sonzogno repertory for the past two seasons. Giordano, too, was familiar with the Neapolitan's performances—he had heard him sing his own *Il Voto*—and believed that Caruso's voice might be well suited to the role of Loris Ipanoff in the new opera. Before agreeing, however, he asked Bellincioni to travel to nearby Livorno to listen to the young man's interpretation of Canio in *Pagliacci*. The soprano did as suggested, and her response was enthusiastic. Though recognizing that a successful Canio did not necessarily mean a successful Loris, she wrote Giordano: "It is my opinion that Caruso has the voice and the intelligence to assure him success in the new role."

In the four months that preceded the première, Giordano patiently coached the singer in his new role. He admired his voice and respected his willingness to learn, but Caruso was inexperienced and by the evening of the première the composer was still troubled by doubts that Caruso's lyric tenor voice was sufficiently robust for the demanding role in *Fedora*. All such reservations soon disappeared.

On the night of November 17, the opera house was filled to capacity. The first performance of the new opera by one of Italy's most promising composers was an occasion of major importance. Cilea and Leoncavallo, Giordano's rivals, were there, as was the young conductor Arturo Toscanini; critics from all over Italy and abroad were also in attendance. The evening began badly. The composer, who himself conducted the opera, was greeted with no more than polite applause. Bellincioni, in spite of her fame, was also welcomed without enthusiasm, and after the first act there were but two curtain calls — an indication of failure for a new opera from which so much had been expected. All seemed lost until the second act, when Caruso stepped forward to sing his short, passionate aria, "*Amor ti vieta*"—"Love forbids you not to love." When he reached the end, the audience rose to its feet in a spontaneous outburst which could not be stopped until the aria was repeated. Even then, the applause was deafening and the performance almost had to be halted. The tenor's voice, his delivery of one aria, had overwhelmed the public and transformed a disappointing evening into a rousing success. This extraordinary personal triumph was later described by the musical historian Carlo Gatti, who was present. "It was a handsome young Caruso, open-hearted, with an ardent intelligence, sturdy, robust, square-faced, with a solid jaw, a row of ivory teeth, shining black eyes and smooth black hair, and olive complexion. He was an authentic 'Vesuvian,' attractive to behold, affable, with engaging ways. And he sang as one of the good Lord's creatures in that happy land can — with the sun and the sky and the stars of the perfumed night in his voice expressing the immense and ever-new marvels of the everlasting universal life."

The press the following day reflected the enthusiasm of the public. "Suddenly, in the midst of the dizzying action, a delightful pause," wrote Achille Tedeschi in *L'Illustrazione Italiana*. "The song of Loris, a sweet melody, sung with an enchanting voice. The melody is one of the maestro's most inspired, and the voice one of the most beautiful tenor voices to be heard."

Gianbattista Nappi, one of Caruso's earliest admirers, agreed. "It was Caruso," he noted, "who awakened the sleepy atmosphere. In his aria . . . he found an enchanting gentleness and a passionate outpouring worthy of the enormous enthusiasm which greeted it and of the insistent cries of 'encore.' It gives me pleasure to repeat that with his success of last night Caruso rises to first rank among the tenors of today."

The reviewer for *La Sera* was no less enthusiastic. "Honors go to the tenor Caruso," he wrote, "who can be numbered among Italy's most important singers. . . . I am most happy to take note of his enormous success and to predict a splendid career for him."

Word of Caruso's triumph even reached America. Reporting from Milan, the correspondent for *Musical Courier* reported: "Caruso, the tenor, certainly has the most beautiful voice that has been heard in many a year. His is a voice of the South, full of warmth, charm, and lusciousness. . . . And this Caruso knows how to sing; his *mezza voce*, or half voice, is delicious and charming, is most agreeable and fascinating to the listener. . . ."

Caruso was still — and the correspondent for *Musical Courier* made note of it — a lyric tenor, lacking a certain robust quality, and his voice was still limited in range. As a performer, too, he had much to learn — Verdi had noted, when told that Caruso would create the role of Loris, "They tell me he has a fine voice, but it seems to me his head is not in its place." Nonetheless, he already had the power to move an audience and he brought a sinking *Fedora* to life. Following his performance that night, he was a star. "Caruso sang in *Fedora*," it was said, and *"la fè d'oro"* — made it golden. It could also be said that the role of Loris, which suited his voice so perfectly that it might have been written for him, made Caruso "golden." Sonzogno, to show his gratitude, presented him with a copy of each score published by his house. The public showered him with praise, and, in Caruso's own words, "After that night, the contracts descended on me like a heavy rainstorm."

IV. Growth and Acclaim

The year 1899 marked the emergence of Caruso as an international star — only four years after his first professional engagements. In the course of the year, he would sing for the first time in Rome and establish himself as a favorite in two of the world's music capitals — St. Petersburg and Buenos Aires.

He left for Russia shortly after the end of his season at the Lirico. The appearances in St. Petersburg would constitute his most formidable challenge to date, and when he left his home in Milan — Ada was booked for a tour of South America and the baby was left with her sister Rina, also an opera singer — he did so with a mixture of apprehension and self-confidence. The Russian city, unlike Cairo and Alexandria, was a thriving, culturally sophisticated center with an opera-loving public accustomed to the very best. The company with which Caruso would be singing was also an outstanding one: it included Mattia Battistini, considered the world's finest baritone and already a great favorite with the Russians; the basso Vittorio Arimondi, who had sung the role of Pistol in the world première of Verdi's *Falstaff*; Sigrid Arnoldson, a Swedish soprano who had sung at New York's Metropolitan and had made her Russian debut in 1886 with great success; and Luisa Tetrazzini, still at the beginning of her career and not yet the great star she would become, but already a powerful presence in the theater.

Never before had Caruso sung with such seasoned professionals. As one of the lesser-known members of the company, he might have been intimidated, but the relationship between him and his fellow artists was based on friendly cooperation rather than a spirit of competition. His first role was that of Rodolfo in *La Bohème* — Arnoldson sang Mimi and Tetrazzini Musetta. Many years later, Tetrazzini spoke to Fred Gaisberg, a pioneer in the recording industry, of Caruso's early development. "I remember Enrico as a youth of twenty years, before his voice was yet rounded and the different registers smoothed out. I recall the difficulty he had even with such ordinary notes as G or A. He always stumbled over these and it annoyed him so that he even threatened to change over to baritone; he did not know whether he had a tenor or a baritone voice," she said. Several years later, when she sang with him for the first time in that St. Petersburg *La Bohème*, she was astounded at the remarkable progress he had made. "I can hear that velvet voice now, and the *impertinenza* with which he lavishly poured forth those rich, round notes. It was the open *voce Napoletana* [Neapolitan voice], yet it had the soft caress of the *voce della campagna Toscana* [voice of the Tuscan countryside]. There never was a doubt in my mind. I placed him then and there as an extraordinary and unique tenor. From top to bottom his register was without defect. . . ."

The Russian public agreed and judged Caruso's debut an unqualified success. Audiences were equally enthusiastic at his subsequent performances in *Pagliacci* (with Arnoldson and Battistini), Donizetti's *Maria di Rohan* (his first appearance in the opera), *Cavalleria Rusticana*, and *La Traviata*. This unanimous acclaim gave the young Neapolitan even greater self-confidence. Secure financially as well as artistically, he was able to enjoy himself as he wandered among unfamiliar sights and unfamiliar people, joking with his illustrious colleagues, forever cheerful and playful. He was suddenly famous, and he delighted in his fame. In St. Petersburg, too, he took part in a command performance before royalty, the first of many such experiences and one he would never forget. The setting for the special concert was the fabulous palace of Czar Nicholas II, and at the conclusion of the concert he was presented to the young ruler who was destined to be the last czar of Russia. Caruso remembered him as a "small, almost insignificant-looking man with an anxious face," and he went on to describe the event: "Royalty to me was something to be regarded from a distance. The scene was brilliant. Such color, together with the beauty of the women and the bearing of the men — assembled in so large a space — was wholly new to me. I recall having felt a sense of gratitude for that opportunity, and wondered if there was to be another — and where and when. I could feel people staring as I was received by the czar, who said 'Thank you very much,' and then presented me with a pair of gold cuff buttons set with diamonds."

Only one unfortunate incident marred this season in St. Petersburg. Called out of town for another command performance, the tenor had arrived late for a performance of *Cavalleria Rusticana*. Raffaele Favia, a baritone who had known Caruso from his early days in Naples, warned him to be careful of his voice, cautioning that the unfamiliar climate sometimes played unexpected tricks on a singer and that Caruso—hurried and tired—would be especially susceptible to vocal problems. The young tenor paid no attention. His opening aria, the "Siciliana," went so well that he consented to repeat it three times. Obviously, he reasoned, Favia was wrong. But shortly afterward, in the duet with Santuzza ("*Tu qui Santuzza?*"), his voice did begin to fail. The more he sang, the less voice he had; finally, the stunned public heard little more than a hoarse whisper. Caruso was terrified. It was clear that he could not continue, and it seemed that the performance would have to be suspended when, to the surprised delight of the audience, an elegantly dressed man arose from his seat in the orchestra, went to the stage, and brilliantly finished the opera in place of the heartsick young tenor. Caruso's unexpected savior had been a well-known and much-loved Russian tenor, Leonid Sobinov.

A triumphant Caruso, hoping that this one incident would be forgotten, returned to Milan in high spirits. But he soon learned that the story of the near disaster in St. Petersburg had followed him—worrying his friends and alarming one impresario, Amelia Ferrari. The perceptive Ferrari had been among the first to recognize Caruso's talents. She had had the good sense to reach an agreement with him to join a company of Italian singers for a season in Buenos Aires—before his enormous success in *Fedora* and at a fee far lower than he would have exacted after that performance. (After *Fedora*, Caruso's friends had urged him to cancel the agreement with Ferrari and change the terms to ones more favorable to him, but Caruso had refused on the grounds that a contract was a contract, and that Ferrari deserved to be rewarded for having recognized him before the others had.)

Now Ferrari was worried, uncertain that she had, in fact, made such a good bargain—even at a low price, she didn't want a singer whose voice might fail in the middle of a performance. She summoned Caruso to her office and expressed her fears, which were little relieved by the tenor's insistence that it had been only a minor incident and that his voice was still the voice she had heard sing *Fedora*. Caruso was disheartened—he worried that his career had been seriously damaged—but he was comforted by word from his early and very powerful supporter, Sonzogno, who wrote to assure him that in spite of the rumors that had spread through Milan, his own theaters were open to Caruso at all times, to sing any opera of his choice.

Sonzogno was vindicated and Ferrari reassured when on the night of

March 22 Caruso again sang *Fedora* at the Teatro Lirico, and his success even surpassed that of the previous season. Four performances of Giordano's opera and four of Leoncavallo's *La Bohème* confirmed that the tenor had in no way lost his voice.

Caruso, too, was sure of himself when, shortly after the end of his season at the Lirico, he boarded the *SS Regina Margherita* on the way to Argentina. Following his arrival there on May 7, 1899, he was immediately faced with still another misunderstanding. This time it was due to a confusion of names. An Italian singer who had often sung in Buenos Aires was a baritone named Guglielmo Caruson who, though more than competent, was not highly regarded by the Argentinians. When word of Caruso's forthcoming debut reached the South American capital, members of the press confused the two names and assumed — and reported — that rather than a most promising young tenor, the public would be given the same old baritone Caruson — this time as a tenor.

The reporters, who had incensed the public, were obviously wrong, as the real Caruso proved on the night of May 14. His South American debut was in the role he could rightly call his own — that of Loris in *Fedora*. Singing with him again was Gemma Bellincioni. It was, as it had been repeatedly in Milan, an enormous success. A grateful Ferrari embraced him following the performance and offered him contracts — not at bargain rates this time — for three more Buenos Aires seasons. Before long, the hitherto unknown tenor was the toast of the Argentine capital. In the course of the three-month season, he sang three times in *Fedora*; twice in *La Traviata*; twice in *Sapho* (an opera which found little favor with the public); once in *Gioconda*; seven times as Osaka in the first South American performances of Mascagni's *Iris*; six times in Goldmark's *Queen of Sheba*; and twice in *Cavalleria Rusticana*. In addition, he created the role of the hero in *Yupanqui* — a work by the Argentine composer Arturo Berutti — which failed to take hold with the public and was given but three performances. With the exception of Bellincioni, Caruso's colleagues were not as distinguished as those with whom he had sung in Russia, but he was able to benefit from working with one of Italy's greatest opera conductors, Edoardo Mascheroni, who had conducted the world première of *Falstaff* at the invitation of Verdi himself. The young tenor expanded his repertory, too, and he learned that his generosity — he was always ready to give an encore — and warm charm could seduce the public as much as his voice did. There was no longer any doubt of his international appeal. As he prepared to leave Buenos Aires, he wrote a short autobiographical sketch for a local newspaper, which ended with: "Will end this season by going to Rome to the Costanzi to create the role of Cavaradossi in Sardou's *Tosca*, set to music by Maestro Puccini, pre-selected by the same maestro."

He returned to Italy an established artist and a much-sought-after one.

Offers poured in; his participation in a performance was beginning to assure that performance of success, as opera-lovers all over the world clamored to hear the phenomenal new Neapolitan tenor.

Before proceeding to his home in Milan and to Ada and little Rodolfo (called then and always "Fofò"), Caruso stopped in Naples to visit his family and friends. He was greeted as a hero. Old friends who had once shunned him, fearing he might ask for a loan, offered him money — now that he didn't need it. Even his father, but above all his stepmother, rejoiced in his newfound success.

After Naples he traveled to Milan, there to sift out those offers that interested him and to make concrete plans for his future. If his reception in Naples had been uncommonly cordial, the greeting he received in Milan was even more so. A brilliant new tenor was warmly received in the capital of Italian opera, and suddenly everyone wanted to know Caruso, to be seen with Caruso, to be counted among his friends. With money no longer a concern, he was able to live in the manner compatible with his generous nature. He was lavish in his gifts to Ada and Fofò, he dined at the best restaurants, was seen at the best cafés, and became known for the elegance of his clothing. The somewhat chubby (he had steadily put on weight), poorly educated Neapolitan was adjusting to his new position with surprising ease.

As much as he enjoyed and relished his newfound celebrity and security in Milan, there was little time to rest. Caruso was soon forced to leave for Rome to prepare for his first performances in the Italian capital. He was especially excited at the prospect of creating a role in *Tosca*. Finding suitable lodgings in an apartment at 79, via Napoli, he set to work. For the first time, he realized that he would require a secretary to take care of the huge amount of detail work and correspondence which his success entailed. For this task he summoned Enrico Lorello, a young man whom he had met a few years before in Salerno and who had predicted that Caruso would become the world's greatest tenor. At the time, Caruso had told him that if he could ever afford a secretary, he would call upon Lorello. As always, Caruso never forgot a promise, and the grateful young man hurried to Rome to become, for a short time, the first of many secretaries, official and unofficial, who would aid the tenor during his career.

Not long after his arrival, however, Caruso learned from the impresario of the Costanzi that he would not after all be singing the first performance of Puccini's new opera. It was a major disappointment. Puccini, after the enormous public success of his *La Bohème,* had established himself as the heir to the great Verdi; there could be no higher honor for a tenor than being selected for the leading role of his eagerly awaited new opera. The composer had been enthusiastic about Caruso's earlier appearances in *La*

Bohème, and Caruso had felt certain that he would be chosen to create the role of Cavaradossi in *Tosca*. For some reason, the assignment had instead been given to Emilio De Marchi. De Marchi was a decent, competent singer. He was well established at La Scala, yet he could hardly be numbered among the great singers of the period. No official explanation was given for the rejection of Caruso. Perhaps it was his lack of experience; even more possible was the fact that he had made his mark in operas controlled by Sonzogno, while Puccini and his operas were very much the property of Giulio Ricordi, Sonzogno's very successful rival publisher. In later years, Caruso sadly noted that his rejection by Puccini was evidence that "one's career is neither so brilliant nor so easy as may seem to the casual eyes of the public."

There was, of course, nothing to be done, and Caruso worked diligently toward his Rome debut not in *Tosca* but as Osaka in *Iris*, the role he had first sung several months before in Buenos Aires. Though not the world première of a new Puccini opera, the occasion was an important one, the first Roman performance of a revised version of Mascagni's opera, and the Teatro Costanzi was filled with friends and admirers of the composer on the night of November 4, 1899. The title role was sung by Carelli and the conductor was Mugnone, but the star of the evening was Caruso. The following day, the influential *Popolo Romano* was ecstatic, labeling him "the tenor with the voice of paradise."

In *Cronache Musicali*, the critic Amilcare Laura wrote of the performance: "When I first heard Caruso in *Iris*, I was surprised by the unusual sweetness and purity of his vocal timbre and, along with everyone else, after the '*Serenata*' decided that he had the most beautiful qualities possible in a moderately powerful voice. I was wrong. At the end of the second act, Osaka's feverish, erotic outburst, the voice doubled, then quadrupled in its power and fullness, and the magnificent high notes filled the auditorium."

Caruso's rousing success gave special pleasure to Vincenzo Lombardi, present to cheer on his illustrious former pupil. Years before, when Lombardi had told Mugnone that Caruso would soon be earning one thousand lire per performance, the then hostile conductor had scoffed, answering sarcastically, "Yes, when I become Pope." That evening Caruso was paid fifteen hundred lire, and following the evening's triumph, Lombardi fell to Mugnone's feet as if to kiss them. "What are you doing?" asked an astounded Mugnone. "My duty," answered Lombardi. "You have become Pope."

Caruso's triumph in *Iris* was followed by a tremendously successful *Gioconda*—his "*Cielo e mar*" brought down the house. Even more gratifying was the experience of singing *Mefistofele* in the presence of Arrigo Boito, the composer. Boito was more than just a composer; he was Verdi's librettist, a distinguished critic, and the most powerful figure in Milan's intellectual circles. The mere thought of his presence at the performance terrified the young singer, yet he did not let his nervousness overwhelm his singing. Instead it inspired him, and Boito was unstinting in his praise. "Your voice," he confessed to Caruso, "has qualities which touch my heart; in your singing there is an instinctive virtue which I cannot describe. I congratulate you. And my mind and my heart thank you for the joy you have given both of them."

Caruso sang in eight performances of *Mefistofele* before leaving Rome for his second visit to Russia. Before departing, he was finally able to come to terms with Vergine concerning the unfair contract he had signed in Naples. A lawsuit to annul the agreement (which the tenor had instituted a few years before) had weighed on him emotionally as it had slowly made its way through the courts. Caruso felt a genuine affection for his old teacher and would always be grateful to him, yet he could not hide his bitterness at having been taken advantage of at a time when he knew no better. Thus, when an out-of-court settlement was reached whereby Caruso would pay a sum of twenty thousand lire to Vergine in exchange for the cancellation of the contract, a troublesome psychological—and economic—burden was removed.

✳

When Caruso left Italy for Russia he was especially pleased that he would soon be joined by Ada. Their separate careers had kept them apart too often, and Caruso was eager to share the wonders of the exotic land with the woman who had stood by him and helped him during his early struggles and his newfound success.

The Russian season again promised to be a brilliant one. In addition to Tetrazzini, Arnoldson, Arimondi, and Battistini, the company would include Salomea Kruceniski, a powerful Polish soprano who would gain worldwide fame as the first successful interpreter of Puccini's *Butterfly*, and more important, the great tenor Angelo Masini, then in his mid-fifties, long a personal favorite of Verdi, who had written the tenor role in his *Requiem* especially for him.

It was in one of Masini's best-known roles, that of Radames in *Aida*, that Caruso made his first appearance of the season at St. Petersburg's Myrinsky Theater on the night of December 18, 1899. This was his first performance in the difficult dramatic role—one not meant for the color and range of a lyric tenor, as Caruso had been labeled—and it constituted a major challenge. Caruso worked tirelessly to overcome what had been considered to be the limitations of his voice. It proved to be a highly rewarding experience. "Much of the growth I gained at that time I attributed to the singing of Radames," he was to say later. "The role was of much help because it developed and consolidated my voice and aided toward making secure my top C, which I had been previously afraid to attempt." (A top C was not required for *Aida*, but he had learned how to approach it when necessary.)

Caruso's interpretation of Verdi's hero was a stunning success. In spite of a brilliant cast which included Kruceniski as Aida, Battistini as Amonasro, and Arimondi as Ramfis, the evening was his, and following it and a performance of *La Traviata*, he was reaffirmed as an idol of the St. Petersburg public. His next performance, his first in the equally demanding role of Riccardo in another Verdi opera, *Un Ballo in Maschera*, was equally praised, as was his later appearance in *La Bohème*. Caruso could no longer be conveniently labeled a light lyric tenor; his repertory was expanding beyond any such limitations. He was, he wrote to a friend, a "colossal success."

Feted wherever he went, cheered enthusiastically at each performance, Caruso was jubilant and carefree. But in the middle of the season he was, for the first time in his career, felled by an illness brought on by his own youthful sense of invincibility. He had for weeks anxiously awaited the arrival of Ada, who was traveling from Milan with the wife of Arimondi, but on the day of their arrival, he was so busy with preparations for his first Russian *Mefistofele*, which he was to sing that night, that he was unable to go to the station. In his place he dispatched the faithful Lorello to meet their early morning train. In a few hours, a distraught Lorello returned with the news that the train had not arrived; furthermore, because of his inability to speak a word of Russian the secretary had been unable to find an explanation for the long delay. Caruso and Arimondi were both desperate, their fears unallayed by a telegram from Signora Arimondi, since it had been transmitted in Russian. Their attempts to find a competent translator were fruitless, and both men feared the worst. Finally, Caruso, dressed inadequately for the harsh Russian winter, stormed out of the hotel and into the icy streets. When he returned, he was chilled to the bones—but he had at least learned that the delay was due to a derailment and that no passenger had been seriously injured. The two women, shaken and suffering from exposure, arrived late in the afternoon. Caruso, apparently recovered from his chill, sang in *Mefistofele* that evening, but the following day he awoke with a cough and a high fever; his illness was diagnosed as bronchial pneumonia.

The tenor was confined to his hotel, bedridden for one month. Happily, Ada was at his side to minister to his needs, and friendly messages and visits of his colleagues relieved his boredom and despair. Nonetheless, the time hung heavy, though some good did come out of this long and dangerous illness. It allowed him at last a chance to rest, to take stock of his career and the direction it was leading him, and to come to terms with the responsibilities attached to his whirlwind success. That success had been achieved at a comparatively early age, without the long struggles which mark so many artistic careers. A young man of unbridled enthusiasm, he had been careless and carefree. He had, of course, studied hard—his achievements would have been impossible without that—but his impulses for a good time and his almost immediate acceptance by the public had caused him to pay too little attention to the rigorous, highly disciplined life required of a great artist.

He had acknowledged the problem before. A few months earlier, in Rome, he had attempted to set a schedule for himself, marking down on the back of envelopes the hours of the day and the use to which he intended to put them. There was time set aside for exercising his voice, for studying new roles, as well as fixed times for meals and for amusements. If these schedules were at first flexible, and all too frequently ignored, they at least served as a reminder of his responsibilities, and his month-long illness in St. Petersburg reinforced his awareness of the need for a more cautious and methodical approach to his art, and to his life.

In spite of his illness, Caruso's appearances in St. Petersburg had added further to his steadily growing reputation, as had other appearances in Moscow and in Warsaw. In the Polish capital, he sang with the Polish soprano Janina Korolewicz-Waydowa, who wrote in her memoirs: "The timbre and color of his voice was so enchanting that it is difficult to find words to describe it. He was very impulsive and subject to nervousness but full of impressive temperament. . . . I can still hear the sound of the 'Czar of Tenors.' "

When the tour came to an end in the spring of 1900, Caruso was more than satisfied. He had mastered new roles which would become part of his repertory, and his experience with some of the greatest singers of the period, before a series of discerning audiences, had taught him a great deal not only about the art of singing but also about the necessity for a convincing dramatic presence. He was, in every way, growing as an artist.

✳

Back in his own country, he barely had time to visit his family in Naples and Milan before embarking on another trip—his second visit to Buenos Aires. Though still worn out from his illness and his stay in Russia, he was convinced that the long ocean voyage would provide the rest he badly needed to regain his strength.

Unfortunately, he had miscalculated his recuperative powers, and his first performance of the Buenos Aires season (on May 10, as Faust in Boito's *Mefistofele*) was a disappointment. His vocal problems, undoubtedly caused by fatigue, were obvious from the start. He was visibly nervous, and the coldness of the audience only increased his anxiety. Though aware that he was not at his best, he was both hurt and angered by the reaction of the public. He had become accustomed to ovations, to cheers and cries of "encore" following each big aria, and the cool response to his appearance disturbed him to such an extent that he seriously contemplated giving up the entire Buenos Aires season. It was not a matter of artistic temperament — Caruso was deeply aware of the need to honor his commitments. But he also believed that if he was not giving audiences what they wanted it was best that he withdraw, leaving the dissatisfied public free to hear singers more to their liking.

Withdrawal, however, was not necessary; his second performance of *Mefistofele* was met with the enthusiasm and warmth to which he was accustomed, and to which he responded by singing at his best. Two more performances in Boito's opera followed, and in the course of the season he also performed — with complete success — in *The Queen of Sheba*, *Iris*, *La Bohème*, *Cavalleria Rusticana*, and Massenet's *Manon*. Once again, however, the prized role of Mario in *Tosca* had eluded him; Emilio De Marchi, its creator, was part of the company and it was he who, with Emma Carelli, introduced the opera to South America on June 16, 1900. Caruso must have derived some special satisfaction, however, when he achieved notable acclaim as a substitute for the indisposed De Marchi as Des Grieux in *Manon*, a role he sang for the first time on July 28, near the end of the Buenos Aires season.

Caruso and the rest of the company proceeded from the Argentine capital to Montevideo, where performances were given at the Teatro Solis from August 16 to September 10. There the young tenor once again sang in *Manon*, as well as in *Iris*, *Bohème*, and *Cavalleria Rusticana*. By the time he embarked for Genoa, he had, after a shaky beginning, reestablished himself as a favorite with the South American public.

❋

Caruso's most important debut to date was to take place at Milan's La Scala in December 1900. Before that, he was finally given the opportunity to sing the role of Mario Cavaradossi in *Tosca*. His first performances in

Puccini's newest opera took place in Treviso's small Teatro Sociale in October, where his partner was Ada Giachetti. Following Treviso, the couple moved on to a far more important engagement in Bologna. The sophisticated capital of Emilia was as famous for the harsh judgments of its demanding audiences as it was for the high standards of its operatic performances. A difficult and often cruel test for any singer, Bologna presented a special challenge for the young Caruso, for he would be competing with two of Italy's leading tenors, scheduled to sing there during the same season. One of them, Giuseppe Borgatti, had already distinguished himself at La Scala, singing Wagner under Toscanini and creating the title role of Andrea Chénier in Giordano's opera. The other, Alessandro Bonci, had gained considerable popularity for the sweetness of his voice and the refinement of his singing. Both singers, though only a few years older than Caruso, were better known to Bologna's public and seemed to have the advantage over him in what the press had publicized as a battle of the tenors.

Both the press and the public thoroughly enjoyed the combat. There were no disappointments, and all three men sang brilliantly, but in the eyes of the critics the winner was clearly Caruso, who thrilled all present with his interpretation of Cavaradossi on the night of November 17, 1900. It was a gala performance, with Eugenio Giraldoni re-creating his original role of Scarpia, and Mugnone conducting, as he had at the opera's première. Bologna's most important newspaper, *Il Resto del Carlino*, proclaimed Caruso's triumph, its critic noting that he was "at the height of his splendid vocal powers." Puccini, too, who had supervised rehearsals, wrote his publisher, Giulio Ricordi, that Caruso had been "divine," and following the last of twelve performances he declared that he had never heard a finer interpretation of the role. Ever the cautious diplomat, however, he never said what he must have believed—that he had been mistaken in passing over the Neapolitan tenor when choosing the cast for the world première of his opera.

V. La Scala and San Carlo

Caruso had proven himself in St. Petersburg and Buenos Aires; he had won honors, too, in his own country — in Bologna, Rome, and at Milan's Teatro Lirico. However, he had not yet met the approval of the audience that regularly filled Milan's legendary La Scala, which had reigned supreme among Italian opera houses since its construction in 1778, after the destruction by fire of the city's Teatro Ducale, and was unquestionably one of the world's most distinguished lyric theaters.

His first appearance there was scheduled to take place a few weeks after his triumph in Bologna. Still relatively inexperienced, he had every reason to be intimidated, for the great opera house's roster in recent years had included two of the greatest tenors of all time — Tamagno and De Lucia — as well as De Marchi and Borgatti. Few tenors — Masini and Stagno were notable exceptions — had achieved international fame without winning the approval of La Scala's public. In addition, Caruso would be facing for the first time the company's brilliant and temperamental thirty-three-year-old musical director, Arturo Toscanini, already notorious for the extraordinary demands he placed upon his orchestra and his singers.

The season would open on December 26, with a performance of Wagner's *Tristan und Isolde* starring Borgatti. This was to be followed the next night by Caruso's debut as Rodolfo in *La Bohème*. The tenor was understandably nervous as he began his first rehearsal, unsettled all the more by malicious reports that he was not worth the high fee that had been offered

him. When he reached his first-act aria, he sang his high C in falsetto
rather than in full voice. Toscanini, annoyed, asked him if he could make
the high C somewhat stronger; Caruso replied that he could, but that he
preferred not to do so during an early rehearsal.

The problem persisted throughout the next rehearsals, with Caruso
courageously defying Toscanini's wishes that he sing the full high C. The
tenor later told an interviewer:

> At last came the date for the general rehearsal, which at La
> Scala begins at nine in the evening with a large audience; it is
> almost a regular performance. The day had not gone far — it was,
> I remember, only nine in the morning — when the man who
> summons the principals to the theater (the *avvisatore*) arrived at
> my house to inform me of a "small" rehearsal. Both the compos-
> er and the librettists had attended all the rehearsals; many
> changes had been made; now someone had thought of new
> changes. Shortly after I reached the theater we began with the
> third act of *Bohème*. There were many stops; many suggestions;
> finally we finished and took up the fourth act. After a time I
> began to wonder when this "small" rehearsal would end. At
> half-past one we were still at work and no mention had been
> made of lunch, nor was there any when this act had been dis-
> posed of, for immediately we began on act one. By this time I was
> becoming angry over the thought that my soup at home was
> getting cold. I began to sing this first act with all my voice and
> continued in this through the romanza, including the much dis-
> puted high note near the close. When I gave it without any vocal
> restraint Toscanini (and everybody else also) appeared relieved.
> For a reward we were put to work upon the second act, in which
> I also used all the tone I had. Having sung with complete
> strength the entire opera, I was astounded when the *avvisatore*
> called out, "Signore, Signori — tonight at nine o'clock the general
> rehearsal."
>
> It was my intention to object, and I should have done so had
> not the soprano stopped me. "Don't worry," she said, "tonight
> we will sing in only half-voice."
>
> Having reached home at five o'clock, I had little rest when, at
> seven-thirty, the *avvisatore* called with a carriage to take me to
> the theater. There was present an invited audience of distin-
> guished persons: the critics, privileged subscribers, La Scala art-
> ists who were not taking part in the performance, and some of
> their friends. I began the opening act in demi-voice. Presently I

noticed that the soprano who had told me in the afternoon that we would all sing that way was using her entire voice. At the first opportunity I inquired why she did so. She answered, "I want to put the part in my throat."

At the end of the first act, while resting in his dressing room, Caruso was visited by Scala's young managing director, Giulo Gatti-Casazza, who had taken over the direction of the distinguished opera house two years before, when he was not yet thirty years old. Gatti-Casazza was worried and asked the tenor to give a little more of his voice during the next act. Caruso politely excused himself, explaining that he was unable to do so so soon after having eaten.

During the second act he had hardly the strength to summon up the half-voice he had used before. Toscanini was furious; he stopped the orchestra and pointed his baton at the tenor, warning him that the rehearsal would not go on if he did not give his all. Caruso repeated his excuse, but the enraged conductor put down his baton and suspended the rehearsal. Finally, at the urging of the Duke of Modrone, the president of La Scala's board of directors, the rehearsal was resumed, ending at one in the morning.

Caruso was distraught; during the restless night that followed he took sick, his weary body racked with fever. Though in a state of panic, he managed to hide his despair and his illness from La Scala's management, certain that he would recover in the few days remaining before his first performance. He had, however, fewer days than he had anticipated: on the morning of December 26 he was informed that Borgatti had taken ill, and that *La Bohème* had been substituted for *Tristan und Isolde* and would be sung on the opening night.

There would be little chance to regain his strength, psychological or physical, yet it was impossible for Caruso to turn away from the unique opportunity to sing at a Scala opening. It was the dream of every singer, and he felt that he might somehow rise to the occasion. His performance, however, was disastrous. To the astonishment of the elegant public and the horror of his colleagues, who knew nothing of his illness, Caruso sang badly. Each aria and each act was greeted with silence; Puccini, who had come to the performance eager to hear the tenor whose performance in *Tosca* had so pleased him, left the theater before the last act, too upset to stay until the end.

Critics the following day were devastating in their appraisals. Giovanni Borelli of *L'Alba* was particularly harsh. "The tenor Caruso was a disappointment. The public expected extraordinary surprises from his golden throat and was left baffled; mortified at having been rewarded so poorly for its hopes," he wrote. "The fact is that Caruso must not have been or must not be in full possession of his powers, or else he was paralyzed by fear." He concluded by calling him "the little tenor from the Lirico who wanted to take a step too long for his leg, and broke it."

Giovanni Pozza of the *Corriere della Sera*, too, was disappointed, questioning whether the part of Rodolfo was simply not suited to Caruso or whether he had been ill. Even Nappi of *Perseveranza*, Caruso's early supporter, admitted sadly that the "result did not live up to the expectations." He wondered if the acoustics in La Scala were to blame or whether the singer had been paralyzed by the lukewarm reception to his first aria; but he concluded charitably that poor health must have been the cause of his dismal performance.

This time Caruso did not respond to a cold audience and a poor press by threatening to withdraw. Instead, recovered from his indisposition, he proved in the following nine performances of Puccini's masterpiece, each enthusiastically acclaimed, that he had merely had one off-night, and that he had by no means taken a step too long for his leg.

His second role at La Scala was that of Florindo in Mascagni's new and eagerly awaited opera *Le Maschere* on January 17, 1901. Rarely had a new work been heralded by such publicity — the première took place simultaneously in six Italian opera houses (at Milan, Venice, Rome, Verona, Genoa, and Turin) with another "first performance" a few nights later in Naples. The opera was a complete failure, and survived three performances at La Scala only because of Caruso's performance. It was widely agreed that it was only when he was singing that the listless work showed any signs of coming to life.

In spite of another false start, Caruso had proven beyond doubt that he was a valuable addition to La Scala's distinguished roster of tenors; "official" recognition of this came to him two weeks after his first performance in the doomed Mascagni opera. On January 27, 1901, Giuseppe Verdi had died, mourned by his countrymen as a national hero. To mark the loss of the beloved composer, a special concert at the opera house was arranged by Verdi's friend Toscanini. The conductor asked for the participation of Tamagno and Borgatti, La Scala's most distinguished tenors. The former was to take part in a duet from *La Forza del Destino* while the latter was chosen to sing in the popular quartet from *Rigoletto*, and in a duet from *Un Ballo in Maschera*. Carelli, who was scheduled to join Borgatti in the duet from *Ballo*, suggested that the newcomer Caruso be selected for the *Rigoletto* quartet, and, after what seems to have been very little hesitation, Toscanini agreed: thus, La Scala's *three* great tenors would be represented in this unique tribute to Verdi.

The great composer's funeral—silent, as he had requested—took place on a chilly February 1. That evening at nine a heartbroken Toscanini climbed solemnly to the podium to conduct the memorial concert. It began with the overture to *Nabucco,* continued with the great chorus from *I Lombardi,* and then came the quartet from the last act of *Rigoletto.* The hushed audience listened in amazement as Caruso sang. Borelli of *L'Alba,* once so scornful, wrote the following day: "The quartet had to be repeated. The tenor Caruso with his marvelous voice, unique for its warmth and smoothness, persuaded all that he would be an incomparable interpreter of the Duke of Mantua." Time was to prove Borelli right.

Though Caruso had by this time established himself as worthy of Italy's greatest opera house and its difficult audience, it was not until his performance in a rather hastily prepared production of Donizetti's *L'Elisir d'Amore* that he established himself as a genuine star. Following the third performance of *Le Maschere* it became clear to Gatti-Casazza and Toscanini that there was no public for Mascagni's opera—a substitute had to be found at once to satisfy the subscribers. The two young men pondered the problem at length, agreeing that they needed a light comic work to take the place of Mascagni's hopeless comic opera. Finally, Gatti came up with the idea of producing Donizetti's delightful *L'Elisir d'Amore,* which had not been heard at La Scala for many years. The conductor enthusiastically agreed—only the question of casting remained. For the romantic young couple, there were no problems. Regina Pinkert was engaged for the role of Adina, and Caruso, though he had never sung it, agreed to study the role of Nemorino. But casting the key comic role of Dulcamara, the quack-medicine salesman, presented a serious problem, for the role required a basso buffo with a mastery of a comic style no longer in vogue. Finally, an aging basso, Federico Carbonetti, was suggested. Once a notable Beckmesser in *Die Meistersinger,* Carbonetti had in recent years been reduced to singing roles in minor provincial opera houses. Desperate, the directors of La Scala reluctantly agreed to summon him to Milan.

Rehearsals began in an atmosphere of gloom. The news that the distinguished opera house would be mounting a production of the lightweight *L'Elisir d'Amore* was met with derision, critics claiming that, charming though it was, it was hardly suitable for Italy's grandest opera house. A fiasco on the scale of *Le Maschere* was predicted. Toscanini, though firm in his belief in the opera itself, nonetheless found it difficult to disagree with those who found the choice of Carbonetti unworthy of La Scala standards. The elderly basso's voice irritated him, and the success of the opera depended in large part upon his portrayal of the role.

On the morning of the première, the maestro, not known for his even

disposition, was in a worse mood than usual. He was convinced that he and
Gatti had made a serious error and that the production would be a disaster.
Gatti-Casazza described that first performance of L'Elisir d'Amore, on the
night of February 17, in his memoirs:

> In the evening, it was not a large audience that attended the
> première, but to make up for its lack of number, those who did
> come were ill disposed and ready to teach me a lesson — also the
> artists and even Donizetti if necessary.
>
> Toscanini appears with his face still dark. He takes his place at
> the desk and the opera commences. The chorus sings its
> strophes; Adina relates with grace and feeling the story of the
> love of Queen Isolde and the magic philtre; Nemorino in a song
> sighs deliciously; but the public takes no interest and remains
> cold. Not even Belcore, whom the baritone Magini-Coletti
> impersonates in a masterly manner, succeeds in winning approv-
> al of those terrible subscribers of the Scala. The second act with
> the concerted scene of Adina, Nemorino, Belcore and the chorus,
> ends almost in silence. An ugly state of affairs. Back on the stage
> I feel my blood freezing and I begin to fear that the evening will
> end disastrously. Through a peep-hole I watch the public and I
> see that it is in ill humor and bored. I glance at Toscanini. He has
> regained his composure and is directing with his customary ele-
> gance and masterly style.
>
> The duets begin and Adina is delivering her phrases delight-
> fully, but when she finishes some murmurs of approval are sud-
> denly repressed. Now it is Caruso's turn. Who that heard him
> would not remember? Calm and conscious that at this point will
> be decided the fate of the performance, he modulated the reply,
> "Chiedi, al rio perchè gemente," with a voice, a sentiment and an
> art which no word could ever adequately describe. He melted the
> cuirass of ice with which the public had invested itself, little by
> little capturing his audience, subjugating it, conquering it, lead-
> ing it captive.
>
> Caruso had not yet finished the last note of the cadenza when
> an explosion, a tempest of cheers, of applause and of enthusiasm
> on the part of the entire public saluted the youthful conqueror.
> So uproariously and imperatively did the house demand repeti-
> tion that Toscanini, notwithstanding his aversion, was com-
> pelled to grant it. When the curtain fell, Nemorino and Adina
> had a triple ovation. During the intermission only Caruso was

talked about and the old subscribers compared him to Mario, to Giulini, to Gayarré, and recalled their glory.

To Toscanini, who came upon the stage with a face less gloomy, I remarked, "It seems to me that the battle is won."

"All right," he replied, "provided the quack doctor doesn't upset the basket."

Carbonetti did not upset the basket; his richly comic interpretation of the role, his mastery of the style needed for it, made even the most skeptical members of the audience cheer. The greatest acclaim, however, was reserved for Caruso, toward the close of the opera, after his stirring rendition of "*Una furtiva lagrima*," which almost had to be repeated a third time.

Following the performance, Toscanini warmly embraced the tenor; and, in a burst of enthusiasm, he predicted to Gatti, "By God, if this Neapolitan continues to sing like this, he will make the whole world talk about him." At the same time he wrote Boito of the young tenor "who sings like an angel." (Toscanini's enthusiasm soon cooled. Though the two men were to work together often in the future, the maestro confided to a biographer, B. H. Haggin, many years later: "But in 1901, is already change; and in New York—! I tell him, 'Yes, you make much money—but no! no! NO!!!' ")

Any reservations on the part of Milan's critics concerning La Scala's new tenor now disappeared. Pozza in *Corriere della Sera* wrote of Caruso's triumph, adding that "the role of Nemorino seems to have been written for him. He sang with a grace, a sweetness, and an incomparable facility of voice." Achille Tedeschi, writing in *L'Illustrazione Italiana*, noted: "This *Elisir* has in the tenor Caruso a champion, by now rare and precious, of the Italian school of singing which we have taught the whole world."

Caruso's final role that season was that of Faust in *Mefistofele*. Though generously applauded by the audience, he was faulted by the press for what seemed to them an awkwardness in his interpretation. Quite possibly this was due to the overpowering stage presence of Feodor Chaliapin, the great Russian bass and polished actor, who was making his La Scala debut—in fact, his first performance outside of Russia—in the title role in Boito's opera. Compared to the masterful Russian, all performers seemed awkward, and Caruso felt no jealousy toward, but only admiration for, his colleague. The two singers became friends, and on March 16, following the first of nine performances together, the bass proclaimed Caruso's the perfect voice, one he had waited years to hear. Following that performance, too, the venerated Masini joined other tenors in proclaiming the young Neapolitan his one and only heir.

*

The trying La Scala season successfully concluded, Caruso embarked once again for South America with a company led this time by Toscanini, who would be conducting in Buenos Aires for the first time. The tenor's rise to fame had been rapid, and he was learning that maintaining his position would require long periods of hard work, with little time for rest between engagements.

Caruso opened the new Buenos Aires season with a performance of *Tosca* on the night of May 19; starring with him was the Rumanian soprano Hariclea Darclée, who had created the role at its première in Rome. The evening was a rousing success, with Caruso forced to repeat his third-act aria, over the angry objections of the fiery maestro, who always believed that an encore violated the integrity of the composer's score.

When, three months later, on August 17, the season came to a close, Caruso had sung many of his familiar roles — *The Queen of Sheba*, *Rigoletto*, *L'Elisir d'Amore*, *Iris*, and *La Traviata*. He also participated in a special performance of Rossini's *Stabat Mater*, as a memorial to King Umberto of Italy. In addition, the season was notable for the tenor's first and only appearance in a Wagnerian opera, *Lohengrin*. The opera, conducted by Toscanini, was performed in Italian three times. Apparently it was not a great success, for Caruso never repeated the experience. A few years later, during his early years in New York, he spoke of this to Adelaide Louise Samson of *The Morning Telegraph*. While he claimed that he hoped to sing again in Wagnerian operas — at least in *Lohengrin*, *Tristan und Isolde*, and *Die Meistersinger*, which he considered "Italian" — he expressed his reservations. "Wagner did not write his musical dramas for the voice, but for the orchestra," he said. "The latter is all important, the voice is merely considered as an instrument. . . . I personally should fear the effect of a season of Wagner; not only the strain of vocalization, but the strain of the German language upon my vocal chords."

*

At the end of the summer, upon his return to Italy, Caruso was ready for what he was certain would be the most satisfying engagement of his career to date: his debut at the Teatro San Carlo, the most distinguished theater of his native city of Naples. He was returning home in triumph, a star with an international reputation. Inevitably, he had changed since his early days. His trim figure had expanded; he had learned to eat and drink well but had never found the time for exercise. Through travel and experience in some of the world's great opera houses, he had gained self-confidence — it was reflected in the way he held himself and in the care he took in the selection of his clothing. Most important, he knew that he would be returning to his home a far more polished artist than the pleasant, velvet-voiced young tenor who had left there only a few years before.

Before going to Naples in December, he had only two commitments to fulfill — at Bologna and Treviso. He was able to spend the rest of the time tirelessly preparing for his San Carlo debut. Work constituted no sacrifice for him; it was the essential part of his existence. He found little pleasure in ordinary intellectual pursuits — "I learn from life, not from books," he was to say many years later; and life to him was a pleasure, immeasurably enriched by his artistic pursuits.

Well rested and in buoyant spirits, Caruso had every reason to expect a hero's welcome from his fellow Neapolitans, but his self-confidence and his joy at singing in Naples again had blinded him from the facts of operatic life at San Carlo. The magnificent theater, one of Italy's greatest, was more than an operatic stage — it was, in the words of Daspuro, who was there at the time of Caruso's debut, "a stormy sea, and the artists, even the most famous, when they came to it were in need of a good pilot and a good knowledge of the public so as not to run up against the rocks and not get stranded on some stage by a sudden change of wind."

Caruso, a Neapolitan who had never lost touch with his native city, should have known the complex problems that confronted him. First of all, there was the theater's glorious recent past; he was challenging some of the most illustrious tenors in the history of San Carlo, each of whom still had his devoted partisans. Among these were De Lucia and Borgatti, as well as singers who had specialized in the roles to be assumed by Caruso: Julian Gayarré, renowned for his interpretations of Donizetti's heroes; his new friend, though still a rival, Masini, famous for his singing of Nemorino in *L'Elisir;* and Edoardo Garbin, still remembered by Neapolitans for his triumphant *Manon* of a few years before. Caruso not only had to compete against the remembered triumphs of these great tenors, but he had to do so before one of the most demanding and, unfortunately, corrupt audiences in the world, controlled by a powerful, opinionated group of men who believed themselves to be the custodians of the sacred traditions of San Carlo.

This extraordinary tribunal of opera-lovers, whose influence held sway over each San Carlo performance, had been labeled the *"sicofanti"* — the sycophants. Their leaders were the Cavaliere Alfredo Monaco, Marquise Cocozza, the Baron Savelli, and, most important of all, the tall, elegant, bearded Prince Adolfo di Castagneto. Their subtle signals to obedient followers in the audience, making clear how they felt each artist should be received, would set the tone for the evening.

The leaders of these *sicofanti* could be bought — if not by money, by flattery and by the deference they felt due them by each new artist privileged to sing on the stage of San Carlo. Caruso, intoxicated by his past successes and sure he would be greeted with open arms by his fellow Neapolitans, failed to present himself with bowed head to these opinion makers; he failed to pay his respects in any way to them. He gave out no free tickets, a common practice, and he made contact with none of the city's influential newspaper critics before his first appearance. If a good pilot — as suggested by Daspuro — had offered his services to the tenor, the latter had rejected the offer, certain that he was in no need of help.

The eagerly awaited San Carlo debut took place on the night of December 30, 1901; the opera was the familiar *L'Elisir d'Amore*, conducted by Mascheroni. The soprano was Regina Pinkert, who had appeared with him the night of his tremendous success at La Scala, a success he felt certain could be duplicated at San Carlo. When a smiling Caruso, with Pinkert at his side, came to the front of the stage, he was heartened by the warm reception accorded him by his friends from all parts of the theater; all parts, that is, but the first few rows of the right side of the orchestra, where the leaders of the *sicofanti* sat. From that part of the house, there were sustained hisses, cries of "Enough, enough . . . we want to be the ones to judge him." Daspuro described the experience: "Caruso, so sensitive, so susceptible, froze; pale, perturbed, perplexed. He probably felt the best way to win the public was to display his powerful vocal skills. And indeed, in a short time the *sicofanti*, the critics, and the friends of other tenors began to insinuate that that was the way to sing *Otello* but not a sweet idyll like *L'Elisir d'Amore*."

During the intermission and after the performance the judgment of the unofficial tribunal was spread throughout the lobby. Yes, Caruso had a good voice, but it could hardly be compared to that of the really great tenors. No matter what the general public felt or what Caruso's old friends believed, he had not, according to the *sicofanti*, been a successful Nemorino.

The press the following day echoed the judgment expressed in the lobby, reviewers agreeing that a lighter voice was required for Donizetti's comic masterpiece. Baron Saverio Procida, critic for *Il Pungolo*, was especially severe. He not only found Caruso's "not beautiful" voice too "baritonal and throaty"; he also felt that the tenor's acting had been unconvincing.

Caruso's San Carlo debut, though not a triumph, was not really a disaster. Audience response had been mixed, and not completely hostile. Nonetheless, he was deeply hurt by the reception accorded him in the city of his birth. He had desperately wanted to emerge triumphant before his friends and family. Disappointed and bitter, he cut out Procida's stinging review and carried it with him so that he would never forget his humiliation.

Caruso sang four more performances of Donizetti's opera as well as five performances of Massenet's *Manon* — the latter with Rina Giacchetti, Ada's sister. Following that first performance of *Manon*, he was recognized for his true worth by the Neapolitan public, and finally even by the *sicofanti*. However, he was unable to forgive the San Carlo public for spoiling what he had hoped and expected would be a memorably happy night. At his later performances, he sang with technical brilliance but refused to give all of himself, to share with the audience that unique warmth which set him apart from other singers of his time. His performances could not be faulted — they were good, solid, and professional, but no more than that. He gave the Neapolitan audience his voice and his mind, but not his soul.

When on January 21 he sang *Manon* for the last time, Caruso bitterly told Daspuro that Naples would never again hear his voice. "I will come back to Naples only to see my dear stepmother and eat spaghetti with clams," he said. He kept his word. He also, according to a story he later told Richard Barthélemy, his accompanist, had his revenge on the *sicofanti*, arranging a conciliatory meeting with their leaders for the afternoon of his departure and abruptly leaving town before the appointment.

VI. Covent Garden: "A Leap into Popularity"

Caruso could well afford to turn his back on San Carlo in anger; if he hadn't been properly appreciated in his own city, he had ample proof that he was appreciated and sought after elsewhere. He was negotiating with New York's Metropolitan Opera, a Covent Garden debut was in the offing, and, before either of these, he was to sing at the Monte Carlo Opéra, an engagement that was sure to add to his growing reputation as an international star.

Monte Carlo's opera house was a small one, with a capacity of only six hundred, but under impresario Raoul Gunsbourg it had achieved worldwide recognition for its inventive productions and its distinguished casts. For the winter season of 1902, Caruso was part of a company which included one of the world's greatest tenors, the fifty-two-year-old Jean de Reszke, past his prime but still an artist of impeccable refinement. More important to his future, the young Neapolitan was to make his debut, as Rodolfo in *La Bohème,* opposite the undisputed queen of opera, the Australian Nellie Melba. Melba was the *prima donna assoluta* wherever she sang, and she knew her worth. While Caruso was to be paid three thousand francs for each performance, she would receive eight thousand, four hundred. There was no doubt that the self-confident, strong-willed soprano was the star, and she played the role brilliantly both off the stage and on.

Melba had sung the role of Mimi—which she said was her favorite—

with her friend De Reszke and, at Covent Garden in 1899, with De Lucia; she had created it at the Metropolitan première of *La Bohème* in 1898. The role was hers, and she approached the Monte Carlo production with a new tenor confidently—he had to prove himself, not she, though even the great Melba admitted that she was afflicted with nervousness before every performance. "It's when you are the diva," she once said, "that you have to become nervous. When you are climbing up, you just do your best. When you are the diva, you have to be the best always." (Caruso, the new divo, was also learning this.)

Nonetheless, if Caruso was nervous—and he must have been—he showed no trace of it to the glittering audience that filled the jewel-like opera house on the night of February 1, 1902. In attendance for the gala evening were Prince Albert and his entourage, as well as Puccini, who, because of his own nervousness, refused the prince's offer to join him in the royal box during the performance. Caruso was not fazed. Soon after conductor Arturo Vigna climbed to the podium and began the opera, he proved himself as worthy to sing with the great Melba as had her previous Rodolfos. The soprano remembered the occasion in her memoirs: "Caruso absolutely captivated Monte Carlo," she wrote. "As a voice—pure and simple—his was the most wonderful tenor I have ever heard. It rolled out like an organ. It had a magnificent ease, and a truly golden richness."

It was the beginning of a legendary partnership—"never clouded for an instant," Melba wrote later, noting that in the third act of *La Bohème* she felt that their two voices had merged into one. They made a curious pair: the elegant, ladylike Australian and the rather awkward, stocky Neapolitan, twelve years her junior, only then beginning to feel at ease among the international society that adored Melba. Apparently, however, Caruso already felt sufficiently at ease to begin playing the onstage jokes that often delighted but sometimes irritated his colleagues. "Never shall I forget one night at Monte Carlo, before an audience 'thick' with grand dukes and princesses and marchesas, how I was suddenly startled in the middle of the death scene by a strange squeaking noise which seemed to come from Caruso as he bent over me," Melba wrote of one *Bohème* performance. "I went on singing, but I could not help wondering at the time if Caruso was ill, for his face was drawn and solemn, and every time he bent down there was this same extraordinary noise of squeaking. And then with a gulp which almost made me forget my part, I realized that he had a little rubber toy in his hand, which at the most pathetic phrases he was pressing in my ear."

At another performance of Puccini's opera, Caruso pressed a hot sausage into Melba's frozen hand during the aria *"Che gelida manina,"* causing the startled soprano to hurl the sausage into the air. Though she professed to believe that he was "a simple, lovable creature," it is doubtful that Dame Nellie fully appreciated her young colleague's childlike playfulness—she was far too serious for that. In spite of their differences in temperament, however, the couple caused a sensation that season in Monte Carlo (during which they also appeared together in *Rigoletto*) as they did whenever and wherever they sang together.

✳

Caruso and Melba were to be reunited at Covent Garden within a few months. Before that, the tenor had promised to return to La Scala to create the role of Federico Loewe in Alberto Franchetti's new opera, *Germania*. The Baron Franchetti, who had once wanted to set Sardou's *La Tosca* to music but had been outmaneuvered by Puccini, was a composer of some talent; but, because of his great personal wealth and important connections, his new opera was more eagerly awaited than it might ordinarily have been. Because of Franchetti's influence among Milanese operatic circles, the work's première on the night of March 11, 1902, was a gala event, attended by a large number of dukes, duchesses, counts and countesses as well as prominent figures in the arts—Puccini, Giordano, and Gabriele D'Annunzio among them.

The opera achieved a moderate success—it was performed fourteen times during the La Scala season and sporadically thereafter—and Caruso was praised for his interpretation of the new role, which he later repeated in Buenos Aires and New York. Most important, however, the tenor's appearances in Franchetti's opera led to a meeting with Fred Gaisberg, the manager of London's Gramophone and Typewriter Company, and a pioneer in the new medium of sound recording. Gaisberg and his brother Will had come to Milan in search of artists for a series of records the English company planned to press. Upon Gaisberg's arrival, the firm's local representative, Alfred Michaelis, informed him that two tenors—Caruso and Bonci—were causing a sensation at La Scala, and that either or both of them should be immediately engaged. Though he failed to get tickets for the première of *Germania*, Gaisberg managed to find seats for the second performance; overwhelmed by the power and beauty of Caruso's voice, he immediately dispatched Michaelis to find out what the tenor's fee would be. Caruso had briefly experimented with the new medium in 1901, and he welcomed this opportunity to try again. The following day an agreement was concluded. He would sing ten arias for one hundred pounds; because of his busy schedule, all ten selections would have to be sung in the course of one afternoon. Gaisberg enthusiastically transmitted these terms to his main office in London. The reply, cabled at once, was disappointing: "Fee exorbitant, forbid you to record." Nonetheless, Gaisberg went ahead and a recording session was arranged for April 11 in his suite at the Grand Hotel di Milano. It was a memorable occasion, the birth of a great recording artist and that of a fabulously successful industry. Gaisberg recalled it with admirable simplicity in his memoirs. "One sunny afternoon, Caruso, debonaire and fresh, sauntered into our studio and in exactly two hours sang ten arias to the piano accompaniment of Maestro Cottone. . . . Not one *stecca*, blemish, or huskiness marred this feat."

The ten arias had included selections from *Rigoletto, Manon, Tosca, L'Elisir d'Amore, Iris, Aida, Germania,* and *Mefistofele,* and the release of these historic recordings was timed to coincide with Caruso's first appearance at Covent Garden. He had been engaged for a season there at the suggestion of his good friend and fellow Neapolitan, the baritone Antonio Scotti, who had been a favorite in the London opera house since 1899. Scotti had never sung with Caruso, but he had met him in Milan in 1898 and had greatly admired his voice. When Henry Higgins, manager of Covent Garden, told Scotti that he urgently needed an outstanding new tenor for his company, the baritone at once suggested Caruso, assuring Higgins that he would cause a sensation at England's greatest opera house. Higgins, having already heard favorable reports of the tenor from the continent, asked Scotti to relay a firm offer to Caruso. The fee suggested was lower than that paid Caruso by La Scala, however, and only Scotti's insistence on the prestige of Covent Garden and the desirability of singing with more of the world's greatest singers convinced Caruso to undertake the London season.

It was a wise decision, and it led to the beginning of an extraordinarily affirmative relationship between Caruso and the English-speaking public. He quickly became and remained for that public the quintessence of the Italian tenor: jovial, well-fed, with a rich, full, sensuous voice, somehow the embodiment of the sunshine of his native land.

His first performance, on the night of May 14, 1902, as the Duke in *Rigoletto,* with Melba and the distinguished French baritone Maurice Renaud, was a rousing success and an indication of what was to come. The warmth and sweetness of his voice easily won over the audience, which included Queen Alexandra, and the following day the critics cheered the auspicious debut of the Neapolitan tenor.

"Signor Caruso," the *Illustrated London News* reported, "has a vitality and exuberance of expression that carries the audience with him, and a voice that, though powerful, is always melodious." For the critic of the *Sunday Times,* he was "the most gifted vocalist that Italy has sent us for some years past." The reviewer for the *Daily Telegraph* agreed. "His value was at once perceived and acknowledged," he reported. "Mr. Caruso has an ample voice, round and resonant, and he employs it with the discretion and skill that only an experienced artist can claim." News of Caruso also reached America, and the correspondent for New York's *Musical Courier* wrote: "The success of the evening was scored by Caruso, the new tenor. From the moment that he first opened his mouth his fate never hung in the balance, and Covent Garden has evidently brought us at last a new tenor who is really worth hearing. . . ."

On May 24, the London public was given its first and eagerly awaited opportunity to hear Caruso and Melba together in *La Bohème*. They were not disappointed. The *Illustrated London News* reported: "Caruso made a leap into popularity," while the astonished correspondent for *Musical Courier* noted that Melba "seems to act all the better with Caruso to play to."

On June 4, he sang the role of Edgardo in *Lucia di Lammermoor*. The dramatic role of the heroine, sung by the Portuguese soprano Regina Pacini, of course, dominated the evening, and Pacini's success was tremendous. Nonetheless, Caruso sang so well that critics noted with surprise that the audience remained in their seats to hear the final scene, instead of abandoning the theater as they customarily did after Lucia's spectacular Mad Scene.

On June 6, Caruso scored again, this time as Radames in *Aida*, opposite the great American soprano Lillian Nordica in her last London season. *The Daily Telegraph* reported that Caruso's Radames "was a figure fully worthy to stand beside those with which he has already graced the Covent Garden boards," and the *Musical Courier* reported that as Radames he proved again to be "a singer with a glorious voice and dramatic powers of no mean order."

It was an unbroken string of dazzling achievements. On June 14, Caruso captivated audiences with his portrayal of Nemorino in *L'Elisir d'Amore*, an opera not heard as part of the regular season of Covent Garden for almost a quarter of a century. Two weeks later, he was acclaimed for his performance in *Cavalleria Rusticana*, singing with Emma Calvé, and on July 4, he appeared with Melba in *La Traviata*.

The night of July 19 was of special interest, for Caruso made his first appearance in a Mozart opera, singing the role of Don Ottavio in *Don Giovanni*. He was part of an illustrious cast that included Renaud as the protagonist, Antonio Pini-Corsi as Leporello, Marcel Journet as the Commendatore, Fritzi Scheff as Zerlina, and Félia Litvinne and Suzanne Adams as Donna Anna and Donna Elvira. Caruso was not then—or ever—thought of as a Mozart singer, and he never sang Mozart outside of London, yet his success was extraordinary. "He sang his role magnificently," the critic for the *Pall Mall Gazette* reported, and the Russian-born soprano Litvinne wrote in her memoirs that he was an "incomparable Don Ottavio, with a luminous voice." Litvinne mentioned, too, that Caruso was unable to refrain from playing his little jokes, even during the Mozart opera. "When he came on the stage, with Donna Anna and Donna Elvira on his arms, for the trio of the masks, he made me laugh by saying, 'I am a samovar,' " she wrote. Later performances in *Don Giovanni* won equal acclaim. In 1905, when Caruso again sang the role of Don Ottavio, the reviewer for the *Pall Mall Gazette* noted: "Quite a feature of the performance was the impersonation by Signor Caruso of the part of Don Ottavio. . . . Caruso proved that a really great tenor is needed to sing with complete success the very difficult songs allotted to Don Ottavio. For example, it is rare enough that one hears '*Il mio tesoro*,' save in its lovely opening passages, made extremely interesting; for some reason or another the latter part of the song very often falls flat. Caruso showed how it should be sung, and achieved a very great success." The following year, when he sang the small but demanding role for the last time, critics again commended him for his complete understanding of and sensitivity to Mozart's intentions.

Caruso's triumphant season at Covent Garden came to an end on the night of July 28, when he was again paired with Melba for a performance of *Rigoletto*. The evening was colorfully described by the correspondent of the *Musical Courier*:

> The house was one of the most brilliant of the season. Hours before the curtain rose every seat in the theatre had been taken and people were being turned away from the doors, while the cheaper part, such as the gallery slips, which is really the best part of the house for hearing, was crowded three deep. The audience was quite extraordinary. In addition to the customary array of dukes and duchesses, there was a large sprinkling of Oriental potentates in picturesque costume — the Maharajah of Jaipur occupied a box and took a keen interest in the proceedings. . . . Lesser potentates in really remarkable raiment filled the stalls and the only notability whom we missed was King Lewanika. Doubtless, however, he feared trouble with his twelve little wives at home if it came to their ears that he had gazed on the attractive maidens who constitute the Covent Garden chorus. At the end of the opera a startling innovation was introduced by a number of Australian and New Zealand troopers in

the boxes, who gave vent to their enthusiasm by a series of cat calls, the like of which can never have been heard in Covent Garden before. . . .

Caruso loved it all. He was growing accustomed to royalty, to contact with the upper strata of society, and he took a special delight in his acceptance by the London public in view of what he still looked upon bitterly as a rejection by his own people in Naples. On stage, he delighted audiences with his impassioned, resonant voice and his unforgettable interpretations of roles which had not been sung so brilliantly in London in many a year. Backstage, he enchanted appreciative stagehands with his jovial good humor and his childlike pranks, and he entertained them — and himself — with his improvised, increasingly perceptive caricatures; his skill as a caricaturist had developed effortlessly since his childhood and he practiced it with enthusiasm.

Away from the theater, he established a firm friendship with Paolo Tosti, the Italian composer of popular songs, who was a darling of English society and singing teacher to the royal family. Caruso frequented the Tuesday luncheons at Tosti's house near Oxford Street, and in time he, Scotti and Tosti presided over a long table at Pagani's, a small restaurant in Great Portland Street behind Queen's Hall. The walls of Pagani's were covered with autographed photos of Tamagno, Calvé, Sarah Bernhardt, Richard Strauss, Tchaikovsky, Melba, Mascagni, Leoncavallo, Fritz Kreisler, Puccini, Paderewski, and Maurice Maeterlinck — all of whom dined at the Italian restaurant during their stays in the British capital.

During this first visit to London, too, Caruso made the acquaintance of the beautiful and wealthy Sybil Seligman, Puccini's closest confidante, who was hostess to every visiting Italian of note and whose elegant home on Upper Grosvenor Street became an unofficial salon throughout the opera season. In his book *Puccini Among Friends*, her son Vincent Seligman recalled Caruso's visits to their home that first year:

My mother had met Caruso shortly after his first appearance at Covent Garden in the summer of 1902, when, like everybody else, she had promptly fallen in love with his voice. Thereafter he became a constant visitor at our house in Upper Grosvenor Street during the Opera Season; when he was not rehearsing or resting his voice preparatory to singing in the evening, he would come to lunch and then — how well, as a little boy, I remember it! — would follow the usual comedy of enticing him towards the piano. Not that my mother ever *asked* him to sing, or even suggested it; with Society hostesses tumbling over each other and offering him fabulous sums to sing a couple of songs at their parties, not even a liberal helping of his beloved macaroni could be regarded as a fair return for the privilege which we were all secretly longing to enjoy. Fortunately his affection for his hostess, his extreme good nature and the lure of the piano nearly always proved sufficient; my mother had only to show him some song with which he was not familiar—it was, incidentally, through her that he became acquainted with many of the numbers which he afterwards sang so successfully at concerts or for His Master's Voice—and the trick was done; for hours on end he would continue to sing, partly to give us pleasure and partly for the sheer joy of singing. Not that the pleasure was confined to my mother and the few friends gathered together in our tiny drawing-room; on these occasions all work was indefinitely suspended in the house, and the servants would congregate together on the stairs outside; moreover, since it was essential in such a small space to have the windows wide open when he was singing, passers-by in the street would stop and listen, spell-bound by the glorious notes that issued forth through the open windows.

❊

A jubilant Caruso returned to his home in Milan in August 1902. His "glorious notes" had carried him to the top of his profession, but his travels had allowed him little time for his beloved Ada and their young son. He was deeply attached to both, but his career would always come first and would deny him—as it inevitably denied most performing artists— many of the pleasures of family life.

He passed the rest of the summer agreeably, enjoying his family and basking in the recognition and esteem accorded him by the Milanese public wherever he went. Happily, his first commitment for the fall—to create the role of Maurizio in Cilea's new opera *Adriana Lecouvreur*— would keep him in Milan for several months. By agreeing to sing the role, he was repaying a debt. Caruso never forgave his enemies—the opera-going public of Naples, for example—but he also never forgot the many friends who had helped him early in his career. Prominent among these had been Cilea and Sonzogno who, when he was little known, had offered him a chance to create the tenor role in *L'Arlesiana*. Now, though sought after by many of the world's greatest opera houses, he could not turn down their offer to participate in the première of the new opera, even if it meant singing again at the Lirico, a theater second in importance to La Scala. His feeling of indebtedness was so great that he even proposed to Sonzogno that he perform without pay. The offer was rejected, but Caruso agreed to the small fee of three thousand lire for six performances, also agreeing that he would provide his own costumes, which cost him at least twice the fee paid by the impresario for the entire engagement.

The première of the new opera took place on the night of November 6, 1902; singing with Caruso were Angelica Pandolfini and his old friend De Luca, and the conductor was Cleofonte Campanini. The opera was more enthusiastically received than the composer's earlier works had been, and Caruso's performance was highly praised. Critics spoke now of his golden voice — it was no longer velvet — and his exquisite diction and unique vocal strength. "Caruso sang divinely," wrote the reviewer for *Perseveranza*. "He delighted the public," noted the critic for *Il Tempo*; "He performed with intense emotion and intense excitement," was the comment of the reviewer for *Lega Lombarda*.

Caruso's triumph had been an apparently easy one, and those who had followed his career were impressed by the progress he had made since his last appearances in Milan. Daspuro, who hadn't heard him sing for some time, was present at the première of *Adriana Lecouvreur* and visited the tenor in his dressing room following the performance. He expressed astonishment at the ease with which Caruso managed the high notes that had troubled him in the past. Caruso explained that he had achieved this ease by simply doing the opposite of what he had been taught. If his answer betrayed a degree of arrogance, it was also based on fact, for he had, in large part, learned to sing by singing; his own instincts, through experience, had been a reliable guide to the proper use and control of his marvelous vocal instrument.

After Milan, Caruso traveled to Trieste for two performances of *Rigoletto*, and then to Rome for his second season at the Costanzi. The highlight of the season was his first performance there in *Manon Lescaut*. The distinguished conductor Vittorio Gui, then a seventeen-year-old student at the Conservatory of Santa Cecilia, recalled, many years later, one of the rehearsals of Puccini's opera.

> I remember Caruso wearing a bowler and holding a cane in his hand. He rehearsed singing *mezza voce*, and he didn't seem to be involved. But suddenly something unexpected and wonderful happened. It was near the end of the third act when Manon is about to board the ship that will take her and the other poor prostitutes to their exile in America. Des Grieux suddenly decides to join his beloved in the hard life of exile and throws himself in front of the captain, begging him to let him come aboard, perhaps as a cabin boy. . . .

Caruso has thrown his hat and cane behind the wings; he is no longer there, in his place the living character of Des Grieux, who explodes with his cry of desperate supplication. A great wave of emotion has overcome all of us—musicians, chorus, conductor. We, the students, dry our tears in the dark. . . . Finally, the rehearsal had to be interrupted: the poor old supporting singer Gironi, who was supposed to answer, "Do you want to go to populate the Americas, young man?" could not go beyond the word "populate" before he burst into tears. The conductor Vitale, the good father figure to us all, took a large white handkerchief from his pocket and, pretending to dry his perspiration, dried his eyes.

The Caruso magic—more than just a brilliant voice or a dazzling technique—was making itself felt wherever "the Emperor of Tenors" (as *Musical Courier* had already described him) sang. The Rome season was followed by his first engagement in Lisbon where, over the period of one month, he delighted Portuguese audiences with his brilliant performances in *Fedora, Aida, Tosca, Adriana Lecouvreur,* Donizetti's *Lucrezia Borgia,* and *Rigoletto.* A few performances of *Tosca,* with Darclée, followed in Monte Carlo, after which the indefatigable tenor embarked on his fourth trip to South America. Before doing so, however, he took time out to buy his first home, the sumptuous Villa alle Panche in the Tuscan countryside near Florence. It was a significant step: the purchase of a home he had dreamed of as well as a symbol of his final separation from the crowded streets of Naples.

*

When Caruso left Italy on April 15, 1903, he was again part of a star-studded company which included Darclée, Krusheniski, De Luca, Giraldoni, and, as principal conductor, Toscanini. He was greeted as an old friend by his enthusiastic admirers in Buenos Aires and Montevideo, after which the company traveled to Rio de Janeiro, where Caruso would make his Brazilian debut. One incident marred his succession of triumphs during the Rio season. At the last moment, it was announced that Caruso would be joined in a performance of *Manon Lescaut* by a local soprano whose previous appearances at the Teatro Pedro II had been considerably less than successful. The public showed its disfavor with the casting of the little-esteemed soprano by staying away. As a result, the opera house was half empty—already a rarity for a Caruso appearance—and the performance was a dispirited one.

The following day, the tenor was as usual lunching at the Hotel dos Extrangeros; at a nearby table sat the opera house's impresario. Caruso approached him, saying he noted that he was in a bad mood. When the impresario denied this, Caruso admitted that he himself was in a bad mood because he was unaccustomed to singing before an unenthusiastic audience in a half-empty theater. He proposed a solution: that the uninspired performance should be forgotten and an extra performance scheduled, for which the tenor expected no pay. In that way, the failure would effectively be forgotten, a strong performance erasing that failure from the memories of all concerned with it.

Apart from that one unfortunate evening, the Rio engagement had been a satisfying one. Dorian Gray, *Musical Courier*'s correspondent in Rio, reported: "The grand attraction this year has been Enrico Caruso. From the time of Gayarré, Mario, and Tamberlik, there had not been heard such a voice. He was heard in *Tosca, Rigoletto, Manon Lescaut*, and *Iris*, enchanting all who heard him with his marvelous effects." The reporter ended, prophetically: "Caruso goes to New York, and I am sure will occupy the vacant place of de Reszke."

VII. New York

New York's Metropolitan Opera desperately needed a tenor to take the place of Jean de Reszke, who had reigned as the company's "Italian" tenor for most of the past decade. The charming, elegant Pole — whose good manners, impeccable taste, and splendid voice had won the hearts of the members of New York society who patronized the opera house — was reaching the end of his career. His last performances at the Metropolitan had taken place at the end of the 1900–1901 season. In spite of this, the management of the Metropolitan seemed in no hurry to find a tenor to take his place.

Caruso had been dealing with various officials of the New York opera house for a number of years. As early as 1899, an elderly Milanese agent named Fano, who represented the Metropolitan's managing director, Maurice Grau, in Italy, had offered the young tenor the astoundingly small sum of two hundred dollars a week for a twenty-week season, and Caruso, still little known and eager to have the opportunity to sing in New York, had agreed. But Fano had difficulty in reaching Grau to confirm the agreement, and after two months Caruso gave up. He could no longer turn down other engagements while waiting for the New York company to make up its mind.

The Metropolitan came through with another offer after Grau had learned of the tenor's enormous success in Monte Carlo. By that time, however, Caruso was sought by opera companies all over the world and no longer willing to sing anywhere for a mere two hundred dollars a week. After a great deal of bargaining back and forth, with Fano as intermediary, it was agreed that the tenor would come to New York for the 1903–1904 season to sing forty performances for a fee of approximately one thousand dollars each. Before he had a chance to make plans for New York, however, Caruso learned that Grau had resigned due to poor health. The contract with the Metropolitan, under a unique arrangement whereby the singer was tied to the managing director and not to the company itself, was thus no longer valid.

Grau's successor was named on February 14, 1903; he was a Viennese-born actor and manager named Heinrich Conried, who had come to New York in 1877 and had quickly made a name for himself in the theater. A strict disciplinarian, he was known primarily for his tremendously efficient sense of organization as manager of the Irving Place Theater, which had won plaudits for its diversified repertory and brilliant stagings. Though he had an undeniably brilliant instinct for the theater, Conried was ignorant of both the opera and of opera singers; for this reason, his engagement by the Metropolitan had come as a complete surprise to him and to the New York public.

Caruso's agreement was on the new managing director's desk when he took over the reins of the opera company. He was interested—he knew that the company badly needed a new tenor—but though he had heard reports of Caruso's success, he had also heard of the growing fame of Alessandro Bonci. There was, he felt, no reason to engage two new Italian tenors for his first season at the opera house, but he was not prepared to make a choice.

✳

Caruso had learned of the Metropolitan's change of management while singing in Lisbon. Though puzzled by the complexities of his contract, he was still eager to sing in New York and he asked an acquaintance, Pasquale Simonelli, president of the Italian Savings Bank of New York, to act as his representative and discuss the validity of his old Met agreement with the new managing director. Simonelli called on Conried. The latter, having been told of Caruso's remarkable talent by the baritone Scotti, who had become a leading singer at the Metropolitan following his Covent Garden triumphs, agreed to engage Caruso—but for twenty performances and not the forty previously agreed upon. A compromise of twenty-five performances was reached, and the tenor made plans to come to New York. By the time Conried finally heard Caruso's voice—via a recording of "*Vesti la giubba*"—he was prepared to return to his previous offer of forty performances, but it was too late. The tenor, who learned of the new offer in Buenos Aires in May 1903, had already committed himself to sing in Monte Carlo following his twenty-five performances at the Metropolitan.

Nonetheless, Conried had hired an Italian tenor after all. When he had taken over the management of the Metropolitan, he had repeatedly boasted that he would build a company that would never be dependent upon stars. Without realizing it at the time, he had engaged a singer who would be the greatest star of the new twentieth century.

The Metropolitan roster had been rich in sopranos for many years. Melba had been a favorite there, as had the Yugoslav Milka Ternina and two great American singers, Emma Eames and the extraordinary Lillian Nordica. Among those engaged for the 1903–1904 season were some of the greatest names in the history of opera: Calvé, Olive Fremstad, the German Johanna Gadski, and the remarkable Polish soprano Marcella Sembrich. The great Italian tenors, however, because of the dominance of German and French works during the leadership of Grau, had been neglected since the last days of Italo Campanini twenty years before. De Lucia had sung in New York for only one season, that of 1893–1894; and Tamagno had met with little success at the Metropolitan — the influential critic Gustav Kobbé had called him "a mere shouter of high notes." With the retirement of De Reszke, who had assumed the important Italian roles during his years in New York, the time was right for the appearance of a tenor who could restore the Italian repertory to its proper place at the most important of American opera houses.

De Reszke himself had, upon hearing Caruso in London, predicted that the Neapolitan would one day be his successor, and the American press had reported the tenor's astounding successes in Europe, yet no more than the ordinary amount of fanfare surrounded Caruso's first visit to America. Accompanied by Ada, he arrived aboard the *SS Sardegna* on November 11, 1903 — only twelve days before his scheduled debut at the Metropolitan. The couple — Caruso made much of his happy "marriage" and ideal family life to questioning reporters — were taken at once to their apartment at the Hotel Majestic at 72nd Street and Central Park West. Orders were given that for the period of his stay there, no visitors would be allowed access to the apartment on those days when he was to sing; to make certain that this would be enforced, a list of performance dates was presented to the hotel's chief clerk.

Before his debut, however, there was the inevitable round of interviews with various members of the press. "He is a wholesome good-looking person, this young Neapolitan," a reporter for the *Telegraph* informed his readers. "Deep-chested, full-throated, square-shouldered, a fine upstanding specimen of a man, not far from thirty either way. . . . He looks as if he ate and fully digested three square meals a day, besides a snack at bedtime."

In spite of a certain sarcasm concerning his waistline—de Reszke, whom he was to replace, was a strikingly handsome man with a trim figure—Caruso favorably impressed journalists at a press conference held on the afternoon of his arrival. Through an interpreter—he knew little English—he regaled them with humorous stories of his early trials and tribulations, taking special pleasure in recounting the unfortunate incident at Trapani. After playing one of his recordings, he advised the members of the press that his voice onstage was "not as worn as it sounds on the machine." Reporters enjoyed making fun of his stoutness and his lack of "refinement," but they were charmed by his warmth and boyish exuberance and they were enchanted by his quickly drawn caricatures of them and of himself.

That day, too, was Caruso's first chance to meet the man responsible for his coming to New York—Heinrich Conried. The two men had little in common, least of all a language (the banker Simonelli acted as interpreter at their meeting), yet a close bond, built on mutual respect, was quickly formed between the stern, iron-fisted manager and the new tenor. Caruso praised the interior of the opera house, its stage and technical equipment, and Conried was impressed by Caruso's apparent willingness to adhere to the discipline which would be imposed upon him.

✳

Caruso's debut on November 23, 1903, the opening of the Metropolitan season, was also the first performance of the company under its new managing director. Always an occasion for elegance—it was a highlight of the New York social season—this first night was even more festive than usual, for the theater itself had been extensively redecorated. Dull-gold plaster reliefs had been added to the faces of the boxes and balconies, and deep-red upholstered seats had been newly installed as had red velvet drapes. The edge of the stage had receded several feet, enabling the artists to make their curtain calls more gracious, and the orchestra pit had been lowered to allow the audience a more complete view of the stage. Only the glamorous audience, with its plethora of Astors, Vanderbilts, Belmonts, Blisses, Roosevelts, and Morgans, remained unchanged from that which habitually attended the season's opening; it was an audience notoriously more interested in fashion and jewels than in whatever might be happening onstage.

Caruso always maintained that nervous tension preceded each of his appearances—that it was even an essential prelude to a good performance—but he was especially tense as he faced his debut at the Metropolitan. He was tired and not yet used to New York, or its pace. His first days in the city had been exhausting—long hours of rehearsals, followed by meetings with strange people in unfamiliar surroundings. He felt very far from home—he knew European audiences, and those he had encountered in South America had differed little from their European counterparts—and he was burdened by what he sensed to be the extraordinary importance of his American debut. Admittedly, that debut seemed to be taking place under the best of circumstances. His role was a familiar one, that of the Duke in *Rigoletto*—it had served him brilliantly as his introduction to the demanding public of Covent Garden. Singing with him would be his good friend Scotti and Marcella Sembrich, with whom he had established a harmonious rapport during rehearsals, and the conductor, Arturo Vigna, also making his debut that evening, was a musician with whom he had worked before.

As he left his dressing room and the objects which had long served him as good luck charms—a rag doll, a figure of a Zulu warrior, a number of pictures of Madonnas—Caruso had every reason to believe that the New York audience would accord him the enthusiastic welcome to which he had become accustomed. Instead, only scattered applause greeted his first entrance onto the stage as the lecherous Duke. Somewhat taken aback at the public's indifference, his nervousness increased, causing him to crush the fan held by the soprano (Helen Mapleson) playing the minor role of the Countess, as he awkwardly clutched her arm. His first aria, the difficult *"Questa o quella,"* sung immediately afterward, was received politely, but the public reserved whatever enthusiasm it could muster up for the ever-popular Sembrich.

The audience at last warmed to Caruso in the second act; and in the third, the crowd-pleasing *"La donna è mobile"* roused the apathetic public to call for an encore (a not uncommon response to almost any singer's interpretation of the well-known aria). At no point during the entire performance did Caruso receive anything that might be called an overwhelming ovation; there was no indication, in the audience's response to the new singer, of the importance of this debut to the history of the Metropolitan Opera.

Nonetheless, Caruso's first appearance in New York, overshadowed as it was by the circumstances under which he sang, was in no way a failure, though it was far from the memorable triumph that might have been expected. Historians of music who have expressed disappointment over Caruso's rather lukewarm reception at his debut often forget that he was competing with the popularity of one of the most beloved of all sopranos in one of her finest roles, and that his first appearance in New York took place before a public that knew and cared little about the art of singing.

The press the following day was for the most part more appreciative and enthusiastic than the audience had been. Because of the importance of the occasion, these reviews are worth citing at length. The critic for the New York *Times*, Richard Aldrich, while reserving his greatest praise for Sembrich, termed Caruso's debut a success. "He is an Italian in all his fibre," Aldrich wrote, "and his singing and acting are characteristic of what Italy now affords in those arts. His voice is purely a tenor in its quality, of high range, and of large power, but inclined to take on the 'white' quality in its upper ranges when he lets it forth. In mezza voce it has expressiveness and flexibility, and when so used its beauty is most apparent. Mr. Caruso appeared last evening capable of intelligence and of passion in both his singing and his acting and gave reason to believe in his value as an acquisition to the company."

"Mr. Caruso, the new tenor, made a thoroughly favorable impression, and will probably grow into firm favor with the public," wrote W. J. Henderson in the *Sun*. "He has a pure tenor voice of fine quality and sufficient range and power. It is a smooth and mellow voice and is without the typical Italian Bleat. Mr. Caruso has a natural and free delivery and his voice carries well without forcing. . . ."

Henry Krehbiel of the *Tribune*, like many of his colleagues, devoted most of his review to praise of Sembrich and Scotti, though he wrote of Caruso that "musically he was the finest Duke that New York has heard for a generation." Some reservations followed. "Signor Caruso has many of the tiresome Italian vocal affectations, and when he neglects to cover his tones, as he always does when he becomes strenuous, his voice becomes pallid. But," the critic concluded, "he is generally a manly singer, with a voice that is true, of fine quality and marvelous endurance."

The reviewer for the *Post* commented on the coolness that greeted the tenor on his first appearance but noted that enthusiasm grew from act to act, culminating in an ovation after his third-act aria. "True," he wrote, "he exaggerated its catchpenny effect by his vocal flourishes at the end; but the changes of pace he introduced in the melody made it seem less offensive than usual, and his phrasing, here as in the other numbers, was remarkably artistic and refined. . . ."

Even Gustav Kobbé of the *Morning Telegraph*, while cool and cautious, had a few kind words. "What about Caruso?" he asked. "That is the question everyone interested in opera wants answered today and answered quickly and without equivocation. Answer: Not a great tenor, but an eminently satisfactory one. Not a second Campanini but a tenor who, it is safe to say, will make it possible for Italian opera to have a fair share of the representations at the MOH this season. . . . He is the nearest approach to the popular ideal of what an Italian opera tenor should be that has been heard here for many seasons. . . . Taking into consideration the conditions existing on the operatic stage today, Caruso's debut should be recorded as a success."

More serious reservations were expressed over his physique. The reviewer for the *Herald* noted that "disappointment that he should own so generous a girth could be read on many faces, for, to tell the truth, Signor Caruso is no Antinous." The writer for *The Commercial Advertiser*, while admiring his voice, had to admit that Caruso was not much to look at. "He is short and squat, with little or no neck," he commented. The New York critic for *Musical Courier*, anti-Conried, anti-Met, and chauvinistically pro-America, seemed delighted to report that "he is stout and slow in his movements. His acting was conventional, which means that it was unexciting. Up to date, all memories of Jean de Reszke are not effaced." The writer for the *Journal*, also remembering the elegant Pole, noted that Caruso was "a manly fellow but the grave question is whether he will be loved as devotedly by the feminine portion of the opera-goers as some of his predecessors have been. His voice is of rare beauty, but he is stout and what heart that flutters behind new stays could forgive such failure?"

Following this less than sensational debut, Caruso politely informed a reporter for the *World* that he was delighted with his reception. "It was superb, splendid, overwhelming," he said through an interpreter. "I had no idea that such a thing could be in America. . . . Such an appreciation of the wonderful music, such an appreciation of myself — far beyond my wildest dreams. . . . New York has opened its arms to me, a stranger, and I embrace it."

Of course, New York had not yet opened its arms to Caruso, nor had he embraced New York — but that first season was in fact the beginning of an enduring love affair between the stout Neapolitan tenor and the American public.

The beginning was somewhat delayed. The nervous strain which had preceded his debut and had most probably plagued him during his first appearance — together with New York's harsh climate — took its toll following that performance. Caruso's next two scheduled appearances — in *La Bohème* on November 27 and *Rigoletto* on the 28th — had to be canceled because of an attack of tonsillitis. A hurried search for a replacement resulted in the hiring of a little-known Italian tenor, Giuseppe Agostini, who interrupted his trip from San Francisco to Italy to serve as a substitute but who proved to be no threat to the ailing Caruso — he never returned to the Metropolitan after those two performances.

Caruso felt well enough to sing again by the evening of November 30.

The opera was *Aida*, and in the cast were Gadski, the American Edyth Walker (making her Metropolitan debut as Amneris), the renowned French bass Pol Plançon, and Scotti. From the start, it was clear to many that Caruso was still not in full possession of his vocal powers. His singing of "*Celeste Aida*" at the beginning of the opera was tentative, and for two acts he showed unusual restraint, saving himself for the dramatic Nile scene in the third act, when he unleashed the full force of his voice to stunning effect. The press the following day was, with some reservations, pleased. Henry Krehbiel, writing in the *Tribune*, was more than that, noting that his performance stirred "keener appreciation of his knowledge of the art of singing and invited still greater admiration for the superb beauty of his voice. . . ." The critic for the *Times* commented at length:

> The greatest interest was felt in Mr. Caruso's assumption of the part of Radames, and though he evidently had not fully recovered from the troubles that put so sudden a check upon his career here after his first appearance, he materially deepened the favorable impression he then made. He was clearly singing with circumspection and care, especially in the first acts of the opera, and seldom ventured to put forth the full power of his voice. But in the very manner in which he did this he proved the remarkable mastery he possesses over his organ, and the skill of his vocal technique, the manifold resources he possesses to make every effect count, even against the most unfavorable influences. . . . There were passion and conviction in his interpretation of the fated lover, and everywhere the marks of the adept in stagecraft. It was an admirable performance and commanded not only the enthusiastic plaudits of the cooler portions of the audience, but also the frenzied "bravos" of his compatriots who were present in large numbers. After the third act there were scenes of tumultuous enthusiasm.

There were comparisons, both favorable and unfavorable, with other tenors — de Reszke, Tamagno, and Campanini — and though it was obvious that Caruso had made a highly favorable impression on the press, he had not yet won it over entirely. The audience, however, was already beginning to show signs of the tremendous affection it would lavish on Caruso for the rest of his life. *The Herald* reported that "he had not sung halfway through the '*Celeste Aida*,' tenderly phrased, before the audience was impatiently waiting for him to finish, that it might break into applause. The last note had not ended before 'bravo!' rang out from all parts of the house." Audience reaction to the new tenor was summarized in the December 1 issue of *The Press*:

> Thunderous was the applause that came from every part of the crowded auditorium. It may be predicted safely that Caruso will be this year's popular idol. The public has not made a mistake in offering this honor to him. It was apparent again last night that New York has acquired a singer who is unsurpassed in beauty of tone production and exquisite artistry combined, unless it be by Jean de Reszke. Caruso's singing of the first aria *'Celeste Aida'* showed, perhaps, a little reserve, due no doubt to his recent indisposition, but it was given with intensity of feeling, depth of expression and lusciousness of tone-color and was withal so artistically finished in enunciation and phrasing that there was no resisting the natural impulse to approval. The house burst out with an amount of applause that seldom is heard. In the third act Caruso "let loose." His fire is unbounded. He hurls his heart at his listeners. . . .

Caruso revealed to New York audiences, perhaps for the first time, the full force of his vocal strength on the night of December 2, when he sang Cavaradossi opposite the Tosca of Milka Ternina (who created the role in New York) and the Scarpia of Scotti. While duly noting the beauty of his singing, the reviewers, however, severely criticized his dramatic interpretation of the role. "Caruso sang Mario excellently," the *Evening Post* commented, "but dramatically he hardly filled preconceived conceptions of the part. There was something common about it. It lacked, altogether, aristocratic flavor, and therefore seemed to be out of the picture." Henderson in the *Sun* was even more severe: "Mr. Caruso's Cavaradossi was bourgeois. It was difficult to believe in the ardent passion of the aristocratic Tosca for this painter of hack portraits at job prices. His clothes were without distinction and his carriage was less so. His anger at the laying on of hand by the police officer was petulant. No wonder the Italian policeman paid no attention to it. . . ." The critic for the *Tribune* also made note of the tenor's shortcomings. Complaining that he acted the role with "far less fire and distinction than his predecessor," the reviewer continued: "His musical instincts are as perfect as his voice is luscious; but neither his instincts nor his voice is at the service of that dramatic characterization which is so compelling in Mme Ternina's performance of every part she undertakes." The *Times* concurred, praising his singing while objecting to his "bourgeois air, with little distinction of bearing. . . ."

Although the critics quibbled about his appearance and bearing, audiences increasingly showed uncritical enthusiasm for the new star. The reviewer for the *Press* lamented this, condescendingly blaming it on the Neapolitan's appeal to Italian members of the audience. "He indulged frequently in the '*voix blanche*,' dear to the Italians but disagreeable to the Americans," he wrote. "He achieved some fine climaxes, however, especially in the early part of the third act and so worked upon the feelings of the Italian contingent in his audience that he was forced to repeat a whole passage, greatly to the detriment of the dramatic integrity of the scene. The applause continued even after his concession to popular feeling and it was several minutes before the orchestra could be heard."

It was the reporter for the *Telegraph* who pointed out the significance of the tenor's first *Tosca*. "Caruso leaped into the hearts of the audience. Henceforth he will probably be as popular as idols of years gone by. Caruso sang for the third time in this country last night and only last night he arrived," he wrote.

For most reviewers, however, Caruso did not really arrive until December 5, when he sang for the first time in *La Bohème*, again with Marcella Sembrich. This time the critics were jubilant. "Mr. Caruso showed yesterday afternoon for the first time since he has been in this country the supreme beauty of his voice, and the perfection of his style when he is at his best," the critic for the *Times* wrote. "Now we know what Mr. Caruso's voice really is. As it was displayed yesterday afternoon, it was such a one as has not been enjoyed here for a long time. . . ." Henderson of the *Sun* agreed. "Music of the fluently melodious and sentimental style of *La Bohème* is admirably suited to Mr. Caruso's voice and method of singing. All the lovely qualities of his uncommonly beautiful voice are brought into prominence. . . ." The critic for the *Herald* found the tenor's singing tremendously exciting and claimed that because of Caruso even Sembrich surpassed any previous performance. "Mr. Caruso outdid himself and fairly inspired his fellow artist," he wrote. "Even those who had followed his singing in each new role since his debut were unprepared for the electrical surprises his voice provided at every point during the afternoon. . . . Mme Sembrich's recognition of his great singing was gracefully shown when at the curtain call she impulsively plucked a blossom from her bouquet and pressed it into his hand."

Sembrich and Scotti again joined Caruso, this time in *Pagliacci* on the night of December 9. Once again, the audience cheered him enthusiastically, forcing him to repeat his aria at the end of the first act. "He was in admirable voice," the *Times* noted, "and put a magnificent vehemence of passion into his acting and singing." The influential critic Henry Finck noted that "the opinion prevails generally that he is the best Italian tenor New York has heard since Campanini retired from the stage."

On December 23, Caruso sang his first *La Traviata*, but Sembrich sang so sublimely in what was her favorite role of Violetta that he was overshadowed. This was not the case with the *Lucia di Lammermoor*, sung on the night of January 8, 1904. As had happened before, Caruso transformed what had generally been considered a soprano's opera into a work for tenor as well. Once again, the audience did not leave after the Mad Scene. The "lost" last scene was restored, according to the *Times'* critic, who added: "Mr. Caruso was quite in his element, and put passion, vehemence, and glowing rhetoric into his interpretation. He made Edgardo seem a living and real personality." The initially skeptical critic Gustav Kobbé noted: "As for Caruso, rarely have I witnessed such excitement as followed the singing of the sextet the evening of his first appearance as Edgardo at the Metropolitan Opera House. It is a fact that the policeman in the lobby, thinking a riot of some sort had broken loose in the auditorium, grabbed his night stick and pushed through the swinging doors—only to find an audience vociferously demanding an encore."

The tenor's popularity was by now secure, but his greatest success took place on the night of January 23, when he assumed his final role of the season, that of Nemorino in *L'Elisir d'Amore*. Singing once again opposite Sembrich, an ideal partner, his "golden" voice, as it was already called, dazzled the audience. This was the first performance of the new Metropolitan production of Donizetti's opera, and, as had happened at La Scala, Caruso's singing made the work one of the most popular of the entire repertory. Henderson of the *Sun* wrote of Caruso's "splendid success," adding that "he has never done anything better here than his beautiful singing of the air in the last scene. The audience rose at him and literally compelled him to repeat the number." The reviewer for the *Times* wrote:

> Mr. Caruso's part of Nemorino represents one of the futile, subdued, despairing class of operatic lovers who cut a very poor figure on the stage, but there is much music for him to sing, in which he reveled with all the graces of the Italian tenor superimposed upon the truly beautiful voice and style and pleasing that he can command. What could be more captivating, more melting, more flowery in its old-fashioned rhetorical passion than his singing of the famous air "*Una furtiva lagrima*" in the last act? Rapture is no fitting expression for the state of mind into which it threw the audience, and he was instantly called upon to

unfold that tale of amorous longing again. So, too, in his "*Quanto è bella*," which was, however, given in a less exaggerated, and hence in some ways more artistic style.

Caruso began to show some signs of fatigue toward the end of his first visit to New York. He seemed especially tired at his last performance of *L'Elisir d'Amore* on the night of February 8 when, in the course of a duet with Sembrich, his voice broke. The public, for whom he could by now do no wrong, seemed unconcerned, and the tenor quickly recovered, singing his last act aria with his customary brilliance. In spite of his protests—he pointed to his throat in discomfort—he was forced to oblige the cheering crowd by repeating the aria.

Caruso had in a short time established a unique, almost confidential rapport with the New York public. What he might have lacked in elegance and style, he made up by the sheer force and beauty of his voice and by the magnetic warmth of his personality. De Reszke had been greatly admired, but, ever the aristocrat, he had kept himself at a distance from his public. The Neapolitan, with his simple charm and ready wit, was a popular tenor in the true meaning of the word, one with whom the people who filled the upper balconies of the opera house could identify.

Caruso, too, had learned to enjoy life in what had at first seemed to him an alien city. After a few weeks, he and Ada had left their hotel and moved to an apartment in Murray Hill, where they could entertain their friends—fellow artists and members of the city's large Italian colony—in a more relaxed and informal atmosphere. The open, uncomplicated friendliness of New Yorkers was congenial to the tenor's own spirit; he responded to the city and its people warmly, as they had responded to him. His first season at the Metropolitan had been a short one—it ended with a performance of *Lucia* on the night of February 10—but he looked forward eagerly to his return the following year for a longer stay.

An enormous gathering of his new friends and admirers crowded the pier on February 14, 1904, as Caruso and Vigna—who had conducted every Caruso performance at the Metropolitan—prepared to embark for Le Havre and on to Monte Carlo. The tenor, genuinely moved at the outpouring of affection shown him, was gracious in his farewell remarks. "My audiences have been everything to me, and I am sorry I could not have gone on singing in answer to their desire," a reporter for the *Telegraph* quoted him as saying. "Of course, I love my dear America—she is beautiful, generous, and I shall come back to her next year.

"The critics—they were kind, except about my fat and my clothes. I shall train down next year and wear better—what you call them?—pantaloons and coats. Then the critics will have nothing to criticize."

VIII. King of Song

By 1904, word of Caruso's resounding triumphs and of his uniquely intimate rapport with his audiences had spread, and opera companies all over the world vied for his services. A Caruso appearance had become a guarantee of a full house. Composers, too, sought him to create roles in their new operas; among them was Ruggero Leoncavallo, who tried in vain to persuade him to sing the role of Henning in *Rolando*, his new work which he hoped, also in vain, might duplicate the tremendous success of *Pagliacci*.

The Monte Carlo engagement which had forced Caruso to leave the Metropolitan in midseason was an unqualified triumph. He was greeted as an old friend, and his reception for his first performance of the season, in *Rigoletto* on the night of March 3, was succinctly described by the *Journal de Monaco*: "Delirious applause, recalls, ovations, nothing spared."

Equally delirious applause followed his other performances during the month-long season: in *La Bohème*, *L'Elisir d'Amore*, and *Aida*. Most significant, however, was his first appearance of the season in *La Bohème* on the night of March 10. The 1902 Monte Carlo production of the Puccini opera had marked the beginning of Caruso's partnership with the great Melba; this 1904 performance of the same opera in the same theater would signal the start of his equally brilliant partnership with another soprano, the American Geraldine Farrar. Unlike the Australian prima donna, Farrar was young — she had just celebrated her twenty-second birthday — and she was strikingly beautiful. At the beginning of her career, she had made her debut at Berlin's Hofoper in 1901, and had not yet sung in opera in her own country. Her appearance as Mimi in *Bohème* marked her Monte Carlo debut; it was also her first opportunity to sing with a tenor of Caruso's stature.

She approached her introduction to the celebrated tenor with a degree of apprehension, but she was soon put at ease. "Never shall I forget the apparition that walked into the first rehearsal," she wrote in her memoirs. "Clad in shrieking checks, topped by a grey fedora, yellow gloves grasping a gold-headed cane, he jauntily walked onto the stage. A happy smile illumined a jolly face, which was punctuated by the two largest black eyes I had ever seen."

Jean de Reszke, then retired and teaching voice at Nice, was among those present at that first rehearsal, but Caruso did not sing with his full voice for him or for anyone else then or at later rehearsals. Because of this, Farrar was astounded when she heard him on the night of the first performance. "When I heard those rich and glorious tones rise above the orchestra, I was literally stricken dumb with admiration," she remembered. The performance was a tremendous success, a milestone in the soprano's career. The tenor, too, was delighted with the magic that he and the beautiful young American had generated, and he made no secret of it. "After the third act, and in full view of the audience," Farrar wrote, "Caruso lifted me bodily and carried me to my dressing room in the general wave of enthusiasm."

Caruso's Monte Carlo season was followed by another enormously successful debut — this time in Paris where, with the Gunsbourg company, he made his first appearance on the night of April 14. The opera was *Rigoletto*, and singing with the tenor was the dazzlingly beautiful Lina Cavalieri, a one-time flower seller and star of the Folies Bergère. It was a gala occasion, a benefit in aid of Russian soldiers injured in the Russo-Japanese war, and in spite of the high prices charged for tickets, Parisians filled the Théâtre Sarah Bernhardt to hear the celebrated new tenor in his first and only performance in the French capital that year.

Within a short time, Caruso had conquered audiences wherever he sang: Monte Carlo, London, Lisbon, New York, and Paris. No challenge seemed too great for him as he left France for Barcelona and his first appearance in Spain; yet the Catalonian city proved to be the setting for one of the few complete failures of his career.

Contemporary accounts of his brief stay in Spain differ in detail, but all agree that Caruso's Spanish debut was a disaster, and that the cause most probably was not to be found in the performance itself, but rather in the enormous publicity buildup that preceded it. It was only the first of many times this would happen to him. Caruso's arrival had been widely heralded, and along with word of his extraordinary talents there had been reports that he would be receiving the enormous sum of seven thousand pesetas for each of two scheduled performances of *Rigoletto*. This news was greeted with special rage by the proud Spanish public, for Spain was the home of the great tenor Julian Gayarré, and even he had never made such exorbitant demands. In addition, the high fee paid to Caruso meant that there was little money left to pay other members of the cast (another common occurrence later in his career), so that second-rate singers were hired in support of the new tenor.

Because of the public's resentment, the evening was a failure before it started. Caruso was at first received coolly, but before long the indifference of the public turned to open anger. What little applause there was was countered by hisses, and the performance was interrupted several times. Caruso, at first shaken by the unexpected response, soon became enraged. According to Richard Barthélemy, his longtime accompanist and friend, the tenor was so unnerved during the last act of the opera that he brandished his sword at those members of the audience, seated at the front of the auditorium, who had noisily disrupted his every phrase.

The public was stunned, and when the final curtain fell, there was complete silence. The indignant tenor left Barcelona at once. Just as he had vowed never again to sing in Naples, he swore he would never again sing in any Spanish theater.

That Caruso's humiliation in Barcelona was merely an isolated incident was more than amply proven when he sang next, on the night of May 4, 1904, at Prague's Landestheater, considered the finest German opera house outside of Germany. His enormous success there and in Dresden, where he sang a few nights later, restored his spirits and he looked forward with confidence to his next engagement—his second season at Covent Garden.

❋

He felt at home in the British capital the moment he arrived and set up quarters in a luxurious suite at the Savoy Hotel. Londoners accepted him as an old friend; since he had last appeared in their city, his fame had spread, through the sales of his recordings as well as his triumphs in New York, and their earlier judgment of the tenor had been confirmed. On May 17, the opening night of the season, before an elegant audience which included the king and queen, Princess Victoria, and the Duke and Duchess of Connaught, Caruso was reunited with Melba for an ecstatically received performance of *Rigoletto*. Throughout the season, unmarred by even a trace of disappointment, he sang an average of two performances a week before filled houses. He was again joined by Melba in *La Traviata* and *La Bohème*. In addition, he sang *Un Ballo in Maschera*, during which, according to the *Daily Telegraph*, he lifted "his listeners to the supreme heights of operatic enjoyment"; *Pagliacci* ("his superb vocal and dramatic gifts attained such heights in the song at the close of the first act that the audience persisted on an encore," wrote the critic for *News of the World*); and *Aida* with Giannina Russ, one of the most distinguished Aidas of the time.

It was a happy period; Caruso the star now reigned supreme at Pagani's, where he took many of his meals; he was wined and dined by members of British society, relaxed in the company of Tosti and other members of the Italian community, and deepened his friendship with Sybil Seligman, whose home was always open to him.

The tenor's final performance of the season, in *La Traviata* with Melba, took place on the night of July 25; following it, he left for Italy and his first chance to relax in many months. Relaxation for Caruso, then as in the future, was achieved with difficulty. His enormous successes had been the result of intensive hard work; in addition to his performances, which had always drained him of much of his energy, he had been forced by his rigorous schedule to spend much of his free time in his hotel suites, vocalizing and studying new roles. The short periods between engagements rarely allowed him enough time to unwind from the tensions which had come to mark his existence, and his two-month visit to Italy was intended to give him the opportunity to do just that.

Apparently, however, he was not eager to unwind in his newly acquired home outside Florence, for upon his arrival there he busied himself negotiating for and eventually buying a second villa, the lavish Villa Campi, situated near the small village of Lastra a Signa, also near Florence. Though he would later buy still another home in the Tuscan countryside (the Fattoria di Cercina), the Villa Campi — which he renamed the Villa Bellosguardo — would remain his principal residence for the rest of his life.

His short vacation did give him the chance to enjoy his young son, Fofò, but it had already become obvious that the demands of his performing schedule would never allow the singer to assume the role of a full-time father. Giachetti, too, was unable to devote enough time to their child — when not pursuing her own faltering career, she accompanied Caruso on his travels — so a decision was made to send the five-year-old boy to school at the Badia Fiesolana, outside Florence, in the fall. It had been a difficult decision, the recognition that a normal home life could never be theirs, and a decision complicated further (if joyfully) by the birth of a second son, christened Enrico, Jr., but known as Mimmi, on September 7, 1904.

Soon after the birth of the child, Caruso's holiday came to an end, as he prepared for his next important debut—in Berlin on October 5. The setting for that debut—the Theater des Westens, not the city's major opera house—seemed inappropriate for an artist of his stature, and the singers who joined him were in no way the equal of the international stars with whom he had sung in the recent past. Nonetheless, his first performance in the German capital—*Rigoletto* again—was another unqualified success, though reports of the performance vary. The reporter for *Musical Courier* wrote that the house was sold out at three times the ordinary prices. Anna Eugenie Schoen-Rene, a soprano who became an outstanding voice teacher, remembered that "Germany immediately claimed him as the most promising tenor of the day." On the other hand, the soprano Frieda Hempel, then nineteen years old, wrote in her memoirs that the theater was half empty and commented on the sadness she noted in the face of Ada Giachetti as she watched Caruso sing under such unusual circumstances.

All agreed, though, that he sang brilliantly and that he completely won over his audience. The correspondent for the music magazine wrote that Caruso "made a tremendous impression; the beauty, purity, and resonance of his voice are wonderful. It is a voice that combines warm and sympathetic timbre with great brilliancy and penetrating power." Hempel, while expressing shame at the initial indifference of her fellow Berliners, wrote of her own joy as, from her seat in the top balcony, she heard the tenor sing. "When I arrived home in a state of agitation," she remembered, "I attempted to describe my impressions to my parents. 'It is as if I sank into a deep velvet armchair so soft, so tender, so velvety!' I said. . . . 'Caruso's singing was so perfect, so heavenly! It is a true miracle that a man should possess such a God-given voice.' "

Madame Schoen-Rene had first met Caruso in London in 1903 at a luncheon given by Nellie Melba. Though the tenor did not enjoy theoretical discussions of his vocal techniques, he showed interest in studies of male voices which Schoen-Rene was at that time making under the tutelage of the great teacher Manuel Garcia, and he volunteered his own ideas on the subject.

> One of the startling things he told me [Schoen-Rene later wrote] was that he controlled his breath with his back muscles. I demonstrated to him the "lumbar-breathing" for men, which was essential in the Garcia technique, but he seemed to be certain that he acquired all the strength for his singing and for the relaxation of his throat from the powerful muscles of his back. The next time I saw Manuel Garcia I spoke to him of this, and he

told me that it was the most dangerous sort of breathing because it forced every muscle in the body to strain the diaphragm. Many people will recollect, and can even hear today in Caruso's records, that he always had some breath left on the end of every phrase, which was kept between the epiglottis and the vocal cords, and was expelled with a glottic stroke before a new phrase was begun. This over-exertion in breathing weakened his diaphragm support. Another curious practice of his was wearing a belt of canvas and elastic in order to have something to push against, and for the sake of feeling the control of his breath.

Schoen-Rene attended both of Caruso's Berlin appearances that season — he also sang in *La Traviata* — and she was immensely impressed with his performances on the stage as well as his behavior during rehearsals. "He never wished to be treated as a star, or to set himself apart from the other singers," she wrote. "In Berlin I noticed at the rehearsals, that many of the other experienced singers thought it not worth while to go to rehearsals arranged to prepare new soloists; but Caruso was invariably on hand — though he needed extra rehearsals less than any of them — and every newcomer was given his cordial co-operation."

✳

After Berlin, Caruso canceled plans to take a short rest before his early November departure for New York, and, instead, returned to Covent Garden, this time under the auspices of Naples' San Carlo opera company. It was a unique opportunity to get back at the Neapolitans who had rejected him. He had said he would never again sing in Naples, but he had never said that he would not sing again with his home town's opera company. At the urging of impresario Henry Russell he agreed to join San Carlo for its short London season, certain that word of his success would reach the ears of those responsible for that early failure. He took special pleasure, too, in the knowledge that the success or failure of San Carlo's London season was almost entirely dependent on him. The company was a good one, but the star attraction was Caruso, and if London audiences flocked to the opera house, it was in order to hear him and only him.

The tenor's enormous hold on the London public could not be doubted when the season opened on the night of October 17 with a performance of *Manon Lescaut*. The fact that he was suffering from a cold mattered little, and the correspondent for *Musical Courier* reported the reaction of Londoners to the return of their idol. "Of course," he wrote, "the announcement that Caruso would appear was largely responsible for the smartness of the audience, for where Caruso sings there is the fashionable world gathered together. . . . So many eulogies have already been written concerning him as a singer that it is useless to add to the number, and it will be enough to say that his singing on Monday was as finished and as effortless and that his acting was as sincere and as free from conventionality as ever." Caruso was doubly pleased with the opera's reception, for singing the title role, in her very successful London debut, was the twenty-four-year-old Rina Giachetti, Ada's young sister.

In the two weeks that followed, Caruso also sang in *Carmen*, *La Bohème*, and *Pagliacci*. His Don José in *Carmen* was a special triumph. "Both in the lyrical and tragical passages of the part the artist gave of his best," wrote the critic for the *Daily Telegraph*, "and where Caruso is concerned one wants nothing more than that. At the close of the third act, in particular, the singer rose to the full heights of his task, and his hearers, rising with him, indulged themselves with an overwhelming burst of enthusiasm. . . ." John McCormack, the Irish tenor, then twenty years old, was present at one performance of *La Bohème*, his first chance to hear the Italian tenor who would become a good friend. In his autobiography he recalled, ". . . when I listened to the opening phrases of Puccini's music, sung by that indescribably glorious voice as Caruso alone could sing, my jaw dropped as though hung on a hinge. Such smoothness and purity of tone, and such quality; it was like a stream of liquid gold. . . . The sound of Caruso's voice that night lingered in my ears for months, and will doubtless linger there always. It will always be to me one of the memorable moments of my life. . . ."

❊

Caruso's eagerly anticipated second visit to the United States was notable not only as his first full season at the Metropolitan but also as his first introduction to the vast American public outside of New York.

The Metropolitan season was in every way a splendid one. Caruso sang superbly in the company of some of the greatest artists in the history of the opera house. On the opening night, November 21, 1904, when he appeared with Emma Eames in *Aida*, he was, as Richard Aldrich of the New York *Times* wrote, "acclaimed with an outburst of genuine enthusiasm that came to him as a spontaneous greeting." The critic noted that Caruso returned in excellent voice. "Its resonant purity, its lyric beauty and fullness are such as have been heard from no other singer of his school for years."

It was only the beginning of a season during which Caruso dazzled the New York public by singing a total of twelve roles—nine of them during the first five weeks alone. His achievement was an astounding one, worth noting in detail.

Two nights after his opening performance in *Aida*, he appeared in *Lucia* with Sembrich; on Saturday afternoon, November 26, it was *La Traviata* with Sembrich and Scotti; and on the night of the 28th, he sang Enzo in an all-star production of *La Gioconda*, with Nordica, the American contralto Louise Homer, Edyth Walker, Giraldoni, and Plançon.

On December 5, he sang the role of Gennaro in the Met's first performance of *Lucrezia Borgia*; December 16, *La Bohème* with Melba (in her only appearance of the season); December 21, *Rigoletto* with Sembrich, Homer, Giraldoni, and Journet; December 24, *L'Elisir d'Amore* with Sembrich; and on December 26, *Pagliacci* with Scotti as Tonio and Bella Alten as Nedda.

In January and February, he appeared in three more roles: on January 16, in *Tosca* with Eames and Scotti; on February 3, in an Italian-language version of *Les Huguenots* with a matchless cast including Sembrich, Nordica, Walker, Journet, Plançon, and Scotti; and on February 6, in *Un Ballo in Maschera*, with Eames, Homer, and Scotti. In addition, he made a guest appearance in the ballroom scene of *Die Fledermaus*; on February 16 he participated in the quartet from *Rigoletto*; and his final Met performance of the season was on the night of March 3, when at a gala performance he sang in the first act of *Pagliacci* and the fourth act of *La Gioconda*.

In the course of the season, Caruso had transformed the character of the austere opera house, drawing to it not only the members of New York society but also masses of people who had never before entered the theater, infusing it with a vitality it had never before known. Everywhere he went he made news, and he enjoyed himself and his fame thoroughly. He sang at private concerts at the homes of the city's rich, just as he instructed Italo-American chefs in the art of spaghetti cooking at restaurants wherever he dined. He continued to enjoy onstage pranks — during a performance of *La Gioconda*, he pressed a raw egg into the hand of a horrified Giraldoni, who did his best to enact the role of the sinister spy Barnaba while wondering what to do with the crushed egg — but he also spent long hours in his suite at the Hotel York, carefully and meticulously studying the nuances of each new role with his accompanist, Richard Barthélemy. There was always time for play, but above all it was his work that absorbed Caruso; each detail, dramatic and historical as well as vocal, became an increasingly important part of his preparation for each performance, as he strove to become a complete artist and not merely a singer with a golden voice.

When the Met season came to an end, Caruso set out for his first encounter with the public that lived far from New York. Through his

Caruso Through the Years

(Peabody Institute Library)

(Courtesy Lim M. Lai)

(Courtesy Lim M. Lai)

(Courtesy Lim M. Lai)

(Courtesy Lim M. Lai)

(Courtesy Lim M. Lai)

His Roles

Canio in *Pagliacci*
(Courtesy Lim M. Lai)

The Duke in *Rigoletto*
(Courtesy Lim M. Lai)

Radames in *Aida*
(La Scala Autographs)

Nemorino in *L'Elisir d'Amore*,
with Frieda Hempel *(Courtesy Lim M. Lai)*

Des Grieux in *Manon*
(Author's collection)

Julien in *Julien*
(La Scala Autographs)

Dick Johnson in *La Fanciulla del West* (*Metropolitan Opera Archives*)

Samson in *Samson et Dalila (La Scala Autographs)*

recordings—he had made five more records for Victor in February of 1905—and with the help of an intensive publicity campaign his fame had spread from coast to coast, but apart from New York and Philadelphia, where he had sung as part of the regular Met season, he had not been seen by the American public. This first tour with the Metropolitan company brought him to Boston, Pittsburgh, Cincinnati, Chicago, Minneapolis, Omaha, Kansas City, San Francisco, and Los Angeles. Wherever he sang, he was ecstatically acclaimed; his kingdom extended from one side of the country to the other. Chicago—where he sang in *Lucia*, *Pagliacci*, and *La Gioconda*—was typical. Each Caruso performance was sold out well in advance; thousands were turned away and the black market for tickets flourished. William Hubbard, writing in the *Tribune*, summarized the reaction to Caruso's Chicago debut performance on March 20, 1905, in *Lucia*: "He began his evening amid applause. He ended it amid applause. The audience welcomed him heartily. It acclaimed him in everything he did before the performance was concluded."

"Enrico Caruso sings just as nature prepared him to sing," Hubbard wrote. "Art and study may have done something toward fashioning and developing the material given him, but nature itself 'placed' his voice and he sings accordingly. The voice is of exceptional sympathy and beauty— the loveliest voice heard in this country since Campanini was in his prime. It is a voice similar in pure tenor quality to that of Campanini, and while possessing all of the lyric charm which made the latter's voice unique in the operatic world, has even more power and intensity in the expressing of the dramatic. The duet with Mme Sembrich in the first act was sung with consummate ease and absolute finish, and in the sextet Mr. Caruso proved his artistic conscientiousness by making no attempt to dominate the ensemble or to throw his own part into undue prominence. . . ."

Two nights later, an incident at the Chicago Opera House indicated that it was not the great tenor's voice alone, but also his enormous fame, that had caused Chicagoans—and others in the course of the tour—to cheer him. Caruso had been scheduled to sing the role of Canio in *Pagliacci*, following a performance of *Cavalleria Rusticana* starring the German tenor Andreas Dippel. The extraordinarily reliable Dippel—always ready to substitute for an indisposed artist and very often called upon to do so— felt he was not in good voice and confessed to Caruso that he feared he might falter in his very difficult first aria. Since the aria was sung before the curtain was raised, Caruso volunteered to sing it in Dippel's place, certain that the audience would have no way of knowing of the substitution. He was right; the public, having learned of Dippel's indisposition and expecting a poor performance, offered little applause following the aria and saved its enthusiasm for Caruso's Canio—unaware that the tenor they so enjoyed in *Pagliacci* was the same one they had greeted coolly in *Cavalleria Rusticana*. Caruso was neither surprised nor hurt; he enjoyed telling the story of this unannounced substitution time and again, as proof of the power of his public image.

The tenor's last performance of the extended tour took place on the night of April 18 when he sang *Lucia* in Los Angeles. He had gained admirers wherever he had sung, and he left for Europe more than satisfied with his long stay in America. This time there had been far fewer comparisons to the great De Reszke, and when those comparisons were made, they often corresponded to the judgment made by James Huneker, who wrote in *Success Magazine* (March 1905) that one note from Caruso's golden throat was "worth, in a purely tenoric way, all of Jean's voice." From that time on, it was other tenors of the past—and the future—who would be compared to Caruso.

✳

Caruso's first European engagement upon his return from New York had been set for Covent Garden in late May. Until then he had planned to take a badly needed short rest, but once again his plans were changed, this time because of an urgent plea from Sonzogno to sing the role of Loris in the first Parisian performance of *Fedora* as part of a six-week Italian season the impresario was presenting in the French capital. Caruso's presence in the cast of Giordano's opera, in the role he had created in Milan, could mean the difference between its acceptance or rejection by the French public, and Caruso found it impossible to refuse his old friend.

The French première of *Fedora* took place on the night of May 13, 1905; singing with Caruso in his second Parisian appearance were Lina Cavalieri and the great baritone Titta Ruffo. The Théâtre Sarah Bernhardt was sold out—as it was for each of the tenor's six performances—and the audience, which included the masters of contemporary French music Massenet, Saint-Saëns, Debussy, and Ravel, gave Caruso a rousing reception. Daspuro, who was in the theater, later wrote: "An occurrence truly phenomenal and outstanding took place during the second act when Caruso, looking like a wounded lion, with voice and aspect transformed by fury, attacked the phrase '*La fante mi avela,*' causing an irrepressible shiver and thrill to run through the theater, the voice breaking with contempt, torrential in its anguish with lightning flashes in its still beautiful outburst. . . ." No one was happier at the success than the composer Giordano, who later wrote Caruso, on December 12, 1906: "You have been and will always remain the greatest, the only Loris."

His obligation to Sonzogno fulfilled, Caruso left for London and still another triumphant season. His first performance there took place on the night of May 22, 1905, when he was reunited with Melba in *La Bohème*. The couple's appeal was undiminished, and the unique experience of the performance was somewhat effusively described by the critic Thomas Burke in his book *Nights in London*:

The stage is in semi-darkness. The garret is low-pitched, with a sloping roof ending abruptly in a window looking over Paris. There is a stove, a table, two chairs, and a bed. Nothing more. Two people are on. One stands at the window, looking, with a light air of challenge, at Paris. Down stage, almost on the foot-lights, is an easel, at which an artist sits. The artist is Scotti, the baritone, as Marcello. The orchestra shudders with a few chords. The man at the window turns. He is a dumpy little man in black wearing a golden wig. What a figure it is! What a make-up! What a tousled-haired, down-at-heel, out-at-elbows Clerkenwell exile! The yellow wig, the white-out moustache, the broken collar. . . . But a few more brusque bars are tossed from Campanini's baton, and the funny little man throws off, cursorily, over his shoulder, a short passage explaining how cold he is. The house thrills. That short passage, throbbing with tears and laughter, has rushed, like a stream of molten gold, to the utmost reaches of the auditorium, and not an ear that has not jumped for joy of it. For he is Rodolfo, the poet; in private life, Enrico Caruso, Knight of the Order of San Giovanni, Member of the Victorian Order, Cavalier of the Order of Santa Maria, and many other things.

As the opera proceeds, so does the marvel grow. You think he can have nothing more to give you than he has just given; the next moment he deceives you. Toward the end of the first act Melba enters. You hear her voice, fragile and firm as fluted china, before she enters. Then comes the wonderful love-duet — *Che gelida manina* for Caruso and *Mi chiamano Mimi* for Melba. Gold swathed in velvet is his voice. Like all true geniuses, he is prodigal of his powers; he flings his lyrical fury over the house. He gives it all, yet somehow conveys that thrilling suggestion of great things in reserve. Again and again he recaptures his first fine careless rapture. His voice dances forth like a little girl on a sunlit road, wayward, captivating, never fatigued, leaping where others stumble, tripping many miles, with fresh laughter and bright quick blood. There never were such warmth and profusion and display. Not only is it a voice of incomparable magnif-

icence: it has that intangible quality that smites you with its own
mood: just like something that marks the difference between an
artist and a genius.

During the remainder of the two-month season, Caruso repeated his
earlier successes in *Aida, Un Ballo in Maschera, Don Giovanni,* and *Rigoletto;* he also sang his first London performances of *Les Huguenots.* Two
evenings were of unusual interest. On June 8, he sang before the most
glamorous audience of his career. The occasion was a gala performance in
honor of the visiting King Alfonso of Spain; Caruso sang the third act of *La
Bohème* with Melba, and the fourth act of *Les Huguenots* with the Czech
soprano Emmy Destinn and Scotti. Covent Garden had been the scene of
many spectacular galas, but none surpassed the spectacle presented both
offstage and on that evening. "During recent years there have been several
remarkable performances at Covent Garden in honour of distinguished
visitors," the *Illustrated London News* noted, "but that given in honour of
King Alfonso was second to none in brilliancy. . . . From floor to ceiling
the house was decorated with roses and draperies in the Spanish colours,
red and yellow. The stalls and boxes were ablaze with diamonds and uni-
forms. . . ." In addition to King Alfonso, who escorted Queen Alexandra
to her place in the royal box, there were countless other members of the
aristocracy present: the King of England, the Duke and Duchess of Connaught, Prince Arthur and Princess Victoria of Connaught, Princess Christian, the Prince of Wales, Princess Henry of Battenberg, Princess Beatrice
of Saxe-Coburg, the Prince of Siam, and the Duchess of Fife. Reigning on
stage, unfazed by the splendid audience, was the portly tenor from Naples.
Several weeks later he was summoned to Buckingham Palace, where he
Visited the king and queen and was presented with a diamond and ruby
pin bearing the king's initials.

The second occasion of special interest in which Caruso participated was
the July 10 London première of *Madama Butterfly,* with Destinn, one of
the tenor's favorite partners, as the tragic heroine. Thomas Burke noted:
"He worked up the love duet with Butterfly at the close of the first act in
such fashion that our hands were wrung, we were perspiring, and I at least
was near to fainting. Such fury, such volume of liquid sound could not go
on, we felt. But it did. . . . As the curtain fell we dropped back in our
seats, limp, dishevelled, and pale. It was we who were exhausted. Caruso
trotted on, bright, alert, smiling and not the slightest trace of fatigue did he
show."

Dettmar Dressel, a noted violinist, commented in his memoirs: "The
impression made was so deep that a complete silence followed the fall of

the final curtain. Nobody stirred in the huge auditorium and it seemed minutes before the applause, long and continued, broke out."

Caruso left London at the end of July; before he could return to his home in Italy, he had one more commitment to fulfill — at the popular gambling and beach resort of Ostende, Belgium. A distinguished audience attended his first performance there — it also marked the inauguration of the Théâtre Royal — on August 3. It included the King and Queen of Belgium, and, apparently, many other members of the European aristocracy. Caruso made no attempt at modesty when he told a reporter from the New York *Times* that the authorities at Ostende had informed him that the opening performance in their city had been "graced by the presence of a Persian sovereign, a European Prince, and a King of Song, meaning, I believe, myself."

Following his single operatic appearance, he gave a series of concerts at the Kursaal, delighting the crowds not only with his singing but also with his generosity; he had agreed to sing no more than two arias or songs, but in response to the public's enthusiasm he sang many more. He was in a lighthearted mood; during the intermission of one of the concerts, he went to the Kursaal's gambling room and found himself standing behind the German lieder singer Elena Gerhardt, who was seated at the roulette table. In her memoirs, Gerhardt remembered his asking her age. She replied "Twenty-two," and Caruso then placed his money on that number. To his obvious pleasure, it came in, adding further to his earnings during his stay at the Belgian resort.

✳

In August, Caruso was finally able to enjoy the material fruits of his triumphs and return to his new home, the Villa Bellosguardo. The imposing villa stood in the midst of a huge park; there were formal gardens, many acres of vineyards, and — something he had learned to appreciate but not play on in America — several lawn tennis courts. The "castle" itself, as Caruso called it, had an illustrious history, having once belonged to Dante's friend Guido Cavalcanti. Originally built of roughhewn stone, it had been renovated and modernized in a manner worthy of a twentieth century king of song, and Caruso took great pride in showing it off to the members of the press who visited him during his stay there. On the ground floor were two salons, a chapel, a forty-foot-long drawing room, kitchens, a baggage room, and a completely separate servants' quarters. On the second floor there were twenty more rooms, among them a gallery of arms, a gallery of paintings, an Arabian conservatory, a special room for his growing coin collection (reflecting one of his few diversions), and an immense studio.

Caruso liked to complain to reporters that because of his work he could spend far too little time in his "castle" with his two small children; but in fact he was born a boy of the city, and a teeming city, and it was obvious that gardens and vineyards were of no real interest to him—except for the food and wine they might produce—and family life was relatively unimportant. The magnificent Villa Bellosguardo was a potent symbol of his success and not a source of satisfaction, and as much as he cared for his family and found pleasure in their company, his satisfaction came largely, if not solely, from his work. A holiday in his elegant home allowed him to spend time with those he loved, but above all it granted him a peaceful period in which to study his operatic roles, refreshing the old ones as well as learning the new, and an interval during which he could catch his breath between his exhausting engagements.

IX. Caruso Fever

The glamorous audience that attended the opening night of the Metropolitan's 1905–1906 season for a performance of *La Gioconda* (with Caruso, Nordica, Homer, Scotti, and Plançon) greeted the tenor's return for his third New York season with an overwhelming ovation. The stunned Caruso was not even permitted to finish *"Cielo e mar,"* his crowd-pleasing second-act aria, before thunderous applause broke out. Though visibly annoyed by this interruption, he was delighted with the spontaneous warmth of the welcome accorded him. "I never saw the auditorium so white with diamonds," he told a reporter from *Musical America*. "Were not Nordica, Homer and the others admirable? They were inspired by the audience, as I was. That is the secret. New York is fascinating by its faculty to be quickly impressed. I like immensely to sing here, and this evening has made me happy."

Throughout the long season, New York audiences again proved that they liked immensely to hear Caruso sing. In the course of the season, he sang fourteen different roles, among them his first Metropolitan appearances in *La Favorita*, *La Sonnambula*, *Martha*, *Faust*, and *Carmen*, never failing to please his devoted public. However, for the first time since his early days at the Metropolitan, the critics expressed serious reservations, especially concerning his interpretations of Faust and Don José in two major works of the French repertory, Gounod's *Faust* and *Carmen*.

Accepted wholeheartedly as an Italian tenor in Italian roles, Caruso had yet to prove himself in a different language and a different style.

The season's première of Gounod's opera, on the night of January 3, 1906, was a most unusual one, for shortly before the curtain was to rise, the Metropolitan Opera chorus put into effect a long-threatened strike. The year's first performance of a familiar, popular opera, sung by an idolized tenor who had never before assumed the title role and would be singing in French for the first time in New York, seemed a perfect occasion on which to force the management's hand. However, the members of the chorus had not taken into account the tenacity of the iron-fisted managing director with whom they were dealing: Conried decided to go on with the performance, even without a chorus.

Under these circumstances, it was, of course, difficult to evaluate the singing of any of the principals—they included Eames, Scotti, and Plançon as well as Caruso. The audience, admiring their courage in singing under such trying circumstances, was sympathetic and responded enthusiastically. The press, however, was less kind—especially toward the Italian tenor. The critic for the *Tribune* bluntly stated that Caruso as Faust was "a flat and irredeemable failure." The *Telegram*'s reviewer was primarily distressed by Caruso's appearance: "Mr. Caruso appeared in a yellow cropped wig insistently suggestive of the comic little boys in Sunday papers, and he wore up-to-date white gloves with his velvet costume of romance."

Richard Aldrich of the *Times* was somewhat more compassionate:

> Of course, such an evening was not one to bring out the best in any of the singers who were concerned in the representation. Every one of them felt the nervous strain and the unnatural and unaccustomed surroundings, from Mr. Caruso, who was making a debut, through the whole list.
>
> Mr. Caruso's Faust suffered from an exaggeration, by all these things, of the nervousness natural to his first appearance. It would not be fair to estimate what he can do by what he did last night. He was evidently singing with circumspection and allowed himself very few of those tours de force that he is often so fond of. There was much of great beauty in his singing, for it is often most beautiful when he restrains his tendencies to exaggeration; yet often, too, his voice seemed not under perfect control, and his effects were not always fully achieved. . . . Mr. Caruso's embodiment of the character is not distinguished. The figure he presents has little allurement or grace. His conception is not uplifted with chivalrous devotion nor fired with impulsive

ardor, so far as he made it known last night. It is through his voice that he will impress it deeply upon this public, and it is likely that he will do much more toward effecting that end under less disturbing conditions than those that prevailed last evening.

Caruso's second French role of the season was that of Don José in *Carmen*. He had sung it with considerable success on February 20 in Philadelphia, but the reception of the critics following his first New York appearance on the night of March 5 was decidedly mixed. Writing in the *Times*, Aldrich commented: "Mr. Caruso is not made by nature for parts that have the suggestion of the cavalier in them, and Don José is such a part. There have been more convincing impersonations of the Spanish soldier, so far as appearance and action are concerned, but he showed a much stronger dramatic conception and more adept method than might have been supposed. It is true that in the highest pitch of the emotional tension at the close of the opera he cannot refrain from some of the lachrymose manifestations that usually accompany his denotements of great passion. But in this and in the third act as well he showed some powerfully temperamental traits in his acting. He sings the music, of course, with much beauty of tone."

Other members of the press were more critical. The writer for the *Journal* noted: "Caruso was not Don José for an instant. He sang divinely. But he was a Calabrian brigand all the time. And once, the pain of reconciling Spain and Italy made him falter. His notes grated a little! Oh, he was not Don José!"

Such reservations on the part of the New York press in no way dampened the enthusiasm of the audiences which filled the opera house for each Caruso performance. They did not want a perfectly groomed, immaculate, refined French stylist: they wanted Caruso in any guise, the man with the robust, golden voice, the man who sang not only with that voice but with all his heart. Writing in the *Sun*, following the rather poorly received performance of *Carmen*, W. J. Henderson commented that "New York is no longer opera mad, but Caruso mad." And at the end of the season, on March 18, the same critic noted: "The fact now to be recorded is that the public has gone to the opera in the season just ended, almost solely for the purpose of hearing Enrico Caruso. The public has not cared a rap what opera was sung. The invariable request proffered at the box office has been 'Can you let me have seats for Caruso's next appearance?'"

❊

Caruso's celebrity had already spread far beyond the confines of the opera house. He was a personality known to those who had never heard an opera, and his every move, onstage as well as off, no matter how insignificant, was reported by the press. It was news when, during a performance of *L'Elisir d'Amore*, a suddenly lowered drop curtain nearly felled the tenor, just as it was news when, in the same performance, he accidentally broke the bottle containing the elixir of love against his temple, thereby cutting his skin. New York newspapers took special pleasure in reporting what briefly became known as "the Caruso kiss." The version of this "scandal" printed in the New York *American* ran: "Kissed full upon the lips for half a minute, while held as in the grip of a bear, Emma Eames, upon the stage of the Metropolitan Opera House last night, must have felt the sensation of her life. It was in the first act of Puccini's *Tosca*, in which she was impersonating the diva, and it was Caruso, the Italian tenor, who was Mario Cavaradossi, her lover, that stormed and carried by assault the rock-ribbed reserve of the American prima donna, and held her captive while an audience that filled the house from floor to roof tittered and then laughed outright. There was a minute, after Eames freed herself, when her eyes blazed with indignation. She was white and red by turns. Then the humour of the situation possessed her, and by roguish glances and coquettish actions, she saved the situation."

This "marvellous, transcendental kiss," as one writer called it, was talked about for days. There were letters to the editor — for and against this display of Latin passion on the stage of the dignified opera house. A feature writer for the *Evening Telegram* even speculated on the presence or absence of garlic on the tenor's breath, and on its effect on Madame Eames. Though a few New Yorkers expressed indignation, for most the incident only added to the irresistible appeal of the warm-blooded Italian tenor.

Caruso's private life — though with his arduous performing schedule there was little of it — was also subject to close scrutiny. Recognizing the advantages to his career, he was a willing subject of endless interviews. These were not easy — Caruso's English was still poor and he usually spoke in halting French — but his charm rarely failed to delight those journalists who took every opportunity to report details of the offstage existence and habits of the man one reporter called "Herr Conried's thousand-dollar-an-hour tenor."

The popular image of an affable, relaxed family man emerged. Caruso was, according to reporters unacquainted with the facts, happily married and comfortably settled, and his dark-eyed, beautiful wife, Ada, exquisitely dressed in her Parisian gowns, was often at his side as he regaled interviewers with stories of his Neapolitan childhood, and as he both created and refuted legends that had become part of his image. He did not, he declared, fill his dressing room with dolls or fetishes; when nervous before a performance, he thought with love of his dead mother. He denied that he owned several hundred waistcoats, but the dapper, neatly mustached tenor (he was seen with and without the mustache at different times in his career) admitted that he paid great attention to what he wore offstage: if the day was dark, he donned bright colors; if it was sunny, he favored black suits.

Food, he confessed, was important to him, and his own chef accompanied him on his travels through America. American restaurant cooking was not to his taste, and he had been forced to move from his apartment at the Hotel York to his own home at 54 West 57th Street because the hotel would not allow cooking in any of its rooms. According to one journalist, he had "a spaghetti appetite and a voice of gold," but Caruso maintained that he ate lightly and regularly, though well. He noted that he never tried a new dish on a day on which he was to sing, fearing its effect on his voice. He drank moderately, preferring the wine of his own country, but he smoked incessantly, boasting that cigarettes did not harm him in the least.

If Americans loved him, he reciprocated by loving America, finding the skyscrapers "extraordinary," President Roosevelt "great," and American women "fine." His complaints were few — he found New York apartments overheated, he had too little time for social life because of his commitment to the Metropolitan, and he was hurt that Mark Twain was to give a dinner, in honor of cartoonists, to which he had not been invited. Perhaps, he mused, America's great writer only knew of him as a singer and was not aware of his talents as a caricaturist.

He was without a doubt the brightest star in the world of opera — the luxury of his New York home and the flourishes with which his valet, Martino, greeted visitors were evidence of his great wealth — yet Caruso's warm personality, ready wit, and good nature enabled him to project, without apparent effort, the image of a simple and generous man — the people's tenor.

Because of this, his appearances with the Metropolitan Opera Company during the transcontinental tour which followed the regular season in the spring of 1906 were avidly awaited by audiences in every part of the country. He had been popular the year before, but his records, which continued to sell at an enormous rate, had increased his fame immeasurably. His voice was uniquely suited to the new medium, and as a result he became the first truly important recording artist in the history of the growing industry. His latest recordings had been of special significance. On February 11, 1906, he had recorded five more arias for Victor; the company utilized a new and improved technique for these, his first recordings with orchestra accompaniment. Just before leaving New York for the tour, he recorded, on March 13, his first duet — *"Solenne in quest'ora"* from Verdi's *La Forza del Destino* — with Scotti, which proved to be one of the best selling of all operatic recordings.

❊

The long cross-country tour began successfully — too successfully — in Baltimore where more than three thousand spectators crowded into the twenty-three-hundred-seat Lyric Theatre to hear the tenor sing *Martha* on the night of March 19, 1906. During the next stop, in Washington, Caruso was visited in his dressing room by President Theodore Roosevelt, who invited him to the White House and presented him with a large autographed photo. (It proved more valuable than any of the decorations given Caruso by the European heads of state and monarchs who had previously honored him.) Pittsburgh followed, and then Chicago, where the *Tribune's* critic William Hubbard wrote that "this little Italian with the voice of molten gold" was "in excellent vocal form," and sang "like a god." After short visits to St. Louis and Kansas City, the company departed on April 13 for what was meant to be a two-week season in San Francisco.

The entire company showed signs of fatigue when they finally arrived in the Golden Gate city. Over a period of twenty-five days there had been a total of thirty-two performances. Caruso himself had sung six different roles in thirteen of them, and with good reason he was not his usual jovial self when greeted by journalists upon his arrival. Not only exhausted from his demanding schedule, he showed deep concern over reports of the recent eruption of Mount Vesuvius, which had resulted in the deaths of more than two thousand of his fellow countrymen and had left thousands of others homeless. He showed his sympathy by volunteering to sing in San Francisco for the benefit of the victims.

The tenor's visit to San Francisco did not begin auspiciously. Many of the Metropolitan's stars, including Caruso, were taken immediately to the city's finest hotel, the Palace. A symbol of San Francisco's unique elegance and extravagance, the beautifully appointed hotel was known as one of the most luxurious in America. In the past, it had played host to many of the most illustrious visitors to the city — among them Sarah Bernhardt, Lillie Langtry, Ellen Terry, Oscar Wilde, and Rudyard Kipling. Caruso, however, worn out from his travels, was not easily satisfied. He angrily rejected the first suite offered him, calling it too depressing, but finally accepted more suitable quarters — with a French chandelier, an English marble fireplace, Turkish carpets, a Persian bedspread, and satin-covered walls — which had once been occupied by General Ulysses S. Grant.

The company's first performance, on the night of April 16, was not a promising one. The opera chosen for the opening was Karl Goldmark's *The Queen of Sheba*. Never one of the most popular works of the repertory, it was given a listless performance by its weary cast and was coolly received by the public. Happily, the performance of *Carmen* on the following night proved more satisfactory, largely because of Caruso's presence in the cast. Olive Fremstad, singing the title role, was not in good voice, but the evening was more than redeemed by Caruso's superb interpretation of the role of Don José. So thoroughly did he dominate the performance that Blanche Partington of the *Call* wrote in her review: "*Carmen* rechristened itself for San Francisco last night. For the season, at least, it is *Don José*. Caruso is the magician."

It was a review that few San Franciscans ever had a chance to read. Early on the morning of April 18, 1906, the great San Andreas fault, which extends the length of the California coast, settled violently. The ensuing earthquake and fires nearly wiped out their city. More than twenty-eight thousand buildings — including the opera house which had been the scene of Caruso's triumph — were destroyed, and more than a quarter of a million people were left homeless. It remains one of the greatest disasters in the history of the United States.

The first tremor was felt at 5:13 in the morning, while Caruso slept. He later described his initial reactions to a reporter from *The Sketch* of London:

> . . . What an awakening! You must know that I am not a very heavy sleeper — I always wake early, and when I feel restless I get up and go for a walk. So on the Wednesday morning early I wake up about five o'clock, feeling my bed rocking as though I am in a ship on the ocean, and for the moment I think I am dreaming that I am crossing the water on my way to my beautiful country. And so I take no notice for the moment, and then, as the rocking continues, I get up and go to the window, raise the shade and look out. And what I see makes me tremble with fear. I see the buildings toppling over, big pieces of masonry falling, and from the street below I hear the cries and screams of men and women and children.
>
> I remain speechless, thinking I am in some dreadful nightmare, and for something like forty seconds I stand there, while the buildings fall and my room still rocks like a boat on the sea. And during that forty seconds I think of forty thousand different things. All that I have ever done in my life passes before me, and I remember trivial things and important things. I think of

my first appearance in grand opera, and I feel nervous as to my
reception, and again I think I am going through last night's
Carmen.

And then I gather my faculties together and call for my valet.
He comes rushing in quite cool, and, without any tremor in his
voice, says: "It is nothing." But all the same he advises me to
dress quickly and go in the open, lest the hotel fall and crush us
to powder. By this time the plaster on the ceiling has fallen in a
great shower, covering the bed and the carpet and the furniture,
and I, too, begin to think it is time to "get busy." My valet gives
me some clothes; I know not what the garments are, but I get
into a pair of trousers and into a coat and draw some socks on and
my shoes, and every now and again the room trembles, so that I
jump and feel very nervous. I do not deny that I feel nervous, for
I still think the building will fall to the ground and crush us.
And all the time we hear the sound of crashing masonry and the
cries of frightened people.

It was the beginning of a nightmare for Caruso as it was for all San
Franciscans. The tenor's ordeal lasted more than twenty-four hours. It is
not surprising under the circumstances that accounts of his behavior vary
from observer to observer. "Some of the papers said I was terribly frightened, that I went half crazy with fear, that I dragged my valise out of the
hotel into the square and sat upon it and wept; but all this is untrue," he
stated. "I was frightened, as many others were, but I did not lose my
head."

Arnold Genthe, a photographer, wrote that he found Caruso at the
Hotel St. Francis, a few blocks from the Palace, wearing a fur coat over his
pajamas and muttering, "'Ell of a place. I never come back here." According to another report, he was found sobbing on the shoulder of the conductor Alfred Hertz, and still another observer heard him trying in vain to
reach a high C in the corridor of his hotel. His friend Scotti told reporters
that he had found the tenor on Union Square, a towel wrapped around his
neck to protect his throat, and the framed photo of Theodore Roosevelt in
his hand. According to Scotti, both he and Caruso took refuge in the home
of a friend, Dr. Arthur Bachman, where they spent the night, with Caruso
choosing to sleep under a tree rather than risk having the house fall on
him. Caruso himself told reporters that he slept in either Lafayette Square
or in the Golden Gate Park. One thing seems certain: throughout the
ordeal, Caruso proudly held on to the signed photo of the American president, which served as his identification as well as a passport through the

barricades erected by the police and army in an attempt to maintain some degree of order amid the overwhelming chaos.

On the morning of April 19, Caruso and the other members of the opera company managed to reach Oakland, where they boarded a train for the long journey to New York. Upon his arrival there, the tenor, still shaken, reportedly told journalists: "Give me Vesuvius." The terrifying experience was not soon forgotten, nor could Caruso ever forgive the city of San Francisco: it joined Naples and Barcelona as cities in which he vowed he would never sing again.

✳

With a great sense of relief, he left New York on April 26, bound for Europe. After a short visit to Paris, where he replaced twenty thousand dollars' worth of costumes destroyed in San Francisco (the loss of sets and costumes to the company itself had been enormous), he proceeded to London for the spring season at Covent Garden. On the opening night of May 15, he put to rest all speculations that the San Francisco catastrophe might have caused permanent damage to his nerves; his appearance in *Rigoletto* opposite the young Canadian soprano Pauline Donalda, a protégée of Melba, was enthusiastically acclaimed, and some critics even felt that he had never sung better. Among these was the correspondent for *Musical Courier*, who assured his readers that "those glorious notes of his seemed to ring out with an even greater ease and brilliance than last season." He went on to say: "He was in wonderful form, and as the Duke sang and acted superbly. I notice, by the way, that very few critics say as much as they ought to about the excellence of Caruso's acting. There was a time when, provided an Italian tenor could sing, no one expected him to act. But Caruso has changed all that, and has set a high standard for those who may follow him."

If most London critics did indeed neglect to mention the tenor's skill as an actor, they nonetheless praised, without qualification, each of his performances in the course of the season. The public agreed and enthusiastically cheered him in *Don Giovanni* (with Destinn and Donalda), *La Bohème* and *La Traviata* (both with Melba), *Madama Butterfly* and *Pagliacci* (with Destinn), and *Aida* and *Tosca* (with Rina Giachetti). The noted record collector P. G. Hurst, who heard Caruso often that season and throughout much of his career, felt that the tenor had reached a high point in his career. This period, according to Hurst, "was marked by a greater steadiness and a closer coordination of his vast resource, resulting in a degree of technical perfection which was recognized as being equal to that of Jean de Reszke himself. The stupendous breath control, the greater regard to note values, and above all the wonderful and massive phrasing placed Caruso on a pinnacle, used as these attributes were with a voice that, as it increased in power, increased also in sensuous and luscious quality."

Once again, Caruso also endeared himself to his fans through his activities away from the opera house—he sang at a concert to benefit Belgian charities; he performed, with his friend Tosti at the piano, at the Theatre Royal Drury Lane on June 12, as part of a tribute to the actress Ellen Terry on the occasion of her jubilee; and he good-naturedly submitted to the usual round of press interviews. Whether dining with friends at Pagani's or having supper in the grillroom of the Hotel Cecil with Scotti, he showed patience and kindness to those admirers who asked for autographs or merely-gaped at the sight of their hero.

※

Caruso's Covent Garden season ended on July 26, after which he again traveled to Ostende for another series of highly profitable concerts at the Kursaal. In mid-August he returned to the Villa Bellosguardo, where he planned to spend some time at leisure with Ada and the children. Complete relaxation, once again, was impossible; he was far too preoccupied with preparations for the long season to come. The season offered one special challenge: his debut in Vienna before one of the world's most discriminating audiences.

The sophisticated Viennese, with their rich tradition of opera, were skeptical. An avalanche of publicity had again preceded Caruso's visit, and prices for tickets to his single performance at their distinguished opera house—then flourishing under the direction of Gustav Mahler—were far higher than normal. Though the proceeds would benefit the Opera's pension fund, the public was understandably resentful of the high cost of attending a Caruso performance. It was a problem he had faced before and would face often again. Because of the fanfare and the large sums charged for the privilege of hearing him sing, the public would be satisfied with nothing less than a brilliant performance.

In spite of the strain this frequently imposed upon him, Caruso rarely disappointed; and his Viennese debut, on October 6, more than met the demands of his audience. His role was that of the Duke in *Rigoletto*, and the cast included Titta Ruffo and a popular Viennese favorite, Selma Kurz. By the time the performance ended, any coolness or reserve on the part of the audience had vanished, and a mob of more than three thousand fans awaited the tenor in the street, hoping to carry him away in triumph and blocking his way until police came to the rescue.

Police also had to break up a crowd in Berlin, after the tenor's performance there in *Rigoletto* on October 10. It was his first appearance at the capital's leading theater, the Opernhaus, Unter den Linden, and Berliners filled the auditorium, cheering Caruso deliriously and calling him before the curtain fifteen times. His second appearance, in *Carmen*, was even more spectacularly received. Kaiser Wilhelm and members of his Court were in the audience, and the sovereign summoned the tenor to his box, spoke to him for ten minutes and, after presenting him with a pair of diamond-studded gold cuff buttons, conferred upon him the title of Imperial Chamber Singer.

An equally tumultuous reception awaited Caruso following his debut in Hamburg on October 16. This time crowds gathered beneath the balcony of his hotel room, refusing to let him sleep for hours on end. It was the first outbreak of a disease the German press came to call "Caruso fever."

The tenor's unprecedented popularity was not, however, limited to Germany, as his final European engagement before leaving for New York proved. The setting was Paris' Palais du Trocadéro, where on the night of October 25 he took part in a concert for the benefit of the Maison de Retraite de Pont-aux-Dames. Once again, the promise of a Caruso appearance filled a theater — more than five thousand people paid one hundred and fifty thousand francs to hear the celebrated tenor, who was given one more official decoration, the Croix de la Légion d'Honneur, for his services. The Caruso fever was spreading throughout Europe.

X. The Monkey House

Caruso sailed for America on November 6. Also on board the *Kaiser Wilhelm II* were Scotti and Farrar. The latter was to make her American debut in *Romeo and Juliet* on the opening night of the Metropolitan season — the first and only Metropolitan opening during his career there in which Caruso would not participate.

He returned to New York in high spirits. He had been feted and praised in Europe, where critics agreed that his performances had surpassed their and the public's greatest expectations. Unanimously acclaimed as the greatest tenor of his time, Caruso was, apparently, invincible. Only a few months before, he had survived the devastating San Francisco earthquake, and he could not possibly foresee that he was about to face the most senselessly humiliating ordeal of his life.

That ordeal began innocently, with a walk through New York's Central Park zoo and a stop in front of the monkey house, but it resulted in an incident that threatened to destroy his entire American career. It became known as the "Monkey House Case," and newspapers throughout the world delighted in reporting, with varying degrees of accuracy, every detail of the trials and agony of the great idol of the operatic stage.

The story broke on the morning of November 17, 1906. Front-page headlines announced that Caruso had been arrested in the zoo for molesting a woman. The arrest had been made at 4:50 on the previous afternoon by Policeman James J. Kane (often spelled Caine), a plainclothesman

118

detailed especially to the duty of watching men who bothered women in the zoo. Kane told of watching a well-dressed man standing suspiciously close to a woman in front of one of the monkey cages and of seeing the woman suddenly move away from the man, calling him a loafer and threatening to have him arrested. At this point, Kane stepped in: he placed the man under arrest and led him to the police station at the Arsenal.

Once there, Caruso vigorously protested his innocence, but the woman, who identified herself as Hannah Graham, insisted that he had "annoyed" her not once but three or four times before she threatened him with arrest. The woman was told to appear at the Yorkville Police Court the following morning, and the horrified tenor was led away to the 67th Street Police Station, where he was arraigned and ordered locked up. Confused and near hysteria, unable to understand fully the charges made against him and unable to make himself understood, he was restrained by two policemen and forced into a cell.

Caruso remained there a short time. Once he had regained his composure, he asked that a note be sent to Heinrich Conried, asking the managing director to come to the police station. Shortly after six o'clock Conried arrived and provided the five-hundred-dollar bail required for Caruso's release. The two men left together in a private cab.

When Caruso returned to his home—he had taken a suite for the season at the Hotel Savoy opposite Central Park—he issued a statement to the press, denying the accusation and complaining of his treatment at the police station. Conried, too, realizing how the press would treat the story of his prize tenor's humiliation, met with journalists and angrily denounced the arrest. "Ridiculous, absolutely ridiculous," he declared in answer to questions. "Who would ever believe such a story? I have known Caruso for many years and he is a man of honor and dignity. Such conduct is beneath him; he would not be capable of it. Would a man of his distinction go to Central Park to flirt? No, he could have almost any woman he wanted to flirt with—at least he could have many beautiful women at his heels if he gave them the slightest encouragement. . . .

"As I understand it, she simply says that Caruso touched her on the hip. Well, what of that? Maybe he did. That happens thousands of times every day in public places. If he touched her on the hip, it was an accident, pure and simple. Why, it is absolutely ridiculous to even discuss this absurd affair. . . ."

The following morning, neither Caruso nor Hannah Graham—no one named Graham lived in the Bronx building she gave as her address—turned up as ordered for the formal charge at the Yorkville Police Court. A certificate was presented which stated that the tenor was unable to leave his home because of a painful attack of sciatica; Mrs. Graham was simply missing, but the zealous Patrolman Kane declared that he would find her by the following Wednesday, the date set for the next hearing.

Kane was obviously enjoying his role as defender of American woman-hood. After filing an affidavit officially charging Caruso with rubbing against and annoying Mrs. Graham, he made a statement to the press claiming that the tenor was an habitual offender who had been watched by police since the previous winter and that he himself had once, several months before, warned him to stay away from the park. Furthermore, the policeman proudly declared that his specialty for thirteen years had been catching men, among them prominent actors and Wall Street brokers, who molested women in the park's animal houses.

In the days that followed, Caruso recovered his equanimity. The charges were unsubstantiated, there was no trace of Mrs. Graham, and he felt confident of his vindication. At the same time, Patrolman Kane continued to enjoy himself. While presumably searching for the missing accuser, he managed to spend hours near the monkey house, the scene of the "crime," talking of the case to all who would listen and boasting that he was accustomed to making at least twenty arrests a month, and that some of those arrested were "folks worth millions."

The press was having a field day, reporting each and every development (or nondevelopment) in the scandal, and as the time for Caruso's appearance in court approached, public opinion began to shift toward his side. There had been too many charges of dubious validity, there had been too many unfounded rumors, and most important of all, Mrs. Graham was still missing.

Despite stories in the press that she had finally been located (and that she and her husband, a baseball player, were old friends of Patrolman Kane), the mysterious Mrs. Graham was still missing on the afternoon of November 21, when official hearings in the case began. Caruso entered the courtroom with Scotti and Conried at his side; according to some reporters, he seemed bored and self-confident, though others found that he was nervous and flustered. Witnesses, at least one of whom was thorough-ly discredited by Caruso's attorney, were produced by the prosecution, but all their testimony was contradictory and the case against the tenor was unconvincing. Nonetheless Deputy Commissioner Mathot, representing the police, argued his case passionately, frequently taking advantage of the singer's poor knowledge of English (he answered questions through an interpreter) and railing against the crowd of Italo-Americans who filled the courtroom, some of whom he labeled "curs and perverts."

At four o'clock on the afternoon of the second day, the verdict was announced: Caruso was found guilty and fined ten dollars, the minimum fine allowable for the charge of disorderly conduct. Given the flimsy evidence against him, it was a shocking verdict, one that resulted in cries of indignation not only from his lawyer, who immediately filed an appeal, and the tenor's loyal supporters, but even from such an unlikely source as the former Chief of Police William S. Devery, who told reporters that "the arrest of Caruso was an outrage, and his conviction was based upon no evidence at all." Devery summed up the feelings of most of those who had followed the case from the beginning: "I hope that people who go and hear Caruso sing will cheer him every time they can," he said. "It won't do to abuse foreigners just because they are foreigners. The police have more to do than to hang around the monkey house and look for victims for purposes that are not on the level."

Caruso was as profoundly disturbed by the unexpected verdict as he was by the number of totally unfounded rumors that were circulated by the press following the court's judgment. Reporters, eager to hold their readers, wrote that his voice had been ruined by the emotional turmoil he had undergone; that Sembrich, who was to sing with him, had refused to share the stage with a man convicted of molesting an innocent woman, and that he was about to be evicted by the Hotel Savoy and would leave at once for Europe.

Outwardly, at least, Caruso remained calm, encouraged by messages of support he received from all over the world. In New York, a resolution adopted and sent to him by a large number of principals of the Metropolitan Opera Company expressed full confidence in his innocence, ending with the paragraph: "Our regard and respect for you, both as a man and as an artist, remain unchanged, and we feel it our duty, no less than our pleasure, to assure you now, in your hour of trial, of our heartfelt sympathy." Individuals, too, gave statements in defense of the tenor. Andreas Dippel, who had reportedly been told to prepare to replace Caruso, denied the report and added: "I feel sorry for Caruso and am sure he will be vindicated." Emma Eames told reporters: "None of us artists can feel any but the deepest sympathy with Caruso. I do not read the newspapers, but I am sure these charges are untrue."

Europeans, too, rallied to the tenor's support. Puccini wrote from Paris deploring the incident and expressing the certainty that Caruso would emerge triumphant. The well-loved soprano Mary Garden, interviewed in the French capital, commented that though she did not know Caruso personally, "we have, in common, many intimate friends in London and Paris society. We are all of one opinion — that Caruso is as far away as possible from being a man of such character." Jean de Reszke's secretary told the press: "I know M. de Reszke would wish me to express all the friendliness he had always entertained for M. Caruso." Jules Claretie, director of the Comédie-Française, approached the matter in French fashion: "The exuberant Southerner's gaiety, his gallantry, have been misunderstood in America," he said. "He would be ashamed, when a pretty woman smiled at him, not to smile in return. I know hundreds of honest gentlewomen who would never feel hurt by such an insult as the smile of a jovial tenor. If Richelieu were alive today and voyaged to New York, he would stand a good chance of being locked up."

Members of the British press rushed to the tenor's defense, finding the handling of the case to be still one more example of the corruption of justice in the United States. "Certainly it seems to us," the *Star* commented, "that Caruso, whether innocent or guilty, has not had a fair trial and the American people ought to be ashamed of allowing justice to be degraded into buffoonery." The *Pall Mall Gazette* agreed: "We should think that this is probably the first case recorded in any civilized court of justice in which the defendant has been convicted when the principal witness against him has not appeared and there has been no evidence to corroborate the charge against him. But with a Tammany Hall magistrate and a Tammany Hall police strange things may happen in New York. . . ."

The Italian press took the matter somewhat less seriously; it was merely one more indication that Americans simply could not understand the sophisticated European mentality. A writer for the influential *Il Tempo* of Milan noted that Italian ladies "are eager to be rubbed against by tenors, because, like hunchbacks, they bring good luck." Some American reporters, too, found the whole matter a source of humor. New York's *Morning Telegraph* reported that Caruso had had a picture removed from his suite at the Savoy because it was titled "The Monks of St. Simian," and had had a bellboy fired for whistling "I've Got a Feeling for You." *Musical Courier* noted that the betting was one thousand to one that the muff Musetta would hand Mimi in the last act of *La Bohème* (a performance of which would mark the tenor's return to the Metropolitan stage) would not be made of monkey fur.

Even one of New York's leading Italian-language newspapers, the *Bollettino della Sera*, found the episode amusing, though the target of the newspaper's sarcasm was not Caruso, but rather the puritanical American way of life. "Enrico Caruso has been condemned to pay a fine of ten dollars," the article began —

> May the Lord be praised! May St. Ursula with her thousands of little angels exult in the heights of the heavens! Justice is done. The modesty of the Americans is saved. The great tenor has paid the penalty of his depraved appetite. The angel of innocency, who had folded his wings over his eyes to shut out the sight in

the monkey house at Central Park, is now singing a hymn of victory and exalting in the presence of the Almighty the delicacy and purity of American life.

Caruso is condemned. The police have triumphed. The police, who are blind to the infractions of law, by day and by night, in saloons, hotels, concert halls and the innumerable places that corrupt the young and scandalize all. These honest police may be satisfied, for they have convinced a judge and a puritanical people that they caught Caruso patting a modest American woman, who has not been found.

O Europeans! O Italians! O journalists beyond the ocean! When you hear of civilization, of liberty, of justice in New York, turn away your eyes; when you take up your pen to magnify American virtues, write instead a hymn to Venus, to vice, to barbarism, to the most refined hypocrisy masquerading in the public welfare.

It was, however, no laughing matter for Caruso or for the management of the Metropolitan Opera. Caruso had been deeply hurt and embarrassed by the episode; it had been an assault on his dignity, and he suffered from it. As for the Metropolitan, its season and its immediate future depended on public acceptance of the tenor who was the foundation and the main attraction of the opera company. Worldly, sophisticated colleagues and fans of Caruso had come to his defense, but there had been genuine anger from a part of the public over what was considered his "obscene" behavior. The extent of this anger could not be measured until the singer actually appeared on the stage, but there was no doubt that it existed, and that the incident had brought to the surface a smoldering hostility toward the "dirty foreigners" who roamed the streets of New York in search of innocent American women. As evidence, there had been numerous indignant letters to the editors of New York newspapers from women who expressed their gratitude to the police for its handling of the case. One woman commented in a letter to the *Times* that "every woman and child in this city owes Patrolman Kane a debt of gratitude," while another, who signed herself "A New York Business Girl," wrote to express her "admiration for the persistency with which the police follow up such cases as Caruso's."

Both Conried and Caruso knew that the final verdict of the public would be made known on the night of November 28, when the tenor was to make his first appearance of the season at the Metropolitan. The opera was *La Bohème*, and singing with Caruso would be Sembrich, a loyal friend and supporter, and Scotti, who had been at the tenor's side throughout his ordeal. This ensured a friendly atmosphere onstage, but the reaction of the opera-going public remained in doubt. There had been extraordinary interest in the performance; in the hours preceding it long lines had formed at the box office, with tickets being sold by speculators for three and four times their normal prices as the merely curious joined the genuine opera-lovers in the clamor for seats. Inside the auditorium, adding to the tension that pervaded the atmosphere, was a special detachment of twenty-five plainclothes policemen (the irony should have been noted) ready to maintain order in case of a hostile demonstration.

When the curtain rose on the Bohemians' Parisian garret, Caruso was already onstage, his back to the audience as he gazed out over the city's rooftops — Puccini's opera called for no grand entrance, thereby robbing the audience of a chance at an immediate demonstration for or against the tenor. Several anxious moments passed before he was to turn and face the public, but when he finally did, he was greeted with one of the most tremendous ovations in the history of the opera house. There was no longer any doubt of the verdict of the audience. Caruso, overcome with emotion, seemed almost unable to go on; but, though singing somewhat tentatively at first, he and the other members of the cast concluded the first act in triumph. As the public cheered, Caruso and Sembrich were called before the curtain eight times; each time the gracious soprano tried to leave the tenor alone so that he might enjoy a solo bow, but each time he clutched the sleeve of her dress, refusing to let her leave his side. Finally, on the ninth call, Sembrich, a smile on her face, managed to detach herself from her colleague, to the immense satisfaction of the audience, which filled the house with cries of "bravo."

When the curtain calls finally came to an end, Caruso was near collapse, and the scene backstage was an emotional one as he laughed, cried, embraced, and was embraced by his friends and colleagues.

The following evening, he quietly celebrated Thanksgiving with a few close friends at the Hotel Savoy. He offered his own special thanks to all those who had expressed faith in him and had steadfastly believed in his innocence. Because of the pending appeal, however, the case was not yet completely closed. Further developments included the sudden appearance of the accuser, who claimed her name was Stanhope and not Graham, and who disappeared as suddenly as she had appeared without having offered any substantial testimony; the news of charges against Patrolman Kane for making false affidavits in a similar case; and the resignation from the force of Deputy Commissioner Mathot, who had been so active in prosecuting Caruso. In spite of all this, Caruso's appeal was rejected a month later.

The tenor wisely chose to let the matter rest. He had been scarred by the ordeal and would never forget the humiliation he had suffered, yet he took comfort in the knowledge that, no matter how unfairly he had been treated in the court and, often, by the press, he had been thoroughly vindicated by his devoted public.

✳

The remainder of Caruso's season was brilliant. Before the end of it, he had sung a total of twelve roles, among them his first New York appearances in *Fedora* (at its American première), Meyerbeer's *L'Africaine* (which he had never sung before), and in the first Metropolitan productions of *Manon Lescaut* and *Madama Butterfly*. Puccini, on his first visit to New York, was present for the last two of these. "Caruso was amazing," the composer wrote Sybil Seligman following the première of *Manon Lescaut* on January 18, noting in another letter that he was "singing like a god." In still another letter to Mrs. Seligman, following the first performance of *Madama Butterfly* on February 11, he qualified his praise somewhat. "As regards your *God (entre nous)*," he wrote, "I make you a present of him — he won't learn anything, he's lazy, and he's too pleased with himself — all the same his voice is magnificent."

Caruso had good reason to be pleased with himself. He had not let down either his public or Conried and, though illness had forced him to cancel a few appearances, he finished the season in a blaze of glory, exhibiting astounding energy by singing seven performances in the period between March 13 and March 23. Thanks to Farrar's successful American debut, Puccini's visit to New York, but above all to Caruso's immense popularity, the season — in spite of the failure of the American première of Richard Strauss' *Salome* which had shocked the sensibilities of too many influential New Yorkers — had been a successful one, and a credit to Conried's management.

It had been a difficult time for the managing director, who had stood firmly behind his star throughout the agonizing period which preceded his first appearance at the Metropolitan. Conried had been suffering for months from a painful, and as yet undiagnosed, nerve disease, which had caused him great difficulty in both walking and standing. When the season had opened, he had feared that his poor health would rob him of the strength needed to carry out his fatiguing job, which that year was complicated not only by the possible consequences of the Monkey House Case, but also by the threat of a newly formed opera company which would offer direct competition to the supremacy of the Metropolitan among American opera companies.

The Caruso problem had been satisfactorily resolved at the beginning of the season, but the challenge of the new opera company remained, and it proved far more serious than Conried, who at first tried to ignore it, had anticipated. The creation and the dream of the flamboyant showman, Oscar Hammerstein I, it was named the Manhattan Opera Company, and its impresario, driven by a passion for opera as well as a contempt for the hallowed Metropolitan and an intense hatred for Conried, had personally supervised the construction of a new theater on West 34th Street in which to house his newly formed troupe of singers. For his first season, he had recruited some of the greatest stars in the world of opera. Among these were the conductor Cleofonte Campanini, generally considered superior to Vigna who conducted the Italian repertory at the Metropolitan; the baritone Renaud, making his American debut; Melba, who had not sung in New York for two years; and Calvé. In addition, he brought to his Manhattan Opera House Caruso's old rival, Alessandro Bonci, who he felt would at least be able to hold his own against Caruso in a battle of tenors — a battle which the press publicized with glee.

The Manhattan's first season was a resounding success with both the press and public, giving Conried good reason to worry. The critics especially praised the Manhattan's chorus and orchestra, under Campanini's direction, comparing it favorably to the Metropolitan's. Melba, too, was at her best, as was Renaud, and Calvé's *Carmen* was a sensation. The New York *Times* called Hammerstein's production of *Rigoletto*, with Melba, Renaud, and Bonci, "the best seen in New York for many years" — a direct blow at the Metropolitan, where the Verdi opera, with Caruso, Sembrich, and Scotti, had been a favorite.

Bonci was Caruso's special problem, and much was made of the rivalry between the two men; the press even reported absurd rumors that the new tenor had challenged Caruso to a duel — or vice versa, depending on the newspaper. The Metropolitan's star was not unduly worried by this challenge — he had faced it successfully before — but, though he was known for his ability to get along with his colleagues, he made no secret of his contempt for Bonci. Certainly the extent of the feud between the two tenors was exaggerated by the Manhattan's imaginative and energetic press agent, William Guard (who would later work for the Metropolitan), but Caruso's hostility toward his rival could only have increased when Bonci told an interviewer that he had looked the other way while sitting opposite a pretty woman in a subway for fear the police would do to him what they had done to Caruso.

The star of the Metropolitan could find little pleasure, too, in Bonci's reception by New York's music critics, who praised the newcomer and insisted upon making comparisons between the two singers. After his debut in the Manhattan's opening night performance of Bellini's *I Puritani*, Henry Krehbiel of the *Tribune* wrote: "In nearly all things which enter into the art of vocalization he is inescapably finer than his rival. . . ." Richard Aldrich of the *Times* also found him to be a much subtler artist than Caruso, praising his artistry, phrasing, and diction, while conceding that the new tenor's voice lacked the richness and fullness of Caruso's. Comparisons between the two were, however, useless. Bonci excelled in the bel canto roles provided by the operas of Bellini, Rossini, and Donizetti, most of which were not part of Caruso's repertory. Furthermore, the Neapolitan tenor's hold on his audiences was secure — as long as he sang there could be no "rival" as far as the public was concerned. Nonetheless, Bonci was clearly a thorn in the side of both Caruso and Conried; and the only way to eliminate the thorn was to hire him away from the new company by offering him a higher salary. By the end of the season, in spite of threatened lawsuits on the part of Hammerstein, this was done. Bonci, an excellent tenor, would add luster to the Metropolitan, and Conried, undoubtedly with Caruso's approval, could control his American operatic career.

The elimination of Bonci from the Manhattan company had not lessened the challenge the new company posed to Conried's Metropolitan — Hammerstein, eager to do battle, had promised an exciting repertory and distinguished casts for the next season. However, by the spring of 1907, there were no further doubts that Caruso himself had emerged triumphant from the monkey house scandal and that he remained the idol of the New York public. After his final performance in New York, he joined the Metropolitan in a month-long tour that took him to Baltimore, Washington, Boston, Chicago, Cincinnati, St. Louis, Omaha, St. Paul, Minneapolis, and Milwaukee — San Francisco was conspicuously absent from the list. Wherever he sang, his reception was warm, and his performances were inevitably sold out; when he sailed for Europe following his last appearance in Milwaukee on April 27, he did so with the knowledge that his reputation throughout the United States was unblemished.

XI. The Battle of the Opera Houses

Caruso had emerged successfully from his encounters with San Francisco's earthquake and with New York's police. No such disasters were in store for him as he began his first European engagement of 1907 at Covent Garden. He was given a tremendous ovation there on the night of May 15, his first appearance of the season. The British press had been outraged by the tenor's treatment at the hands of American justice, and the opera-going public shared this indignation, showing it by greeting him even more warmly than usual.

The season proceeded smoothly, the only novelty being Caruso's first appearance in the title role of Giordano's *Andrea Chénier*. There was only one hint of scandal, and that was quickly dispelled. During a curtain call which followed a performance of *La Bohème*, the tenor was seen blowing a kiss in the direction of a mysterious blonde, seated in an upper box. The identity of this mystery woman was a subject for speculation the following day; apparently, neither the British press nor the audience at Covent Garden had noticed that the kisses had been meant for a small child, Caruso's younger son Mimmi, seated next to the unknown blonde, who was the boy's governess.

Caruso and Giachetti had settled their older child Fofò in the boarding school near Florence, while Mimmi, not yet three years old, had been entrusted to the care of a governess. Miss Louise Saer, a most proper and serious Welsh lady, was to look after the young boy conscientiously for many years. Caruso had recently established a home for them in London, not far from Miss Saer's own home, and the child and his governess spent most of their time in the British capital. The entire family, including Giachetti, was only briefly united at the Villa Bellosguardo during the tenor's annual summer holiday. It was by no means the ideal solution to a complex family problem, but it seemed the wisest one possible under the circumstances.

Caruso was relaxed and cheerful throughout the entire three-month season. He was again playing jokes on his colleagues, often to their amusement and sometimes to their embarrassment. Melba, not often amused, told a reporter from the *Daily Mail* of one relatively harmless incident which occurred during her last Covent Garden performance of *La Bohème* with the tenor. "Signor Tosti was sitting in the front row of the stalls, wearing a false moustache," she recounted, "and every time I looked his way, he waggled it at me in a most grotesque manner. Signor Caruso saw this and tried to imitate him. You can imagine how I felt when, as Mimi, I was supposed to be dying to Puccini's heart-rending strains!"

There had been other stories of Caruso's pranks while singing at Covent Garden. During one of the most solemn moments of *La Bohème*, Pasquale Amato, a Neapolitan baritone who was singing the role of Marcello, was stunned to find that Caruso had sewn up the sleeves of his coat, which he attempted to put on before leaving the Parisian garret to buy medicine for the dying Mimi. In the same act of the opera, Arimondi, having concluded the dignified Colline's tragic aria, started to place his tall hat on his head, only to find that his lighthearted colleague had filled it with water.

According to Sybil Seligman's son Vincent, the management of Covent Garden was none too pleased with their star tenor's playfulness, which offended those accustomed to the dignity and decorum of the opera house. Whether or not this was the case, Caruso's adoring public was disappointed to learn at the conclusion of the season that he would not be returning to London in the near future. The reason given was money. Caruso had recently signed an exclusive four-year contract with Conried, to expire in June 1911, under which he would receive over two thousand dollars a performance. This figure was far beyond the reach of Covent Garden, which was paying him twelve hundred dollars—the highest sum it had ever offered a tenor for a regular season at the opera house. Caruso might have accepted the lower figure, but under the terms of his new agreement no decisions could be made without the consent of the managing director of the Metropolitan, who would not have approved. In an interview given a few months later, Caruso noted with some satisfaction that while he might not be the world's best tenor, he was certainly the world's highest-paid tenor.

✳

When Caruso left London for Italy in early August 1907, he took with him still more official decorations—he had received the Victorian Order from the King of England, and he had been granted the Cross of the Chevalier of the Order of King Leopold of Belgium in recognition of his generosity in briefly interrupting his London stay to sing at a benefit concert for Belgian charities in Paris. Even more important, he carried with him a letter written on July 16 by Edouard de Reszke, a great bass and the brother of Jean, which read: ". . . I have never heard a more beautiful voice. . . . You sing like a god. You are an actor and a sincere artist, and above all you are modest and without exaggerations. . . . You have heart, feeling, poetry, truth, and with these qualities you will be master of the world."

On the return trip to Italy, Caruso was accompanied by Mimmi, Miss Saer, Sybil, and young Vincent Seligman. Giachetti met them at the station in Milan, and Vincent Seligman remembered "how, directly he [Caruso] caught sight of her on the platform at Milan, he had leapt out of the train whilst it was still moving, and thrown himself passionately into her arms."

The reunion was, as always, a short one. The family divided its time between their villa and a home Caruso had rented at the seaside resort of Viareggio, and before two months had passed, he set off for Budapest for his debut in the Hungarian capital, the first stop of a tour organized by his German manager, Emil Ledner. His performance at the Royal Opera House on the night of October 2, in *Aida*, was an unexpected fiasco. The public was cool and the critics the following day were frigid. Newspapers reported that the tenor had sung badly, that he had been ill and had been given an injection of morphine before the performance, and they complained that he refused to acknowledge the applause of the audience at the end of the opera. Caruso angrily denied all these reports, maintaining that he was in perfect health and that he did not appear before the curtain to acknowledge his applause simply because the soprano—a last-minute substitute—refused to join him. He blamed the disastrous evening solely on the excessive prices charged by the management. Ledner, of course, preferred Caruso's version, since he was responsible for the tenor's forthcoming engagements in Germany and was loath to have reports of his ill health precede those engagements. Many years later, in his memoirs, he admitted, however, that he was behind what had become known as the "Budapest Legend," which blamed Caruso's failure on the high prices and subsequent hostility of the audience. Caruso, according to Ledner, was far from his best on the night of the performance. Having only recently recovered from a minor operation, performed in Milan, for the removal of small nodes on his larynx, he was overly cautious and unsure of himself from the very beginning of the opera. By the third act, Ledner wrote, "he tried to force the withheld applause, but it was useless. He forced his voice, determined at any price to make his larynx obey — impossible under the circumstances. . . . The last act dragged wearily to its end; he was convinced that he had failed completely, and he later told me, 'I had only one feeling: to get it over as quickly as possible.'"

Caruso never returned to Budapest — it joined Naples, Barcelona, and San Francisco on his list of forbidden cities — but, to Ledner's relief, he quickly recovered from his bad experience there and was in top form for his next engagement at Vienna's Hofoper a few days later. Bruno Walter, then thirty-one years old, conducted several of the tenor's performances that season and wrote in his memoirs of the enormous enthusiasm of the Viennese public — as well as his own. "I loved Caruso's voice, his vocal talent, the sense of beauty expressed in his tone coloring, his portamento and his rubato, his noble musicianship, and his naturalness," he stated. "I may say there was a perfect understanding between us."

Subsequent performances in Leipzig, Hamburg, Frankfurt, and Berlin refuted any reports that might have circulated concerning his poor health. The demand for tickets to his performances in the German capital was overwhelming — more than thirty thousand applications for four performances. According to Ledner, those fortunate enough to obtain seats for his appearance in *Aida* witnessed one of the greatest of all of Caruso's performances.

> Caruso was in splendid form that night, revelling in his high notes; sure of victory, he sang *"Celeste Aida"* so brilliantly that the applause stopped the show. But that was only a foretaste of what was to come. The third act was truly extraordinary — truly an experience. Destinn as Aida and Caruso as Radames rose to such heights that those privileged to hear them remembered the occasion for years, perhaps to the end of their lives. Both poured forth tones of unearthly beauty in the great duet. It was sheer perfection, a unique and phenomenal event. What occurred at the end of the duet and the conclusion of the act was not merely applause, but an uproar, a cry of jubilation. The audience, which packed the theatre, clapped, shouted, and stamped their feet as one. . . . The duet in the judgment scene was equally fine, and the end of the opera was greeted by a repetition of the excite-

ment which had followed the third act. Over many years, I witnessed many triumphant Caruso evenings, but none like that
extraordinary performance of *Aida* in Berlin.

❊

In early November, immediately following his triumphs in Germany,
Caruso sailed for America; he was returning to New York for the first time
since the troubles at the monkey house. In May, the ten-dollar fine that
had been leveled against him had been paid, and his lawyer's plans for a
further appeal had been abandoned—all concerned believed that the
entire matter was best forgotten and that another appeal would merely stir
up more damaging publicity.

Throughout the summer there had been occasional reports in the press
that Caruso might, under the law, be considered an undesirable alien and
refused permission to enter the United States again. His attorneys laughed
off such reports, and the singer refused to take the threat seriously. Nonetheless, in an interview, he reminded reporters that he would have to be
paid according to the terms of his contract, even if he were prevented from
reappearing at the Metropolitan.

In spite of this show of confidence, when he arrived on the *Oceanic* on
November 13, 1907, it was rumored—but flatly denied—that he was
bringing with him a "certificate of good character," in case of trouble from
the immigration authorities. The certificate, if there was one, was unnecessary, and there was no challenge by the authorities. Instead, Caruso was
warmly greeted at the pier by an unusually large crowd of friends and
admirers. Before leaving for his new residence, a suite at the Plaza Hotel,
he met with reporters, brushing aside all questions concerning the monkey house incident and making it clear that his one concern was the coming season at the Metropolitan, which was scheduled to open on November 18 with the first New York production of *Adriana Lecouvreur*.

Though there was no challenge to Caruso from the U.S. authorities, the
Metropolitan again faced a formidable challenge from Hammerstein's
Manhattan Opera. The energetic, imaginative impresario had gathered
together a star-filled company and an innovative repertory for the second
year of his battle against the older house. His success during his first season could be attributed to the superb singing of Melba and Calvé and to his
excellent productions of operas of the standard, popular repertory. For his
second season, he offered New York audiences an even greater array of
stars and a number of seldom-heard operas. Most prominent among the
latter were works of the French repertory, long neglected by the Metropolitan: Massenet's *Thaïs*, Charpentier's *Louise*, and of great importance,

the United States première of Debussy's *Pelléas et Mélisande*. All three operas starred, in her American debut, Mary Garden, the glamorous Scottish-born, American-raised soprano who had been the sensation of Paris and had created the role of Mélisande in Debussy's opera. Garden repeated her Parisian triumphs at the Manhattan, but an even more sensational debut at the new opera house was that of the dazzling coloratura Luisa Tetrazzini, fresh from her enormous triumph in London. Tetrazzini took New York by storm at her debut as Violetta at the Manhattan on January 15, 1908, and she continued to draw packed houses whenever she sang.

In addition to these two spectacular sopranos, Hammerstein's company again included Renaud, always a favorite, as well as two brilliant tenors new to New York: Charles Dalmorès, outstanding in the French repertory, and the Italian Giovanni Zenatello, the original Pinkerton in *Madama Butterfly* and a leading member of the La Scala company for four years.

For its part, the Metropolitan still offered New Yorkers some of the world's finest singers, but the older company had its problems, too. Sembrich and Eames, its two leading sopranos, were both approaching retirement and would be badly missed, though another soprano, Farrar, was beginning to attain that popularity with the New York public that she would maintain for the rest of her career. The much-heralded appearances of the Russian basso Feodor Chaliapin were disappointing. Audiences who heard his debut in Boito's *Mefistofele*, as well as his later performances in *Don Giovanni* (he sang Leporello), as Don Basilio in the *Barber of Seville*, and in Gounod's *Faust*, found the Russian's Slavic excesses disconcerting; they were too accustomed to the elegance and polish of Plançon and Renaud. In the Met's favor, there were two new tenors on the roster who made good impressions. One was the Kentucky-born Riccardo Martin, a student of Edward MacDowell and Jean de Reszke; and the other was Bonci, who sang superbly and was greeted enthusiastically by the critics, though he seemed unable to catch fire as he should have with the Metropolitan's audiences. On the positive side, too, was the debut of the great conductor Gustav Mahler, who led the season's first performance of *Tristan und Isolde* on January 1 and shared the Wagner and Mozart repertory with another outstanding conductor, Alfred Hertz.

In spite of these considerable assets, the Metropolitan's most effective weapon in its battle against Hammerstein was still Caruso. Singing in two out of every five of the company's performances, he completely dominated the season. One week was typical. On the morning of January 13, he sang at a concert at the Waldorf-Astoria; that evening, he appeared at the Metropolitan in *Il Trovatore*. The following night he traveled to Philadelphia to sing in *Adriana Lecouvreur*. Two nights later, on January 16, he returned to New York for *Tosca*; the following night, he again appeared at the Metropolitan, this time in *Madama Butterfly*. *Musical America* commented that in that week alone, he earned more than the annual salary of a cabinet officer in the United States government.

During the season, he sang three roles for the first time in New York. His opening night portrayal of Maurizio in *Adriana Lecouvreur* was praised, though the opera itself failed to find favor with the public. On December 6, he sang the role of Osaka in Mascagni's *Iris*; again his singing was greatly admired, but the role of a Japanese suitor proved difficult for him dramatically and his Japanese costumes provoked laughter rather than the respect due a Japanese nobleman. His Metropolitan debut as Manrico in *Il Trovatore* on February 26 was, however, an unqualified success, and his singing of the bravura aria *"Di quella pira"* brought forth thunderous applause and insistent cries of "encore." This appearance marked a new phase in the tenor's Metropolitan career; it was a recognition of a change in his voice, now more suited to heavier, more heroic roles than it had been previously. As a result, he gradually began to abandon his lighter roles in *Rigoletto*, *Lucia*, and *Martha* — all three of which were entrusted to Bonci during the 1907–1908 season.

The Metropolitan's total dependence on its star tenor was looked upon with dismay by many observers of the New York operatic scene. The *Evening Post* noted regretfully that an excellent performance of *Martha* — with the American Bessie Abbot, Homer, Bonci, and Plançon in the cast — did not draw a large house, simply because Caruso was not singing, "the plain truth being that without Caruso it is difficult to draw a large audience at the Metropolitan just at present." Reginald De Koven, in *The World* of April 15, 1908, wrote at the close of the season: "The season at the Metropolitan may be briefly summed up in one word — Caruso — for without this single artist I hardly see what would become of the season at all." The conductor Alfred Hertz, too, was aware of the problem. In an interview given to the New York *Times* on April 13, he commented on the apparent decline of interest in the German operas at the Metropolitan, saying: "I can't see that interest in Wagner is decreasing. Rather do I find that the interest in Mr. Caruso is increasing. It is not a great interest in the Italian opera, but a great interest in Mr. Caruso that fills the Opera House. Go to the opera on Italian nights when that tenor is not singing, and you will find smaller audiences than on the German nights."

❊

The 1907–1908 season was notable for the absolute supremacy of Caruso at the Metropolitan, and it also marked the last year of the reign of Heinrich Conried. The managing director's health had continued to deteriorate, the company was losing money, and the success of Hammerstein's Manhattan Opera had forced the Metropolitan's board of directors to question the direction their own company was taking. In the middle of February, it was announced that Conried would be retiring at the end of the season, and shortly afterward it was learned that both Toscanini and Gatti-Casazza would be leaving La Scala to join the New York company—the former as chief conductor and the latter as managing director, sharing responsibility for that task with the German tenor Andreas Dippel, whose title would be that of administrative director.

The announcement of the change at the Metropolitan was greeted enthusiastically—Toscanini and Gatti-Casazza had been enormously successful in revitalizing the Milanese opera house and the same could be expected of them in New York. However, disconcerting rumors soon began to circulate that Caruso, one of the few artists close to Conried (who had been quoted as saying he enjoyed only those performances sung by his star tenor), and said to be on bad terms with Toscanini, would also be leaving the Metropolitan, to join Hammerstein's company. It was pointed out that the tenor's contract was with Conried and not with the Metropolitan, and that he was therefore under no further legal obligation to the company itself. His presence as a spectator at Manhattan performances of *Louise*, *Les Contes d'Hoffmann*, and *La Traviata* had been noted with much interest throughout the season, but little significance had been attached to these presumably routine visits to the rival opera house. His appearance in a box there on the night of February 22, for *Pelléas et Mélisande*, however, caused a furor. According to the press, this was more than a routine visit to the opera, for it was followed by a lengthy backstage meeting with Hammerstein. Coming right after the announcement of the changes at the Metropolitan, newspapers could draw but one conclusion. "Rival opera houses begin a battle for Caruso," the *American* proclaimed, while a headline in *The World* announced, "Opera war waxes hot over Caruso," and the *Telegraph* stated, "Caruso is open to a new deal."

Caruso vigorously denied these rumors. The press had exaggerated his problems with Toscanini and the importance of his visits to the Manhattan Opera House, just as it had underestimated the strength of his ties to the Metropolitan. It was true that the tenor and Toscanini were not good friends. Many singers had come into conflict with the strong-willed conductor over his strict interpretation of a composer's wishes, and Emma Eames was to state that Caruso completely agreed with her that Toscanini never allowed for a singer's freedom of emotion or need for personal interpretation. Nonetheless, Caruso had worked successfully with Toscanini in the past and had no intention of letting any disagreements with the maestro interfere with his own career at the Metropolitan. "We have all received his reproofs, but we none of us blame him," he told a reporter two years later. "He is an artist in the highest sense of the word."

As for his attendance at several performances at the Manhattan, these could be explained by his close friendship with Tetrazzini and by his normal curiosity to hear operas he had never before heard and singers he had never before seen perform. His meeting with Hammerstein was most probably no more than a friendly one—though the impresario would no doubt have liked to have Caruso on his team.

Most important, though Caruso's contract did bind him directly to Conried, his loyalty was to the Metropolitan itself. He was not, as one observer noted, merely a member of the company; he *was*, in many ways, the company, and he enjoyed his undisputed reign there. He had grown close to many of his associates at the opera house, especially to Otto H. Kahn, a powerful board member who was taking an active part in the management of the company, and it is doubtful that he ever seriously considered abandoning it. At his final appearance of the season on April 4, he was positively exuberant, making it clear that the Metropolitan was and would remain his home. A reporter for *The World* commented that "he was like a boy let out of school. His antics seemed to give nearly as much pleasure to the public as his singing." When the performance ended, two pages came to the stage: first they presented the tenor with a wreath and then each handed him a cluster of American Beauty roses. As Caruso took them in his arms, a thorn pricked his finger. A smile on his face, he took the wounded finger to his mouth, as any boy would, causing the audience to rise to its feet with laughter.

✳

Caruso felt at home at the Metropolitan, but he was far less at ease during his first American concert tour, which followed the company's regular post-season tour. An extended concert tour was an experiment for the singer, who feared he might be lost without his costumes and without the props of the operatic stage. Nonetheless, it seemed a relatively easy way both to earn some money and to make himself better known to the American public outside of New York.

The experiment was not a completely successful one. Joined by a group which included Julia Allen, a soprano; Margaret Keyes, a mezzo-soprano; Henri G. Scott, a bass; and a boy violinist known as Master Kotlarsky, he traveled to Toronto, Detroit, Buffalo, Cleveland, Rochester, and Montreal. A typical program included Miss Allen's rendition of the "Bell Song" from *Lakmé*, arias from *Les Huguenots* sung by Miss Keyes, excerpts from *Faust* by Mr. Scott, and short works of Vieuxtemps and Sarasate played by the boy violinist. Caruso, whose presence guaranteed crowded houses wherever they performed, gave generously of himself, singing familiar arias as well as a selection of popular songs. He also joined his colleagues in singing a certain crowd-pleaser, the quartet from *Rigoletto*. Audiences paid unusually high prices to hear him, and they responded enthusiastically, but the tenor was, as he had feared, uncomfortable. He was more nervous than usual, fumbling with his hands and unable to get on and off the stage effectively. He often sang several arias or songs in a group, in order to avoid the necessity of too many awkward exits and entrances. His cheering public seemed unaware of his difficulties, but at least one critic, Victor Slayton of the Cleveland *News*, while praising the performance, took note of his discomfort. "Out of costume, Caruso makes a strange stage figure," he wrote on May 12, 1908. "His enormous thorax makes his head seem small and his legs spidery. In evening dress he gives a curious effect of an over-plus of linen. He acknowledges plaudits with dignified bows . . . but he never smiles. Instead, he glares fiercely, requiring an awful stretch of the imagination to conceive him as the mischievous Caruso of his leisure hours. The only approach to levity in his stage demeanor is the few little dog trot steps he occasionally adds to his exits."

Caruso was primarily a man of the theater, and he knew it; he laughingly calculated that he was paid two and a half dollars for each note he had sung on the concert stage, but he was relieved of a difficult burden when his first concert tour came to an end in Montreal on May 18, 1908.

XII. *"Ridi, Pagliaccio"*

On May 21, 1908, Caruso left for Europe on the *Kaiserin Auguste Victoria,* accompanied by Martino, his new accompanist Tullio Voghera, and Father Joseph Tonello, an acquaintance of many years. He was, from all accounts, unusually relaxed and happy. He was determined that his summer would be an uncommonly restful one: his schedule included a benefit concert in London, a single appearance — also a benefit — in Paris, a short visit to Naples to visit his ailing father, and, finally, a long reunion at his villa with Ada and their children.

After a few days at sea, Caruso's euphoria came abruptly to an end with the arrival of a cable announcing the death of his father. According to Father Tonello, the tenor collapsed upon receiving the news. Father and son were not close and had never been; nonetheless, Caruso was an emotional man, with close sentimental ties to his past, and now a part of that past was lost forever. Once recovered from the shock, he sent off a number of cablegrams: to friends, informing them of his loss; to Tosti, asking that he cancel the London engagement; and to Gabriel Astruc, the French manager, asking that he be excused from his Paris commitment. He cabled his stepmother: LEARN MIDDLE OCEAN DEATH ADORED FATHER. AM DESPERATE, DESOLATE, HEARTBROKEN, and he further expressed his grief in a letter to a childhood friend, Angelo Arachite, writing, "God wanted to deny me the chance to see him one more time, and I submit to His will. My poor father! What sorrow this is for me. I still can't come to terms with it. . . ."

Once in London, the grief-stricken tenor went immediately to the home he had set up for Mimmi and Miss Saer. Tosti was waiting for him and did his best to calm him and convince him that it was his duty to sing at the scheduled concert, no matter how he felt. Caruso reluctantly agreed. Before long, however, he was faced with even more shattering news: Giachetti, with whom he had lived for eleven years, had abandoned him and run off with Cesare Romati, the family's young and handsome chauffeur.

Caruso was distraught, but according to the soprano Frances Alda, who a few years later recalled the tenor's own account of his relationship with Ada, the news had not come as a complete surprise. Caruso had first learned of Giachetti's affair with the chauffeur while in America more than a year before. When they were reunited in Italy the following summer, according to Alda's version, Caruso had begged Ada to give up her lover, and she had agreed. The reconciliation was, however, short-lived and after a few weeks together the tenor had left for America again, without Giachetti.

The final break had been inevitable. The couple, once so in love, had spent little time together in recent years. Caruso—and he made no secret of it—was completely absorbed in his career; much as he loved his "wife" and children, his career would always come first. Giachetti, though many years his senior, was still a beautiful and desirable woman, and she had, for whatever reasons (it is unlikely that her work was one of them), chosen not to join him in his travels. Although their relationship had steadily deteriorated and had become a source of unhappiness for both of them, Caruso's friends were unanimous in agreeing that the tenor was still deeply in love with Giachetti at the time she deserted him.

The same determination which had characterized Caruso's approach to his career enabled him to put aside, temporarily at least, his profound grief in order to fulfill his two professional commitments in the late spring of 1908. His first engagement, the concert at Albert Hall on May 30, was for him—though the audience was unaware of it—a painfully personal experience. Among the participants at that gala concert were Melba, John McCormack, and the violinist Efrem Zimbalist. Caruso sang two solos: Tosti's *"La mia canzone"* and the heartrending and peculiarly appropriate *"Vesti la giubba"* from *Pagliacci*. The *Daily Express* noted the following day: "The poignant despair with which he invested the words 'Ridi, Pagliaccio, sul tuo amore infranto' (Laugh, clown, for the love that is ended), had a quite thrilling effect upon the audience who applauded him to the echo."

The distinguished audience, which included the king and queen as well as the Prince and Princess of Wales, knew of the tenor's sadness at the loss of his father—the king summoned him to his box to offer his personal condolences—but only Tosti and Sybil Seligman, among those present, knew of the private pain which had gone into Caruso's rendition of the aria, one which movingly expressed the clown's bitterness over his lover's betrayal; it is hard to believe that the aria had ever before been sung with such deep conviction.

Caruso's second and final engagement, before the start of what was once supposed to be a relaxing summer, was equally successful—a performance of *Rigoletto*, with Melba and Renaud, at the Paris Opéra on June 11. It was the tenor's first appearance at the great French theater, and the brilliant audience, which included Armand Fallières, the president of France, gave Melba and Caruso what they agreed was the most enthusiastic reception of their lives.

These ovations, however, usually so important to the tenor, meant little to him during what was to be a lost summer, one veiled in mystery. Able at last to put his career aside and concentrate on his personal grief, Caruso devoted his time to making arrangements for his two—now motherless—sons and to a frantic effort to put together the pieces of his life, which would no longer include Giachetti. His boys were well taken care of, with the aid of Miss Saer (already accustomed to act as Mimmi's surrogate mother), and Rina Giachetti, who took over much of the burden of her sister's responsibility, but Caruso, without Ada, was frantic. Heartbroken, he sent telegrams to every city where he thought she might be, but to no avail. The man whose every move had been followed closely by the press suddenly disappeared from sight as he commenced his lonely crusade to understand what had happened, and, perhaps, to convince Ada to return to him. It is impossible to trace his movements during the early months of that summer, but he apparently spent most of his time traveling throughout France and England, with occasional stops at his villa. Martino, who was with him throughout the ordeal, reported later that he was so worried about Caruso's state of mind that while at Bellosguardo he slept outside his employer's bedroom, fearing that the tenor might take his own life.

A public figure, Caruso was also a very private man, never eager to show to the public—or even to friends—what lay behind the mask of the jovial, fun-loving performer. By the middle of August, however, the press had learned of Giachetti's elopement, and while in London the tenor, in an effort to minimize his difficulties, granted a short interview to a New York *Times* correspondent there.

The result, under the headline CARUSO VERY GLAD WIFE HAS ELOPED, was the lead story on the front page of the August 14 issue of the newspaper. "Life with her was impossible," he told the reporter. "I told her so several weeks ago. I expect my wife to be a woman who can sympathize with me—a woman of ability, of understanding, of appreciation. . . . A month ago in Italy I told her how she had fallen below the expectations I had formed of her and bade her begone. . . . The woman did not come up to my standards, and I have no regrets. She has gone off with somebody of her own level."

Despite this angry display of bravado, Caruso could not long hide the fact that he had been deeply hurt not only by Giachetti's desertion, but by the fact that she had left him for a chauffeur. He was, according to some observers, heartbroken. Other dramatic stories appeared in the press throughout the summer and early fall, the most interesting of which was published in *The Daily Telegraph* of London on August 22, 1908. The headline was simply TROUBLES OF A TENOR, and it read:

As some of the Italian newspapers have already made allusions to the family troubles of a celebrated tenor, I consider myself free to send you the complete story. The tenor in question is of world-wide reputation, and is very well known both in New York and London, where he has been for some years one of the attractions of the Covent Garden Opera. The companion of the famous tenor had already given the newspapers something to talk about, and now a fresh scandal has arisen. For many years the tenor had lived with a beautiful singer, who had left for him her house and husband. The tenor had purchased for her a splendid villa near Florence. During last winter her husband threatened to institute proceedings, so the tenor and the lady had planned to go to the United States and take up American citizenship, so as to allow the latter to obtain a divorce from her husband and marry the singer.

After the theatrical season in New York was over, the tenor was to commence a tour through various American towns. The lady then came to England, and went to live in London.

Here the tenor was to have met her. In the meanwhile, however, the fickle dame had fallen madly in love with her chauffeur. When the singer arrived in London for the season, the lady went to live with him again. The tenor was at that time negotiating for the purchase of a beautiful palace at Nice. The lady soon wanted to go to Italy, and went to the tenor's residence at Florence. But shortly afterwards she fled with her chauffeur to Nice, taking with her diamonds and jewellery to the value of £32,000.

News of her flight reached the tenor when he was giving some private concerts. He rushed over to Nice to claim for himself his two sons, and in desperation begged the fugitive to come back with him, but she refused to do so, and preferred to remain with the chauffeur.

The singer tried everything to convince the unfaithful lady to cease this new scandal, and it is said that in his despair he has also had recourse to the legal husband of the lady, asking him to interpose his conjugal authority in the matter and convince the wife that she has gone too far in preferring an obscure chauffeur to a celebrated singer. But it is stated that the philosopher husband contented himself with quietly smiling.

Now the singer, who has got a new motor-car and also a new chauffeur, for the purpose of touring Italy in search of the old ones, has come regretfully to the conclusion that his relations with the lady must be at an end. The most curious part of the affair is this, that, unfortunately, she, for her part, believes that all is not yet finished with the singer, and it is said that she has now instituted proceedings against him.

The sources for this unsigned article were never revealed, but much of its contents—if not all—later proved to be true. The tenor's own feelings seem to have been mixed. He was reliably reported to have had a meeting with Gino Botti, Giachetti's husband, and it is known that he made other desperate attempts to convince her to return to him. On the other hand, he wrote to Puccini (as the composer recounted to Sybil Seligman in a letter of September 21) that Ada had left with only one dress and without a penny and that he was now free "and glad to be able to devote himself to his boys, to whom he hopes soon to give a good mother."

As if to refute the stories of his depression and his frantic search for Ada (he emphatically told reporters that she had never been his wife), Caruso turned up in Naples in an ebullient mood in the middle of September. He was fresh from a pleasure trip to Tunis, where he had traveled in Arab costume in order to soak in local color. Arriving in Naples dressed in a flowing white caftan, with a turban wrapped around his head, he was delighted to be mistaken for a high Turkish dignitary. Once he removed his disguise, he entered into Neapolitan life with a gusto hardly characteristic of a pining lover. He was observed strolling along the city's waterfront, eating huge plates of pasta at seaside restaurants, and enjoying himself immensely—in public, at least.

Most important for his own well-being, the tenor was gathering strength for the opera season to come. The loss of Ada was painful; the loss of his career would have been unbearable. Aware of this, Caruso traveled to Germany in late September to fulfill his first engagements of the new season. The brief tour, which took him to Wiesbaden, Frankfurt, Bremen, Hamburg, and Leipzig, ended with three performances in Berlin on October 20, 22, and 24. Still badly shaken by his turbulent summer, he was comforted by his loyal friends Scotti and Farrar, who sang with him during the tour, and by the extraordinary warmth of the German public, who again packed the theaters to hear their idol. While in the German capital, he was honored by an invitation from one of his greatest admirers, Kaiser Wilhelm II, to join him for a private dinner at the Imperial Palace. Though he had been able to perform with his customary brilliance on the stage, the tenor was not quite certain that he would have the emotional strength to withstand the strains of a formal social engagement, so he agreed to accept the invitation only if his faithful Martino could be present. The kaiser agreed, and at the end of the dinner, as Caruso was about to leave, the sovereign reportedly said: "If I were not the German Emperor, I would like to be Martino."

✳

When Caruso arrived in New York on November 3, 1908, observers noted that he looked drawn and weary—the inevitable result, it was believed, of his emotionally exhausting summer. Upon arrival, he again changed his place of residence, this time moving into a large luxurious apartment at the Hotel Knickerbocker, which would remain his home for several years. Once settled, he began his preparations for the opening of the new season at the Metropolitan.

That new season, the first under the management of Gatti-Casazza and the first with Toscanini as chief conductor, had aroused unusual excitement among New York's opera-goers. The Italian press had complained that these two men had caught Caruso's all too contagious disease, "*dollarite acuta*," but for New York audiences this disease was a blessing. The board of directors of the Metropolitan, too, was optimistic as the new season approached. It was hoped that the three Italians, with the aid of the brilliant conductors Mahler and Hertz, could finally put an end to Hammerstein's formidable challenge.

Though there seemed to be no indication of it at the time, the end was in sight for the Manhattan company; but in the meantime the challenge was very much alive. Hammerstein's season was a distinguished one, its success guaranteed by his three great sopranos—Melba, Garden, and Tetrazzini. His repertory again was imaginative—it included the American première of Massenet's *Le Jongleur de Notre-Dame* and a new production of *Salome*—and his two star tenors, Zenatello and the Spaniard Florencio Constantino, new to New York, were each of the first rank, though neither could hope to compete successfully with Caruso for the affection of the New York public.

Because of the unwavering loyalty of that public, Caruso remained as indifferent to the threat of the Manhattan as he was to the changes taking place at the Metropolitan. Conried was gone, and the tenor had his disagreements with Toscanini, but the real power at the opera house had fallen into the hands of Otto Kahn, the new chairman of the board of directors, and Kahn—a brilliant businessman and banker, a gentleman of superb taste with a deep understanding of music—was Caruso's friend and supporter. Warm and unassuming in spite of his wealth, he admired the tenor even more than Conried had and showed his affection by studying Italian in order to communicate better with his leading singer during the long, informal meals they frequently shared in the far from elegant restaurants of New York's Little Italy. When, late in the season, it was again rumored that Caruso would abandon the Metropolitan to join the then desperate Hammerstein, it was already clear to all who knew the tenor that he would never desert Kahn nor would he ever leave the organization which had been his home for several years.

Caruso showed absolutely no signs of fatigue as he began the 1908–1909 season with an unprecedented—even for him—display of energy, singing in six of the company's first seven performances. It was an astounding record for a man said to be worn out after a disturbing summer. His first appearance took place on November 14 when he joined the company in a special pre-season performance of *Faust*, which marked the inauguration of Brooklyn's new Academy of Music. On the night of the 16th, he took part in the official opening of the season—a gala performance of *Aida*, the first under Gatti-Casazza's regime and also the American debut of Toscanini and Emmy Destinn. The following evening the company traveled to Philadelphia, where the tenor sang in *La Bohème*; two nights later he was back in New York for *Madama Butterfly*, and the following night he substituted for Bonci in *La Traviata*. This almost superhuman marathon came to an end the next day when Caruso sang in the matinee performance of *Tosca*.

A more normal schedule of performances followed, but after he had sung his first New York Turiddu in *Cavalleria Rusticana*, on December 17, two Caruso performances were canceled. The public was shocked, certain that something serious must have caused the sturdy, apparently indefatigable tenor to renounce his commitments. The official reason—strained vocal cords caused by his strenuous activities at the start of the season—was plausible, but a rumor quickly spread that the real cause was far more serious, that he was suffering from an illness that could threaten his entire career. This story was, according to the irate Caruso, absolute nonsense.

His physician, Dr. Holbrook Curtis, concurred, announcing that he had been treating Caruso for nothing more threatening than a cold which had reached his vocal cords.

Voices predicting some dire tragedy were stilled at least temporarily when Caruso returned to the Metropolitan on December 26 to sing *Pagliacci*; they were completely discounted during the month of January when he resumed his usual schedule, singing brilliantly with the company not only in New York but also in Brooklyn, Philadelphia, and Baltimore. At the end of that month, he did suffer a shock. It had nothing to do with his physical well-being, but was caused by a surprise visit from Giachetti, who demanded both money and more control over the future of their children. Caught by surprise while taking a bath in his apartment at the Hotel Knickerbocker, Caruso responded angrily. A loud shouting match in the corridors of the hotel ensued, until Giachetti was evicted. The following day a somewhat calmer meeting was held. Caruso was surrounded by an entourage of friends and advisers to protect him and look after his interests. When Giachetti left, after only a few days in New York, she expressed at least partial satisfaction to curious reporters: she had apparently been paid off, with a promise of further discussions of their differences when the tenor next returned to Italy. Caruso was not among those present when she boarded the French liner *La Lorraine* for Europe on January 28. Instead, he was on his way to Philadelphia for a matinee performance of *Il Trovatore*. Once there, an unidentified friend of his issued a terse statement to the press: "Signor Caruso says he was never married in all his life. He knows nothing of the lady who sailed from New York today. He has nothing further to say."

❋

Caruso recovered quickly from the unexpected visit. He seemed to have recovered, too, from his throat ailment, maintaining an active schedule the first week of February. On the first of the month he participated in a benefit concert at the Waldorf-Astoria, in aid of the victims of an Italian earthquake, playfully drawing caricatures of the participants, who included Paderewski, Farrar, and Eames. On the third he sang in Massenet's *Manon* for the first time at the Metropolitan, earning praise from the critics, who felt that he had mastered, as never before, the French style and diction. Two days later he performed, along with the young violinist Mischa Elman, at a private tea party given at the Plaza. He seemed nervous and ill at ease, but no more so than at any of his other concert appearances.

On February 6, the tenor took part in a gala performance in honor of

Marcella Sembrich, marking her farewell appearance — as well as her twenty-fifth anniversary — at the Metropolitan. As part of the celebration, Caruso sang the role of Alfredo in the first act of *Traviata*, with Sembrich as the tragic heroine and Farrar, Scotti, and Amato in minor roles. He was in good spirits at a post-performance reception given for the immensely popular soprano at the Hotel Savoy, and was among the 150 people who honored her at a dinner the following evening at the Hotel Astor. On that festive occasion, he was seated at a table with the critic Henry Finck, who "enjoyed his naïve, boyish conduct every moment." Caruso, bored by the endless series of speeches, spent his time drawing caricatures of the speakers and other celebrities present, among them Mahler, to whom — in spite of their warm relationship — he refused to show his finished sketch. Instead, he showed it to the conductor's wife, Alma, explaining, "First, one says one doesn't mind; then one sees and is angry. It's happened to me too often."

Although the singer seemed to be keeping up with the hectic pace, it soon became apparent that his public had been correct in fearing that something more than a cold had troubled him. The first indication came after a February 13 performance of *Aida* when he was again forced to cancel a number of appearances. Following a performance of *Manon* on March 4, it was abruptly announced that he would be taking a month's rest. Once again, rumors of a serious throat ailment began to circulate. Though he insisted publicly that he was merely in need of a rest from his heavy schedule, he was privately both worried and frightened by the recurrence of his illness. On April 2, after a month of inactivity, he wrote to his brother Giovanni: "I will resume singing tomorrow matinee, and you can understand how nervous I am, as I do not know if I will be able to give the performances of the full season or quit and rest one entire year at home. Pray for me."

Caruso returned to the stage in *Cavalleria Rusticana* on the afternoon of April 3, before an enormous crowd which greeted him enthusiastically. Some observers noticed that he was looking haggard and pale, but the reviewer for the *Times* wrote: "He sang in fine voice, and disproved the reports that have been in circulation to the effect that it was failing." Immediately following the performance, Andreas Dippel sent a telegram to Chicago, assuring officials that Caruso would be singing there as scheduled during the Metropolitan's annual post-season tour.

Both Dippel and the reviewer for the *Times* had been too optimistic. Caruso's last appearance in New York took place on the night of April 7, 1909, when he sang *Aida*. It was obvious to all that he was not at his best: his voice was dark and heavy, and he was exercising uncommon caution as he sang. The critic for the *Telegraph* spoke for many of his colleagues when he wrote:

> It had been reported that Caruso was suffering from a most grievous infection of the throat, that his voice had gone, that his career was finished, that the earthquake in San Francisco, the famous police court trial in which he was engaged three seasons ago, his losses of money in the panic of 1907, and his recent domestic troubles had dealt a series of blows . . . from which neither he nor his voice had as yet recovered. Mr. Caruso's voice has by no means left him. It has indeed become darker in tone and heavier in volume. But a careful studying of his singing last night showed that while he was not as vigorously certain of himself as he has been in past years, and while his high notes were not distinguished by the exquisite beauty that has made him one of the wonders of the world, his vocal indisposition was temporary rather than radical. It was obvious that he needs a long rest. He has somewhat overworked that frailest and most mysterious of musical instruments, the human voice, for years. Trouble exists, but it is not deep-seated, and eradication of this trouble rests with himself.

Because of this and other similar appraisals of the tenor's last performance, it should have come as no surprise when an official announcement was made that Caruso would not, after all, be joining the opera company on its tour and that he would instead be returning to Italy in mid-April. Nonetheless, the public was stunned; his premature departure for Europe seemed to confirm its suspicions that his illness was a serious one. These suspicions were intensified by a story published in the New York *Times* of April 14. According to the newspaper, he would be going directly to Milan, where he would "place himself under the care of an eminent specialist, in the hope that the climate and a series of operations will restore his throat to something like its normal condition."

The story noted that the problem had come to light a few years before and that Caruso had at that time undergone surgery and had been warned to modify his busy schedule—a warning he had obviously not heeded. "His friends in this country, music lovers and opera-goers," the *Times* concluded, "are hoping that the fear that it is too late to save the voice may be groundless."

When Caruso boarded the *Mauretania* for Europe on April 14, he responded angrily to the newspaper article. "I am very tired," he told reporters, "and I will get plenty of rest while I am away. The idea that I may never be able to sing again is ridiculous. It may be that just at this time my voice is not up to the standard — just at the pitch where it was a few months ago — but then I have been working hard. I assure my friends that the lapse is only temporary." When asked where he would be spending the summer, he joked that he was going to visit Frau Wagner and study Wagnerian roles.

✳

Caruso was not joking when he arrived in Liverpool in late April. Met by a throng of curious reporters eager to know just how seriously his voice had been impaired, he answered that his "illness" had been an invention of the American press and repeated that there was nothing the matter with him that a badly needed rest, which he planned, would not cure. He added that he had hoped to make that clear by singing at the Metropolitan in the days before his departure, but that he had not taken into consideration the stubborn determination of the press to concoct a story.

In spite of this denial, he was, after consultations in London and Milan, operated on in late May by Milanese throat specialist Professor Della Vedova for the removal of a nodular growth on the left vocal cord. At the time that this news was leaked to the press, it was also confirmed that he had undergone a similar operation on the right vocal cord a few years before.

According to the physician, who stated that the singer's illness had been caused by overuse of his voice, the operation was a minor one and a complete recovery could be expected after a short period of rest. As a confirmation of this optimistic prognosis, and to reassure the anxious public, it was announced that the Metropolitan had extended his contract for three years beyond the present one, which was to expire in two years. Caruso was quoted as saying: "I am in love with New York and its people quite as much as with my business arrangements. I never felt better in my life."

Nonetheless, he was bitter over all the publicity concerning an operation he had hoped would be performed in absolute secrecy. The importance of his illness, he felt, had been unfairly exaggerated, to the point of jeopardizing his career. Reports of his declining vocal powers were potentially damaging to his future, and he had learned that these rumors had already hurt ticket sales for his tour of the British Isles later in the summer — his first scheduled public appearances after the operation. "When I had an operation," he later complained to reporters, "I was pestered night and day with reporters, and because I refused to disclose details which I considered absolutely personal the press in general spoke so malignantly about it that serious business complications might have followed. . . ."

Caruso's rest was shorter than anticipated. His problems with Giachetti had been temporarily put aside, his sons were well taken care of for the summer, and he was so eager to prove to the world that his recovery was complete that he agreed to sing at three hastily arranged concerts at Ostende at the beginning of August, a few weeks before his planned tour of Britain. From the moment he sang the opening bars of his first aria on the night of August 1, it was obvious to the more than ten thousand curious spectators who filled the Belgian resort's Kursaal that all was well. If anything, according to the press and the cheering public, his voice was even better than it had been before the operation. Charles Henry Meltzer of the New York *American* wrote, "Caruso's voice has lost much of the baritonic quality which marred it during the latter part of his operatic career, and was more nearly what it used to be — a genuine tenor, lyrical, yet not effeminine."

Word spread quickly of Caruso's return to normal, and sold-out houses greeted him on his short British tour, which took him to Dublin, Plymouth, Blackpool, Glasgow, Edinburgh, Newcastle, Manchester, Belfast, and Liverpool. His buoyant spirits, too, had returned, and he delighted his public by buying a kilt in Edinburgh (for use in his performances of *Lucia di Lammermoor*) and a splendid golden-brown evening suit in London. Fifteen thousand people filled the Royal Albert Hall — while another four thousand were turned away — for his single appearance in the British capital that year, on the night of September 18. There had been none of the "business complications" he had feared.

There were no such complications either on a tour of Germany which followed — his first appearances on the operatic stage since his illness. No country had been more appreciative of Caruso's talents in the past, but this time the German public outdid itself in showing its affection. Once again, Berlin was the high point of the tour. There were riots at the box office on the day tickets for the performances went on sale; more than two thousand people, some of whom had waited since the previous evening, scrambled for positions on a line which stretched twice around the opera house, and a squadron of police had to intervene to restore order. Caruso fever had become epidemic.

Among the many cheering the tenor's return to the stage, as Don José in *Carmen* on the night of October 19, was his loyal friend the Kaiser. Also present was Lotte Lehmann, the great soprano, then twenty-one years old, who later described Caruso's performance that evening. "Thrilling as an actor, quite apart from his singing, he was a revelation to me. Trembling with emotion I followed the destiny that was being enacted before me with overpowering realism. His complete abandonment to his part communicated itself to his audience, breathless under the spell, and I am sure that many who had only come 'because one must have been there' forgot about sensation and remembered only Caruso," she wrote in her memoirs. Lehmann remembered the tenor's kindness and generosity as well. Two nights later the young soprano sang the role of Euridice in Gluck's *Orfeo ed Euridice* on a program that included Caruso's performance of Canio in *Pagliacci*, and was "dazed with joy" when he enthusiastically praised her singing and invited her to be a guest at a dinner given in his honor.

XIII. The Black Hand and Other Problems

The 1909–1910 Metropolitan season (which opened on the night of November 15 with a performance of *La Gioconda* starring Caruso, Amato, Destinn, and Homer, and conducted by Toscanini), was one of the most extraordinary in the history of the New York opera company — or, for that matter, any opera company. Toscanini electrified audiences with a new production of *Tristan und Isolde*, featuring on separate evenings three of the most brilliant Isoldes of all time — Gadski, Fremstad, and Nordica (in her final Metropolitan appearance). The Italian conductor also led, for the first time in New York, performances of *Die Meistersinger* and Gluck's *Orfeo ed Euridice*, and an enormously successful production of *Otello*, which introduced Austrian tenor Leo Slezak to New York audiences. Toscanini was not the only outstanding conductor on the roster: Mahler conducted the first American production of Tchaikovsky's *Pique Dame* (with Slezak and Destinn); and Hertz's repertory included Wagner's *Ring* and Weber's *Der Freischütz* with a cast that featured the great tenor Hermann Jadlowker. The company's list of tenors was equally distinguished: in addition to Slezak, who also sang in *Aida*, *Il Trovatore*, *Die Meistersinger*, *Tannhäuser*, and Flotow's *Alessandro Stradella*; and Jadlowker, who demonstrated the enormous range of his talent by singing also in *Faust*, *Lohengrin*, *Pagliacci*, and *Cavalleria Rusticana*, it included others who could easily have dominated the season of any opera company in the world. Among these were Carl Jörn, a German who sang Wagnerian roles as well as leading roles in *Faust, Manon, The Bartered Bride,* and *Der Frei-schütz;* Riccardo Martin (*Madama Butterfly, Tosca, La Bohème, Cavalleria Rusticana, Il Trovatore, Aida,* and a new American opera, Frederick Converse's *The Pipe of Desire*); the Frenchman Edmond Clément (*Manon, Werther, Fra Diavolo,* and *Falstaff*); and Bonci, who complained that he had not been used to substitute for the ailing Caruso the previous season, but who sang eight different roles during the season of 1909–1910.

Obviously, this was not just another Caruso season, as the press had lamented in the past. Gatti-Casazza and Toscanini presented to New York audiences a brilliant array of artists in a marvelously diversified repertory of operas. Nonetheless, the beloved Neapolitan tenor remained the company's single most important attraction. When he had arrived in New York, he had put to rest all talk about his health. His problems had been as much emotional as physical, he declared, and they had been resolved. He had even gained weight, though not as much as the press claimed; it was, he jokingly protested, his tight collar which made his face seem fatter than it really was. Most important, he stated that his voice was not only back to normal, but in some ways better than it had been.

His performances in the course of the season substantiated this statement. He no longer abused his voice as he had in the past, but he sang nine different roles for a total of twenty-eight performances at the Metropolitan (plus fifteen performances in Brooklyn, Boston, Philadelphia, and Baltimore, considered part of the company's regular season) with unfailing success. His only novelty of the season was his first New York appearance in *Germania,* which was not a great success; but his interpretations of those roles for which he was already well known brought praise from critics who noted a new artistic maturity, an improvement in his musicianship, and a greater vocal refinement. "It was not quite the same Caruso vocally," wrote the critic for *Musical America,* "but it was a new and more mature Caruso histrionically. . . . His artistic stature has grown notably since he last sang here, and there was a distinct gain in finish of style and dramatic effectiveness."

It was not only his voice and his increasingly effective theatrical presence that endeared him to the public, that made him unique among the opera singers at the Metropolitan and elsewhere. It was also his offstage personality, his magnetic warmth, and his unfailing generosity that set him apart from his distinguished colleagues. "He is by all odds the most popular man who has ever stepped inside the opera house as far as chorus members and other members of the institution are concerned," an employee of the Metropolitan told a reporter, after the tenor had played Santa Claus to the entire company at Christmas. "Caruso is always genial, good-humored, generous, and sympathetic. He is absolutely democratic and always ready to pass the time of day with the most lowly of his associates."

Away from the opera house, too, he showed his generosity by spending several hours each day answering his mail, much of which consisted of requests for financial aid. He was a notoriously easy target for such requests — but not always, as illustrated by an anecdote he recounted to an interviewer from the New York *Herald* on December 12, 1909. "One man write me his wife very sick. I send him five dollars. A few days later he say his daughter very sick. I send three dollars to him. When he says his son is sick, that's too much. I write and say I'm sick. I ask him if he wants me to build a hospital for his family. He make me very mad."

Caruso was made very mad too — and far more seriously so — when what had been a brilliant and untroubled season was disturbed on March 1 by an ugly note from the notorious Black Hand, demanding a payment of fifteen thousand dollars and threatening death if it was not received. The organization, associated with the Mafia, had for years been terrorizing a large percentage of New York's Italian population with similar notes, and it was only natural that the tenor, the most famous Italian in America, should receive one. Most members of the Italian community had given in to those threats, but Caruso reacted angrily. The note said that the money should be given to a man who would stop him on 42nd Street while on his way to the opera house the following day; but instead of complying with these instructions, he immediately alerted the police, who provided him with two bodyguards for his daily walk.

Nothing happened during his walk, but two days later another letter arrived. It contained further threats and ordered Caruso to leave the money in a bag by the entrance to a small factory in Brooklyn. This time the still-defiant singer, with the aid of the police, devised a more complicated trap for the blackmailers. A decoy package — real money on top and false bills below — was given to his valet Martino, who carried it to Brooklyn and, with plainclothesmen watching from a distance, deposited it in front of the factory. Before long, three men arrived to claim the money; they were surprised by the police, and though one managed to escape, two (both of whom had police records) were arrested. The arrests, however, did not put an end to Caruso's troubles. The police feared that other members of the Black Hand might seek revenge, and as a consequence he was placed under steady, and unnerving, police protection. When he went to Brooklyn on March 7 for a performance of *La Gioconda*, he was surrounded by police; and plainclothesmen watched every corner of the Academy of Music throughout the performance, for a note had threatened that acid would be thrown in the tenor's face in retaliation for his betrayal of the Black Hand. Similar measures of protection were taken during Caruso's

visit to Philadelphia for a performance of *Aida* on March 10, and he was
under constant surveillance for the remainder of his stay in New York. As
the days passed, the danger did not diminish; a chain reaction set in, and
other threatening letters were received. Caruso, publicly at least, stood
firm in his defiance of the Black Hand. He turned over each new letter to
the police and formally filed charges against the two men who had been
arrested. The press lauded him for his courage in setting an example for
other innocent citizens who might be threatened by the secret organization, yet a rumor persisted that the tenor had, to some extent, weakened in
his resolve by making a payment of between one and two thousand dollars
to the organization. The rumor was neither confirmed nor denied, but
Caruso's signature was on a petition the following year for the early par-
don of the two criminals who had been imprisoned because of his testimony.

✳

Caruso had been shaken — "I can't wait to put an end to this awful life
and go to live in a solitary corner away from the whole world," he wrote to
his Neapolitan friend Arachite — yet he managed to finish the Metropolitan season without showing any ill effects from the nerveracking episode.
It was, in the opinion of New York's critics, the most successful one of his
career. But just as the public delighted in his return at the top of his form
and in the revitalization of the Metropolitan under Gatti-Casazza and Toscanini, it was also saddened to learn that 1910 would mark the end of
Hammerstein's Manhattan Opera. The valiant, colorful impresario had
continued to present New Yorkers with an exciting alternative to the Metropolitan, but he had overextended himself, speculating recklessly in real
estate and attempting to expand his activities outside of New York. In
January, while Hammerstein was in Europe, his son Arthur began discussions with Otto Kahn concerning the possibility of a merger between the
two competing companies. In the end, this solution proved to be impossible, and Kahn, who both admired and respected Hammerstein, bought
him out for a more than generous sum, while at the same time making
certain that there would be no further threat to the supremacy of the
Metropolitan. Under the terms of their agreement, Hammerstein gave up
the right to produce operas in New York, Boston, Philadelphia, and Chicago for a period of ten years, and the Metropolitan acquired the rights to
the operas owned by Hammerstein as well as the contracts with many of
his leading singers. The Metropolitan reigned once again as New York's
only major opera company.

❋

The Metropolitan's annual tour, which began in Chicago on April 4, was an extension of the company's brilliant New York season; but on the road, even more than in New York, the principal attraction was Caruso. The tenor's fame had grown through the continuing sales of his records— he had signed a new agreement with Victor in December of 1909, granting the company the exclusive right to make and sell records of his voice for a period of twenty-five years—and his name on a program was, as always, a guarantee of a full house in Chicago, Cleveland, Milwaukee, St. Paul, St. Louis, and Atlanta, which would be his stops during the post-New York season.

The tour was a special one, for following the last performance in Atlanta, more than two hundred members of the company set out on an unprecedented voyage to Paris for the Metropolitan's first season abroad. A Paris season had been the dream of Otto Kahn, who was anxious to show off his extraordinary American company to a European audience and had carefully planned an outstanding program of Italian operas, conducted by Toscanini, for the occasion. The Parisian public would have a chance to hear Caruso in *Aida*, *Pagliacci*, and *Manon Lescaut*; it would also be given the rare opportunity to hear Toscanini conduct Verdi's *Otello* and *Falstaff*, with brilliant casts that included Slezak, Jadlowker, Scotti, Alda, and Homer. The season offered an embarrassment of riches, but from the moment the program was announced, Parisian opera-goers proved they were no different from their American counterparts; they clamored for seats for Caruso performances but were slow to buy tickets for the performances of Verdi's late masterpieces. To remedy this situation, it was decided that each purchase of a "Caruso" ticket carried with it the obligation to purchase a seat for either *Otello* or *Falstaff*.

Considering the distinguished productions promised for the two Verdi operas, this restriction constituted no hardship for a true opera-lover, yet the French resented the Metropolitan's ruling. The press, too, at the start, was offended at the idea of an American company showing the French how an opera should be done, and many French performers expressed anger at Toscanini for not including any of their countrymen in the company. In spite of this initial hostility, the engagement was a huge success, and the Théâtre du Châtelet was filled for each performance. Though he was greeted by boos on the opening night of May 21, Toscanini was hailed as a genius throughout the season; even Puccini's *Manon Lescaut*, an Italian's version of a French masterpiece, which was given its first Paris production on the night of June 9, was enthusiastically received, with special praise reserved for the twenty-one-year-old soprano Lucrezia Bori, who sang the role of Manon. True to their reputation, French critics had reservations, but even they were virtually unanimous in their enthusiasm for Caruso.

Kahn had achieved his goal: the Metropolitan was recognized as a major opera company by the skeptical Europeans. However, it was Caruso who had carried the season and had become the idol of the Parisian public, not only because of his singing but, again, because of his behavior away from the theater. Curious crowds gathered in front of his hotel, and he acknowledged their interest with unfailing charm and grace. Autograph seekers came to his table at the Café de la Paix, where he lunched with Italian friends (including his brother Giovanni, who had joined him in Paris), and he responded warmly, appreciative of their attention. Newspapers, too, printed stories which served to endear him even further to the skeptical French public. One of these stories concerned his unconventional behavior before the opening of the Metropolitan's Paris season, when he was asked to sing at a benefit concert at the Trocadéro. At first, according to the press, he had kept the committee waiting for his reply; then he had further angered them by demanding that he be paid his usual minimum fee of twenty-five hundred dollars for one appearance. When it was suggested that it was wrong for him to ask for any fee whatsoever for a benefit, he replied that no official member of the committee had given nearly as much as the sum he was expected to donate. The committee reluctantly agreed, and Caruso participated in the concert; following it he demanded that the money owed him be paid him in cash. He carefully counted the money and then, adding a check of his own for one thousand dollars, he returned the pay envelope to the astonished sponsors, telling them that he felt his contribution should be thirty-five hundred dollars.

This was but one of countless anecdotes—true or untrue—that filled the pages of the French press. Caruso was a hero in Paris as he had been elsewhere, and his superb performances at the Châtelet confirmed his eminence in the world of opera, as did his final appearance in the French capital on the night of June 18, when he participated in a special performance at the Paris Opéra for the benefit of the survivors of a tragic accident which had resulted in the loss of the submarine, the *Pluvoise*. The program was a brilliant one: it included the prologue to *Pagliacci*, the second act of *Tristan und Isolde*—its first performance in German in Paris— conducted by Toscanini, the fourth act of *Otello*, with Slezak and Alda, act three of *La Bohème*, with Caruso and Farrar, and, finally, the rousing final scene of *Faust*, with Caruso, Farrar, and the Spanish bass Andrés de Segurola. It was an unqualified triumph for each participant, but, even in this illustrious company, it was Caruso who was given the greatest share of the audience's applause.

The tenor had earned his Parisian triumphs at the expense of his health. He had ignored his promises to his doctors and to himself to use his voice sparingly—he sang six times during his last eight days in the French capital—and he was exhausted at the end of the season. He did what he could to recover his strength during the summer—spending time with Mimmi, Tosti, and the Seligmans in London, visiting other friends in Paris, and finally returning at the end of July with his child and Miss Saer to the Villa Bellosguardo, where they joined Fofò. After a short stay there, he accompanied both of his sons on a family visit to Naples. His brother Giovanni had occasionally joined him on his travels within Europe, but Caruso had spent little time with his stepmother, who had been reluctant to visit him at his villa, and with his sister Assunta, who was too ill to travel (a frail woman for most of her life, she was to die in 1915).

His stay in Italy afforded him little chance for rest. There were painful reminders of the past. He realized that his sons, isolated from any contact with Giachetti, desperately needed maternal affection, and he learned that Giachetti had instituted a lawsuit against him for defamation of character and had accused him of stealing her jewelry (the case did not reach the courts for almost two years). The Italian press hounded him, too. The country of his birth had had little opportunity to hear him sing, and its citizens were curious about the man who had brought so much glory to their country; he was the subject of countless interviews, focusing largely on the two issues most painful to him: his troubles with Giachetti and the condition of his voice. This probing into his personal life upset him, but he fended off the questions with agility—he was used to them—and he consoled the Italian public by announcing that he would be joining the Metropolitan for a season in Rome the following year.

✳

On September 24 and 25 Caruso was back at work—with two performances of *La Bohème* at the Théâtre Royal de la Monnaie in Brussels, his first appearances in the Belgian capital. Shortly afterward, he returned to Germany for what he hoped would be another spectacularly successful tour. In spite of the continuing adoration of the German public, it was a tour marked by signs of his fatigue, as well as by near disaster. It began auspiciously enough in Frankfurt, where crowds cheered him as enthusiastically as they had in the past; but his two appearances in Munich, his second stop, were marred by accidents that caused alarm throughout the world, and even made the tenor fear that there might be some mysterious plot against him.

The first of these occurred on the night of October 8, his season's debut in the Bavarian capital, when, during a performance of *Carmen*, he fell and injured his knee. The sight of Caruso limping with the aid of a cane the following day was so disturbing that the New York *Times* saw fit to devote an editorial to it. "Caruso has suffered bodily injury and a large part of the civilized world awaits eagerly fresh information regarding its extent, and his chances of speedy recovery," the editorial noted. "There is no other living performer in opera or drama whose disabilities would affect so large a number of his fellow-beings," it went on. "We have strong hopes that Mr. Caruso's bad knee will not trouble him long. . . . But Caruso can sing *'Celeste Aida'* and *'M'apparì'* from a wheeled chair if necessary and still move the whole world to rapturous applause."

Caruso recovered quickly from the accident, but a far more serious mishap occurred on the night of October 11 when, during a curtain call following the third act of *La Bohème*, he was struck on the head by an iron bar which had been used to move scenery. He managed to step behind the wings, but once out of sight of the audience, he fell to the ground unconscious. Carried to his dressing room, where he was revived by the house doctor, he stubbornly refused to follow the physician's advice to cancel the rest of the performance; he sang the final act while sitting on the bed of the dying Mimi.

It had been a frightening experience, but, in spite of rumors that his future German engagements would have to be canceled, Caruso, explaining that he had a *"testa dura"* (hard head), continued on to Hamburg, where he appeared, without incident, in *Rigoletto*, *Martha*, and *Carmen*. These performances were conducted by the twenty-five-year-old Otto Klemperer, who, echoing the sentiments of other conductors who worked with the tenor, remembered in his memoirs that "Caruso was an exceedingly musical singer who adapted himself perfectly to the ensemble without showing a trace of the soloist's temperament."

The final stop on the tour was Berlin, now famous for its annual outbreak of Caruso fever. Nothing had changed: there were long lines at the box office, fans fought for the privilege of buying tickets at three times their normal price, and police finally had to be called in to restore order. The Kaiser was again among those present at the opening performance, having this time postponed an official visit to Belgium in order to hear his favorite tenor once more.

For the first time, however, critics — while praising Caruso for his growing skills as an actor — expressed reservations concerning his over-all performances. Some blamed his supporting casts, especially Florence Easton, an American soprano, who sang Aida on the opening night; but many felt that the tenor's voice seemed tired and that his singing was not up to his usual high standard, indicating that he had not yet recovered from his strenuous Paris season a few months before.

Emil Ledner, Caruso's German manager, was unworried by Caruso's performances during his Berlin engagement; he was, however, considerably disturbed by the prospects of another kind of engagement. While in Frankfurt, the beaming tenor had informed Ledner that he had become secretly engaged to marry a beautiful shopgirl, Elsa Ganelli, whom he had met in Milan. He informed the stunned manager that the girl, accompanied by her father, would be joining him in Berlin, where an official announcement of the betrothal would be made, and that he expected his manager to make proper arrangements for the visit. Ledner later described the episode at length:

> I ordered a suite of two bedrooms and sitting-room for the father and daughter at the Hotel Bristol, at some distance on the same floor from my quarters. They arrived in Berlin, and the daughter really was a very lovely girl. The father was an elderly, rather stout man — both of them wore obviously new clothes. I noticed that Signorina Ganelli seemed rather at ease, her father in his "fine clothes" seemed rather uncomfortable, as if unused to his raiment. I felt rather sorry for the poor Italians, unaccustomed to such surroundings so different from their usual modest environment. The father was a minor civil servant and the daughter a sales-clerk; both were somewhat intimidated and diffident. They lived quietly, secluded in their apartment and saw Caruso only in the theatre, the drawing room or in the dining room or when they went for a walk with him. Caruso behaved in an exemplary manner, treating Signorina Ganelli like a Great Lady, acting like a man very much in love and spoke freely of his plans for the future — marriage early next year — and how dreary the time in between would be for him. Father and daughter stayed about ten days in Berlin. I gathered together a group of friends Caruso had made during his visits to Berlin and arranged a little banquet at which his engagement to Signorina Ganelli was "officially" announced. A few days later father and daughter returned to Milan while Caruso and I left for Bremen. An hour before his steamship was to sail, Caruso handed me a telegram, with an urgent request that I have it sent immediately to Signorina Ganelli by some trustworthy person and ordered me to read it myself beforehand so that I would be fully informed of its

content. It read about as follows: "Our wedding cannot take
place. Exigencies of constant travel force me to revoke our as yet
not publicly announced engagement. Let both of us forget all
previous events." I was dumbfounded, and asked: "This telegram
is to be sent?" He answered nervously, and obviously embarrassed: "Yes! And please no questions." The telegram was sent.

When Caruso sailed for New York on the *Kronprinzessin Cecilie*, he felt
relieved, certain that his short-lived engagement would be forgotten. He
underestimated the tenacity of Signorina Ganelli and her father; before
long, they would be heard from again.

XIV. A Trying Period

Caruso was surprisingly relaxed when he arrived in New York on November 8, 1910 — free from any ill effects of his Munich mishaps and free, or so he thought, from his recently discarded fiancée. He convinced his fellow passenger Leo Slezak to join him in taking off his hat to the Statue of Liberty shortly before the ship's arrival in port, and once on land expressed the opinion that the coming opera season would be an especially distinguished one.

The novelties of the season were to be his appearances in the Metropolitan première of Gluck's seldom-performed *Armide* and in the world première of Puccini's *La Fanciulla del West*, an opera set in the American West, based on a play by David Belasco. The Gluck opera opened the Metropolitan season on the night of November 14; conducted by Toscanini, its cast included Fremstad, Amato, and Homer. It was not a typical Caruso opening, since his role, that of Renaud, a knight, was a small one compared to that of Fremstad, who sang the title role. Nonetheless, Caruso accepted this secondary role with enthusiasm; he was grateful for the chance to master a style to which he was unaccustomed. By accepting it rather than demanding — as he might have — a more showy role in an opera more familiar to him, he demonstrated again that he was not merely a "star" but a serious and responsible musician.

By his own admission, he spent most of the evening in his dressing room, working on caricatures, while his fellow artists sang onstage. One of

161

these sketches was a self-portrait of himself as Renaud, reclining on a sofa, eating a sandwich and fanning himself. The caption read, "What I do in *Armide*," and he presented the finished drawing to a greatly amused Fremstad during an intermission of the opera.

Caruso's gesture in agreeing to sing a subordinate role in an unfamiliar opera was not appreciated by many of New York's critics. There were complaints that he looked ridiculous in the role of the romantic knight, that he had gained so much weight that he was a sorry figure, and that he moved about the stage awkwardly. "He was," according to the reviewer for *Musical America*, "a strange and fearsome spectacle." Carl Van Vechten, writing more seriously in the New York *Times* the day after the performance, complained that the tenor had not fully understood the style in which the opera should have been sung. But other critics disagreed. "He deserves great credit," wrote the critic for the *Post*, "for being willing to assume a role lying so far outside his usual sphere. . . . It was not until the last act was reached that the audience heard the real Caruso; and the real Caruso is — well, everyone knows what he is — he is Caruso, that's all." (Many years later, even Van Vechten admitted that he had never heard the role sung better — even by tenors at the Paris Opéra.)

During the next few weeks, Caruso returned to his more familiar roles in *Aida*, *La Gioconda*, and *Pagliacci*, but most of his energies went into the preparations for the première of Puccini's new opera. Puccini and his publisher had passed him by when selecting a tenor to create the role of Cavaradossi in *Tosca*, but this time they were more than eager to have him in the cast of the first performance of the composer's latest opera — the first work by a living European to have its world première in New York.

It was his first chance to portray an American. He was to sing the role of Dick Johnson, a repentant outlaw; the cast would also include Amato as Jack Rance, the evil sheriff, and Destinn, who was to sing Minnie, the golden-hearted but strong-willed girl of the Golden West. This "American" opera was to be conducted by Toscanini, and the composer himself had come to New York to supervise rehearsals. There were no Americans in charge to lend authenticity to the production, but for the good of all concerned, Belasco (who had originally attended the rehearsals out of curiosity) soon took charge of the stage action.

It proved to be an exhausting task for the American playwright and impresario, for it involved transforming a multinational group of principals and an unwieldy chorus into a homogeneous and convincing collection of Western Americans. "Men and women by the score and fifties would troop out on the stage, range themselves in rows, and become merely a background for the principals," he later recounted in his autobiography. "Then for no purpose they would all begin to shrug their shoulders, grimace, and gesticulate with their hands." Caruso at first resisted Belasco's attempts to turn him into an American outlaw, but he finally gave in and delighted the director by learning, among other things, exactly how to kiss a young lady in a bungalow during a blizzard.

When the opera had its première, on the night of December 10, both Belasco and Puccini were more than satisfied with the results of their efforts. The entire cast performed brilliantly in front of the most glamorous audience in the history of the Metropolitan. Caruso's role was not a particularly gratifying one, and he had little opportunity to demonstrate the full extent of his vocal powers until his last-act aria, sung as he was about to be hanged by an angry lynch mob, but he appeared to enjoy the festivities immensely. At one curtain call, he playfully drew a revolver out of his holster; and at his final one, he rubbed in mock pain the spot on his neck which had been touched by the rope used for the proposed lynching. At the very end of the evening, he presented an emotional Puccini with a solid silver wreath, designed by Tiffany, on behalf of the managing director of the Metropolitan.

Though Puccini's new opera never matched the success of his earlier works, the audience at the première was enthusiastic. The critics the following day, though mixed in their opinions of the opera itself, had nothing but praise for the tenor's performance. Puccini, too, felt that Caruso had sung magnificently, and Belasco noted with satisfaction: "Last night, perhaps for the first time, those in the audience forgot they were listening to the great Caruso. What they listened to was 'the voice of the century' lifting from the throat of a Sierra road agent [sic], dressed and acting the part with as much finesse as he sang his lines."

Caruso sang the new opera eight more times that season, with unfailing success. He seemed at his best, too, as he resumed his standard repertory, singing twenty performances in a period of eight weeks. There was no indication that his performance of *Germania* on February 6, 1911, would be his last of the season. Nonetheless, following that appearance, to the astonishment of the public, four Caruso performances were canceled. The public was immediately reassured that the cause of the cancellations was simply a bad cold, yet rumors of a more serious illness again began to circulate when the tenor suddenly left for Atlantic City and a complete rest. Optimistic statements were issued when he returned to New York in early March; Dr. Holbrook Curtis explained that Caruso had been forced to leave New York primarily to escape from the pressures of well-meaning friends and fans, and that his stay by the seaside had achieved its purpose—fully recovered, he would return to the stage within a few weeks.

In spite of Dr. Curtis' predictions, and sporadic reports that the tenor would be soon returning to the Metropolitan, he did not return to the stage during the month of March. Even the report that Caruso, in order to reassure his fans of his recovery, would rejoin the company during the last week of the season proved to be untrue, and on April 5 it was officially announced that he would soon be returning to Italy. A letter sent by his physician to Gatti-Casazza was released to the press. It read: "This is to certify that we have examined Signor Caruso and find that he is still suffering from the effects of his recent attack of the grippe and laryngitis, and that in our opinion it would be advisable for him not to attempt to sing again this season, but to seek a change of climate."

The news came as a tremendous blow to Caruso's fans, confirming fears that his illness might have actually been a recurrence of the far more serious problems which had troubled him in the past. It seemed most unlikely that an attack of grippe would have prevented him from singing for a period of two months, and the announcement of his withdrawal from the post-season tour of the United States, as well as the cancellation of the Metropolitan's eagerly anticipated visit to Rome, only added to the public's fears. Even if the long-range prognosis was optimistic, the immediate loss to the Metropolitan and to the opera-going public had been considerable. "There is no dispute that the temporary voicelessness of Enrico Caruso threatens somewhat to eclipse the gayety of nations," an editorial writer for the New York *Times* wrote on April 21. "The glory of the New York opera season was perceptibly dimmed by the famous tenor's affliction, and the pecuniary receipts sensibly diminished. . . . Geraldine Farrar, Olive Fremstad, Jörn, and Amato are never slighted, but there is no rival of Caruso in popular esteem, no other voice that so deeply touches alike the public heart and the public pocket. If his voice does not return this summer, what can London do and Paris and Rome?"

❊

London, Paris, and Rome, it was soon obvious, would have to manage without Caruso for a while. He arrived in the British capital in late April, determined that this time his visit there would be the beginning of a long period of rest. He planned to lead a quiet, retired life — visiting friends, shopping in the London stores which had always intrigued him, and, most important, spending time with his young son Mimmi. Yet a series of irritating problems, inevitable in view of his enormous fame, prevented him from enjoying the peace he so desperately sought.

First among these was the persistent rumor that because of his deteriorating health, his career was reaching its end. The rumor seemed to have been substantiated by a report from his Italian doctor, Della Vedova, who

His Leading Ladies

Elena Bianchini-Cappelli
(Courtesy Lim M. Lai)

Nellie Melba
(Courtesy Lim M. Lai)

Geraldine Farrar
(Courtesy Lim M. Lai)

Emmy Destinn
(Courtesy Lim M. Lai)

Marcella Sembrich
(Courtesy Lim M. Lai)

Portrait of Ada Giachetti,
painted on the belvedere
of the Villa Bellosguardo
(Courtesy Enrico Caruso, Jr.)

Ada Giachetti, 1909. This photo-
graph was originally inscribed "To
my dear Fofò, his Mammina," but a
few years later Fofò, angered by his
mother's betrayal of his father,
changed the words to "To my dear
Papa, his Child."
(Museo Caruso, Milan)

The tenor's two sons, with his brother Giovanni (taken in 1925).
(La Scala Autographs)

With Otto Kahn
(Courtesy Lim M. Lai)

With Ormi Hawley in *The Great Romance* *(Peabody Institute Library)*

Sheepshead Bay, August 1918 *(Courtesy Lim M. Lai)*

With Scotti in Atlanta, 1920 *(Peabody Institute Library)*

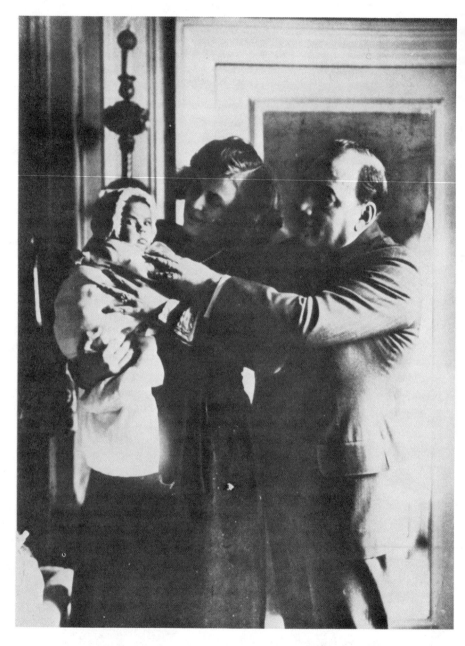

With Dorothy and Gloria Caruso *(Wide World Photos)*

Self-portrait
(*Author's collection*)

As Canio in *Pagliacci*
(*La Scala Autographs*)

He was the subject of songs, during his career and after his death

"Goodbye Caruso"
(Author's collection)

"They Needed a Song Bird in Heaven"
(Author's collection)

had declared that still another operation on his throat would be necessary—an operation so serious this time that it could lead to the effective destruction of his vocal cords. Caruso was furious. He announced publicly that the Milanese doctor's declaration was nothing more than an effort to gain personal publicity, and threatened to take legal action not only against Della Vedova but against all those who made irresponsible comments concerning his health. He produced proof of his well-being in the form of a statement by a noted English physician who affirmed that he had first examined Caruso on April 25 and had found severe catarrh of the larynx, resulting from his long bout with influenza, and then, on May 16, declared that his patient, after several weeks of treatment, was completely cured.

This constant need to combat rumors concerning his health was not the only annoyance Caruso had to face while in London. Another concerned the home that he had established a few years before for Mimmi and Miss Saer. It was only one of his many homes, but in the late spring of 1911 British authorities judged it to be his permanent legal residence and taxed him accordingly. The tenor, who had concerned himself little with minor financial problems—he had more money than he could spend—was this time outraged. Convinced that he had been treated unfairly, he reacted quickly and decisively, emptying the house of its contents and moving Mimmi and his governess into the nearby residence of the latter's family.

Caruso trusted Miss Saer completely, and his mind was at ease knowing his son was in good hands. Though he still hoped that his mother would return, the young boy had grown attached to the rather reserved Welshwoman whom he continued to call "lei"—the Italian for "you," his first word for her when he spoke no English—and he had become fond of her family, whom he identified forever by the colors of the blouses each member had worn when they had first met ("Red" had taught him history and geography). Fofò, Caruso's older son, still at school near Florence, was equally well cared for, and the knowledge of his sons' well-being was a comfort to the tenor. Nonetheless, he knew that both boys needed the special care that only a mother—even a stepmother—could provide, and he was determined to find one for them. Perhaps that was the explanation for his engagement to Elsa Ganelli. In any case, he had already forgotten the young woman he had briefly considered suitable to be a mother to his children. Unfortunately, neither she nor her father had forgotten the celebrated tenor, and while in London he heard again from both of them—it was another problem he had to face while in the British capital. Following his abrupt renunciation of their engagement, Caruso had received—while he was singing in New York—a series of desperate letters from both

Ganellis. Hoping rather naïvely that the entire embarrassing matter could be forgotten, he failed to answer them. Pasquale Ganelli, the father, not surprisingly felt otherwise, and filed suit in Milan for breach of promise, charging that Caruso had misled his daughter by bringing her to Berlin, introducing her to his friends as his fiancée, and then abandoning her. He introduced as evidence approximately sixty passionate love letters that the singer had written his wronged daughter.

When Caruso learned of the action taken against him, he countered by claiming that the suit was nothing more than another attempt to blackmail him. He had, he asserted, no intention of giving in to the threat and hastened to give his own version of the story. He had met the girl two years before while buying a tie at a Milanese store where she was employed. The two had talked, and shortly after their meeting he had offered her a job as housekeeper in his London home. She had declined, stating that it was impossible for her to leave her family in Italy. Before long, while in London, he had received a cable stating that she had changed her mind and asking that he come to get her. He replied that his professional commitments prevented this, and a long correspondence followed. The letters exchanged became increasingly — and foolishly, as far as Caruso was concerned — affectionate, and after a while he suggested that they meet in Berlin; as a proper gentleman, he insisted that she be accompanied by a member of her family. When Signorina Ganelli agreed to make the trip with her father, Caruso generously sent her money, not only enough for the fare but also enough to cover the costs of a new wardrobe for their visit to Germany.

The Berlin meetings were predictably a failure, and Caruso realized there that he had made a mistake; as a result he sent the message formally ending their relationship. The matter might have ended there had it not been for the letters. The Ganellis threatened to have them published unless he bought them back. Caruso wanted them — he was eager to avoid the embarrassing publicity that their publication would cause — but the price demanded by Pasquale Ganelli was far too high. When it became clear that no compromise could be reached, Ganelli filed the suit against Caruso, asking fifty thousand dollars in damages. The enraged tenor put the entire blame for the suit on the girl's father. "Because I am a public character he thought that I would pay fifty thousand dollars in order to avoid a scandal," he told the press. "But I will not be cheated in any such manner."

When the case came to court in Milan several months later, Caruso was legally, if not morally, vindicated. Though he was censured by the judges for "a morally deplorable act" and forced to pay all legal costs, the judges ruled that a promise of marriage did not necessarily involve the obligation of marriage, and the claim for fifty thousand dollars in damages was dismissed.

The prospect of the lawsuit and the embarrassment caused by the publicity did not unduly upset Caruso's stay in London. He felt he was a victim—both of his own poor judgment and of the avariciousness of Pasquale Ganelli—and that he was once again paying a price for his worldwide fame. The tax problem, too, had been no more than a temporary inconvenience, and when he left the British capital in June 1911 he was determined to put these irritations behind him and to follow his doctor's orders so that he might fully regain his strength. His health, he knew, was of paramount importance.

With this in mind, he spent most of the summer in Italy, both at his villa and traveling around the country with his two sons. The complete rest the doctors had recommended was impossible—merely sitting in the sun or exercising were anathema to him, nor could he give up his incessant smoking—yet throughout the summer there was encouraging news, from those who had seen him, concerning the improvement in his health. One visitor to the villa who was impressed with Caruso's physical condition was Maurice Halperson of New York's *Staats-Zeitung*. After telling the journalist that he had limited his singing to one half hour a day, Caruso gave him a sample and Halperson reported that the famed voice "sounded full, healthy, and jubilantly free." Lillian Nordica, too, heard him perform in private and found his voice "more beautiful than ever." And another of his colleagues, Riccardo Martin, wrote to *Musical America* from the Adriatic resort of Rimini in late August to say that he had never seen Caruso looking so well or in such good spirits.

✳

In spite of these optimistic assessments of his voice, considerable anxiety surrounded Caruso's Vienna engagement in late September. It would mark his first public stage appearances in over seven months—he had never before been absent from the theater for such a long period. Extraordinary conditions had been written into his contract with the Hofoper, reflecting not only concern over his health but also worries over the possibility of a recurrence of the accidents that had plagued him in Munich the previous year. No one was allowed to go on the stage or even stand in the wings while Caruso was in either place, unless that person was "necessarily engaged there." No stranger was to be admitted to that part of the theater which enclosed the stage. Absolutely no piece of scenery could be shifted as long as the tenor was onstage or in the wings. Finally, Caruso's physician and private secretary, as well as the impresario and conductor, would have to escort him on all occasions from the stage to his dressing room.

Happily for all concerned the Vienna engagement was not only free from any accidents but also an unqualified artistic triumph, and the tenor — appearing in *Pagliacci, Rigoletto,* and *Carmen* — proved conclusively that he could sing as splendidly as ever. There were absolutely no signs of any deterioration of his voice in Vienna or in the course of his short tour of Germany which followed. His German public, including the ever-faithful kaiser, was elated at what seemed to be a confirmation of his complete recovery. It came as a shock to all who had heard him when, at the end of the tour, it was revealed that their idol had actually been in poor health during the entire engagement, suffering from severe neuralgic headaches as well as occasional irritation of the throat. He had, it seems, been urged by his physicians, his friends, and even the impresario, to cancel his scheduled performances, but he had been unwilling to disappoint the Imperial family and the thousands of people who had paid extravagant prices to hear him. Though he had shown no signs of any indisposition during his performances and had sung as brilliantly as ever, during a farewell luncheon he suffered what was termed a complete physical collapse. Caruso minimized the importance of the "collapse." It was, he assured his fans, merely the result of his somewhat careless overuse of his voice after months of silence, and after boarding the ship for New York he sent the understandably nervous Gatti-Casazza a cable which read: MY HEALTH IS SUPERLATIVELY FINE.

✳

By 1911, Caruso's fame was such that everything he did or said was newsworthy. As he had discovered, to his annoyance, reporters paid great attention to every detail of his physical well-being. Nothing, however, could equal the coverage given to his romances — real or, in many cases, inspired by overzealous press agents. It was not enough that he was facing serious legal problems with Ada Giachetti and Elsa Ganelli; to satisfy the public curiosity, love affairs and "engagements" had to be either exaggerated or simply invented.

In January 1911, it had been revealed that he was "secretly" betrothed to a Canadian singer, Lillian Grenville, who was at the time trying to make a name for herself with the Chicago Opera. When the tenor denied these reports, certain members of the press were indignant. CARUSO REALLY OUGHT TO BEHAVE — HERE HE GOES AND DENIES AN ENGAGEMENT WITH A BEAUTIFUL GIRL IN CHICAGO, headlined the *Morning Telegraph.* The basis for this revelation was not very convincing. Miss Grenville, who had presumably met the tenor in Europe, had written to an American friend, "I can't imagine any woman refusing to become the wife of Caruso. I would rather be the wife of the greatest tenor of the world than the wife of the King of England." Though there was nothing more to the story than that, and in spite of the soprano's own admission that their relationship was based on nothing more than "reciprocal admiration," it was necessary for Caruso to issue an angry public denial, an apparently ungentlemanly one which implied that Grenville was merely using his name to further her own faltering career.

A similar denial had to be made when news stories announced that he was about to marry the twenty-two-year-old daughter of a wealthy Argentinian. This story was somewhat more complicated. At first the girl, then living in Paris, stated that it was she who had rejected the singer's pleas. "While I like Caruso very much," she stated, "I would never bring myself to marry a plumber, even if he is the world's greatest tenor." Shortly afterward, however, it was reported that the girl, who it seems had been left out of her father's will, had been won over by Caruso's persistency and had agreed to become his wife. Once again, Caruso was forced to issue an ungentlemanly statement explaining that the rumor had spread because he had naïvely allowed himself to be photographed with the young girl while they were both vacationing at the Italian resort of Salsomaggiore, and pleading with reporters to "correct this nonsensical error."

There had been and would be other stories of his "romances"—some absurd and some not. In 1909, it was reported that he was about to marry a nineteen-year-old Sicilian peasant and give up his career in exchange for the simple life of a farmer. In 1914, newspapers throughout the world told of his six-year involvement with a wealthy American, Mildred Meffert, which had resulted in a threatened lawsuit—the woman had, it seems, a series of love letters from the singer—but the suit was settled out of court. One story the press failed to report was that of his short but intense courtship of the spectacularly beautiful actress Billie Burke, who met Caruso in 1910 and described the affair in her memoirs. "He made love and ate spaghetti with equal skill and no inhibitions," she wrote. "He would propose marriage several times each evening."

❊

Because of this great interest in Caruso's love life, it is not surprising that the crowd of reporters who greeted him upon his arrival in New York on November 8, 1911, was less concerned with stories of his illness in Berlin than with stories of his latest "engagement." This time his fiancée was, supposedly, Emma Trentini, a fiery Italian soprano who had the year before created the title role in Victor Herbert's *Naughty Marietta*. Trentini's official announcement of their plans to marry the following summer coincided, conveniently, with the start of what was to be a nationwide tour of the Herbert operetta. "Of course," the soprano informed skeptical reporters, "you know Caruso has been engaged so many times and Trentini has not. But this time it is true. And I do not think he will be so naughty when he has a wife." To prove her seriousness she added that she was not only prepared but eager to become a stepmother of his two boys.

When greeted with the news, Caruso refused to take the matter seriously. "She's too small to be a stepmother," he told reporters, noting as well that her press agent was too big with his stories. Pressed to make further comments, he likened her to a little piece of soap and a peanut.

Trentini, then in Chicago, reacted angrily. Supplying eager journalists with a detailed account of his courtship, she announced she was through with him after his public disavowal of their romance. She wondered if he even knew what a piece of soap was and warned that he might well end up selling peanuts on a street corner. He might be a great tenor, she added, but he was really a pig with a face like a sponge.

Caruso wisely refused to continue what was becoming a distasteful exchange, and which served no purpose but to promote Trentini's tour in *Naughty Marietta*. He had good-naturedly gone along with the press agent's game, but it was now time to concentrate on the forthcoming season at the Metropolitan, during which he would once again have to prove that he had not lost his voice.

❋

Caruso's 1911–1912 season at the Metropolitan was a complete success: he proved conclusively in the course of it that his voice had not been impaired by his recent illness. He sang thirty-eight times in New York and eleven times on tour, and, though he essayed no new roles, his first performance of *Manon* with Toscanini, on the night of March 30, was considered — for its display of musicianship and refinement of style — one of the artistic high points of his career to date. It was a season notable for superlative performances and undisturbed by scandals or any startling revelations of any kind.

Following a special concert at the Metropolitan on April 30, to benefit the victims of the *Titanic*, Caruso sailed for Europe. His first stop was Paris, where he made his first operatic appearances at the Opéra, singing three performances each of *Rigoletto* and *La Fanciulla del West*. Critics and public alike agreed that he sang superbly, even more so than usual, perhaps because he was joined by the man who was considered the greatest of all baritones, Titta Ruffo. The two men had sung together infrequently, and during the short Paris season each incited the other to extraordinary heights of brilliance. It was an amicable competition between two giants of the lyric theater, and the remarkable way in which their voices blended can still be heard on their one joint recording, made in 1914, a shatteringly powerful interpretation of the duet which closes the second act of *Otello*. In their Paris appearances, these two singers both emerged triumphant; their friendly battle for vocal superiority was a draw, though for the public there was a subtle difference. Ruffo was frequently called the "Caruso of baritones," while Caruso was never labeled the "Ruffo of tenors."

If the French were overwhelmed by the undiminished beauty of Caruso's voice, the audiences that heard him in Vienna, Munich, Stuttgart, and Berlin in the fall were no less so. His supremacy in the world of opera had been reaffirmed, and he could take satisfaction in the prevailing critical opinion that he was the equal of, or even better than, the Caruso of old. This pleasure, however, was not an unmitigated one, for before returning to the Metropolitan in the fall of 1912, he had to endure one of the most painful experiences of his life — a trial in a Milanese court which finally settled his long-standing differences with Ada Giachetti.

✳

The Monkey House Case, the Ganelli suit, the various reports of his impetuous involvements with a number of women — these were all embarrassing incidents, damaging to Caruso's pride and innate dignity. The Giachetti trial, however, was far more serious — a bitter public airing of his relationship with the mother of his children, a woman many of his friends would continue to think of as the only real love of his life.

Ironically, there would have been no trial had it not been for Caruso's insistence upon a complete vindication of charges brought against him earlier by the soprano. These accusations had been first made in the pages of Milan's *Corriere della Sera*, one of Italy's most distinguished newspapers. Giachetti, while maintaining that Romati, the chauffeur, had not become her lover until after her relationship with Caruso had come to an end, had accused the tenor of doing everything in his power to ruin her career — by making defamatory statements about her, and by paying Maria Carignani, the proprietress of the *pensione* in which she lived, to intercept all letters sent to her from America and give them to Caruso. Among these letters, Giachetti stated, was one which contained a contract to sing at Hammerstein's Manhattan Opera House. In addition, she alleged that the tenor had stolen from her thousands of dollars' worth of jewelry and all of her theatrical costumes.

With public opinion on her side as a result of these newspaper articles, the soprano followed up her accusations by formally filing suit against Caruso. After several months of investigation, involving the cross-examination of almost one hundred witnesses, the public prosecutor dismissed the case. Caruso was held blameless of any wrongdoing, and evidence pointed to bribery and corruption on the part of Giachetti and some of those who had testified in her behalf. In spite of this, Caruso felt the need to pursue the matter even further: he filed a countersuit against Giachetti for defamation of character and also accused Romati, Achille Loria (her agent), and a journalist, Michelizzi, of complicity in the affair.

The proceedings began before a crowded courtroom on October 25, 1912, and continued for four days. Caruso, having interrupted his German tour, was present throughout the hearings, but Giachetti had remained in South America, where she was performing with a traveling Italian opera company.

The tenor and his attorneys carefully countered each of the accusations. They produced letters from the soprano proving that the affair with Romati had started long before her relationship with Caruso had come to an end, letters in which she begged forgiveness and praised Caruso for having always been kind to her while expressing the hope that he continue to be so. While admitting that she could no longer return his love, she asked if he might possibly be able to help her financially in the future.

As to the charge that he had prevented her from singing in New York, evidence was given to prove that there had been no contract from Hammerstein—the impresario himself had confirmed this to Caruso's attorney—and Loria, Giachetti's agent, confessed that he had been bribed to make his statement to the effect that such an offer had been made.

Regarding the alleged theft of the jewelry and other possessions, Caruso's attorneys produced a letter from Giachetti dated June 26, 1909, stating that she was returning all his jewelry, letters, and other effects. Caruso himself testified that he had taken no action until he was convinced "that she was definitely leaving me to take up with the chauffeur," and he added acrimoniously, "I have been accused of theft because I didn't hand over the jewels to Signor Romati."

Testimony from both sides was bitter, and Caruso, seated between his two attorneys throughout the proceedings, was visibly moved as the story of the betrayal was recounted to the court. He himself gave an emotional account of his life with Giachetti and how it had changed after ten years of happiness; their quarrels, her increasing spitefulness, his realization upon returning to Bellosguardo that the chauffeur was not only her lover but the master of the villa. Witnesses told stories of Giachetti's passionate, unreasonable attachment to Romati, and others spoke of Caruso's hope that she might obtain a divorce and finally marry him, and of his unfailing generosity toward her during their years together. When one witness told the court that Giachetti never loved Caruso, "not even during the first years of their living together, and I have proof of that," the tenor covered his face with his hands and sobbed.

At the end of the trial, Giachetti and the others were found guilty—the soprano herself was sentenced to one year in jail (a sentence she never served since she never again returned to Italy). Caruso had been absolved, yet the experience had been a shattering one. As the correspondent for *Teatro Illustrato* commented in the magazine's November issue:

> Caruso reached his goal. He came off very well, his actions were always more than correct and his willingness to behave properly, even when not required to do so, was established. The tenor Caruso carried off a complete victory, but at what a price! I would bet that if he could have imagined that this trial would have been a pretext to delve into his most intimate life, to bare his deepest feelings, he would have gladly given up his suit and been satisfied with the previous verdict. During the trial more than one tear appeared in the illustrious artist's eyes but these tears stemmed not from the trial itself . . . they were tears of pain, of regret, and—why not?—of love. . . . The revelation to the stunned world of his misfortunes caused more pain to the sensitive Caruso than did the sentence to the others.

Caruso and Giachetti never reconciled, though they met again and the tenor continued to send her a monthly allowance until the end of his life. Emil Ledner, who had been with him throughout the trial, commented: "Giachetti was removed from personal contact with Caruso, but not from his life. She was never out of his thoughts, his inner life, his feelings— perhaps as long as he lived." Their children never again saw their mother. A portrait of her, on the belvedere of the Villa Bellosguardo, was stored in the villa's attic. Young Mimmi was fascinated by it, but each time he asked who the woman was he was told that it was none of his business.

His older brother, aware of his mother's betrayal of his father, was bitter. He angrily changed the inscription on a photo Giachetti had given him in 1909 from "To my dear Fofò, His Mammina" to read, "To my dear *Papà*, His *bambino*."

XV. "A Bellows on Legs, and a Jolly, Kind Chap"

When Caruso left for America in late October 1912, he was determined to devote himself singlemindedly to his work. While he realized that as a public figure his private life was of legitimate interest to his admirers, he nonetheless hoped that his accomplishments as an artist might completely overshadow his personal difficulties as a not always wise lover. Only a continuation of his brilliant career could help diminish the pain he had suffered during the Giachetti trial.

Upon arrival in New York on November 6, he brushed aside all questions concerning the trial. Instead, he told reporters that during the summer he had been given the Order of the Red Eagle by the Kaiser; the Order of Arts and Sciences by the King of Würtemberg; and the Order of St. Michael by the Prince Regent of Bavaria. Even more proudly, he pointed to his waistline and asked the members of the press to note that he had lost twenty-five pounds.

Five nights later, the Metropolitan season opened. It was an immensely successful one artistically — again free of scandals, rivalries, and intrigues, just as Caruso had hoped. In excellent voice, he averaged two performances a week — singing ten different roles throughout the season, and overshadowing the other members of the distinguished company. On opening night, November 11, he sang the role of Des Grieux in *Manon Lescaut* opposite Lucrezia Bori, with whom he had sung in Paris. It was the twenty-five-year-old Spanish soprano's American debut, and to some listeners it was a somewhat disappointing beginning—perhaps because of Caruso's presence in the cast. "Mixed with the rich organ tones of Signor Caruso, her voice seemed pallid and infantile," Henry Krehbiel of the *Tribune* wrote of her singing in the first act. Although the critic felt that Bori, later a great popular favorite, showed the "real finesses of her vocal art" in the second act, he noted that Caruso "seemed purposely to have modified his own glorious tones for her sake."

This sensitivity to the needs of a fellow artist during a performance, a great comfort to his colleagues, was rare in a star of Caruso's importance He could well have monopolized the stage, ignoring other members of the cast and singing to his adoring public, yet he was at all times a musician, always aware that he was part of an ensemble. He was often a prankster onstage, but he played his jokes only on friends or other experienced singers—like Scotti, Amato, or Destinn—and never on beginning artists, whom he unfailingly helped and supported. After his death, his close friend Marcella Sembrich told reporters: "He was so courteous to his associates, so generous to all. . . . Also he had that inborn instinct of the true artist—the desire to aid someone else to be as great or a greater singer than he was himself."

The only novelty during the 1912–1913 season was the revival of *Les Huguenots*, performed on the night of December 27, for the first time since Caruso had sung it during the season of 1904–1905. The Metropolitan was again able to provide the stellar cast the opera required: joining Caruso were Destinn, Alten, Hempel (in her Metropolitan debut), Léon Rothier, Scotti, and Didur, in what was described as a brilliant production. For the rest of the season, Caruso sang many of his familiar roles. "Caruso as Canio!" the critic James Huneker wrote after a performance of *Pagliacci*. "Is there ever an end to that glorious organ? He is a bellows on legs, and a jolly, kind chap." Caruso had made the role of Canio his own; and the popularity that Leoncavallo's opera gained during those years, and still maintains today, can be largely attributed to his interpretation of the role of the wronged lover. Yet this role, so identified with the tenor to this day, held no special interest for him. "Canio my favorite role?" he told an interviewer in 1913. "Oh, no, no. I have no favorite roles at all. It is all work, all a part of my business. I do not enjoy hearing myself sing any more than a confectioner would enjoy eating all the sweet things that he concocts."

Once the trouble-free New York season had come to an end, Caruso joined the company for what had become an annual and always a most enjoyable visit to Atlanta. In no other city were they received with more uninhibited enthusiasm. Caruso arrived there in excellent spirits; he strolled from the train, a Scotch plaid hat covering one eye, a cigarette between his teeth, and an irrepressible grin on his face. The warmth that surrounded the arrival of the company each year was fully returned by the traveling opera singers, as they were graciously shown the best of Southern hospitality throughout their short stay. They were cheered in public and royally entertained at private parties and elegant dinner dances; Atlanta papers likened the behavior of the visitors to that of happy schoolchildren out for a holiday. In addition to giving three enormously successful performances, Caruso won the hearts of his Georgia hosts by traveling to the local federal penitentiary to sing for hundreds of curious prisoners. Accompanied by several opera singers as well as by the baseball hero Ty Cobb, he was greeted by a poem written in his honor by Julian Hawthorne, convict No. 4435, which read in part:

> Then in the hush of the great blank wall
> God wrought a wondrous miracle,
> For a voice, like a glorious trumpet call,
> Arose as a soul from the deeps of hell,
> And our souls rose with it on wondrous wings—
> Rose from their prison of iron and clay,
> Forgot the grime and shame of things.
> We were men once again in sunlit day;
> Sin and grief and punishment—all
> Were lost in that human trumpet call

Caruso, moved, if puzzled, thanked the prisoner and expressed the hope that he would soon be freed.

At the end of the Atlanta stay, he wrote a letter to the editor of the Atlanta *Constitution*, expressing his gratitude and that of the entire company:

> We have come to look upon the occasion of our annual visits to Atlanta as rare events in our professional careers. We come to give what there is in us, but we feel that while giving we take away even more in the delightful memory of the association. What noble, whole-souled people you have, both here and in the thousands who are attracted here by the events in which we have been humble participants! And these events are even more than national in their significance—they have attracted the attention of the whole world, so marvelous has been the response of the people!
>
> We, ourselves, wonder how you do it, and we go away to tell the world about it. In my whole experiences I have never seen anything like it in this or any other country, and I challenge the

world to duplicate for a similar event audiences of nearly 37,000 people for seven performances, with cash sales aggregating over $91,000 and this for a city of 200,000 people!

*

Caruso returned to Europe in May 1913. His first engagement was in London, where he was to sing at Covent Garden for the first time in several years. Shortly after his arrival in the British capital, he was irritated to read an extraordinary analysis of his vocal skills, given to the press by his British physician, Dr. William Lloyd. According to Lloyd, the tenor's success as a singer could be accounted for by his unusual physical characteristics, above all the structure of his entire throat machinery. In addition, the doctor found that Caruso had music in his bones, that the simple tapping of the Caruso knuckles resulted in a vibration that was higher and more resonant than that produced by tapping the knuckles of an ordinary mortal. Furthermore, Lloyd noted that Caruso's vocal tube was unusually long and that the distance from his front teeth to his vocal cords was a full half inch greater than normal. He was, one headline writer concluded, a "one-man band."

Caruso was understandably angered by this absurd representation of himself as a kind of machine or freak of nature. Writers throughout his career frequently tried to account for his extraordinary talent by bizarre diagnoses of his throat, his chest, his lungs, and his vocal cords, but no such diagnoses could possibly explain his artistry and musicianship or the intelligence and control with which he used his admittedly remarkable voice. Certainly the crowds that cheered his return to London would not have agreed that what they heard was nothing more than the result of an uncommon physique.

His return to Covent Garden had been eagerly anticipated; his loyal British public had missed him. Even at more than twice the prices ordinarily charged, tickets for his first performance—in *Pagliacci* on May 20, 1913—had been unavailable for weeks, and lines for unreserved gallery seats began to form at 5:45 on the morning of the performance with many hundreds turned away empty-handed.

Caruso was even more tense than usual as the performance marking his return to Covent Garden began. There had been too much excitement, expectations had been too high (he was beginning to fear comparisons with the youthful Caruso), and the overwhelming wave of applause which greeted his appearance seemed to unnerve him. For a few moments his voice was unsteady, but he regained his composure and delighted his public by singing with the brilliance they had remembered. By the end of the first act, however, the strain took its toll; following a few curtain calls, he fell into a dead faint — happily, out of the view of the audience, which never guessed what had happened. Carried back to his dressing room, he quickly recovered and concluded the evening in triumph.

A few nights later, on May 24, he showed no signs of nervousness as he sang *Aida* with Destinn and Scotti. Some reviewers quibbled that his voice was somewhat woolly, but the *Daily Telegraph* echoed the sentiment of the public by proclaiming that "he is an incomparably finer artist now than he even was before," and that his was "a performance of genius." His performance of *Tosca* on June 5 was similarly praised. "The fact seems to grow clearer at each performance," wrote the reviewer for the *Daily Telegraph*, "that if Caruso's voice — the voice of the century — ever fails him, which Heaven forbid, that amazing person will be long admired as actor only, to so great an extent has he developed the histrionic side of his talent in the past few years."

The highlight of the season took place on the night of June 23, when "at the king's request" and in the king's presence, Caruso and Melba once again — after many years — performed their earliest success, *La Bohème*. Osbert Sitwell, who was there, described the two (Melba was fifty-two years old and Caruso forty) as "fat as two elderly thrushes, trilling at each other over the wedge of tiaras," but he confessed that Caruso's voice carried "the warm breath of southern evenings in an orange grove, and of roses caught in the hush of dusk at the water's edge." Critics the following day lauded the tenor's performance: "Not once has he shown his almost superhuman qualities to so great an advantage," the critic for the *Daily Telegraph* wrote. "His voice was in glorious order, and . . . his artistic ability is grown out of all common knowledge." So overwhelming was the success that evening that a repeat performance was arranged for the night of June 28, Caruso's last appearance of the season.

❊

On September 15, 1913, after two months in Italy, where he spent most of his time at the Villa Bellosguardo, doing his best to avoid celebrity-seekers and inquisitive journalists, Caruso began his fall season in Vienna. Once again, crowds gathered at the box office as early as five in the morning to purchase seats, and once again his listeners were convinced that he remained the world's greatest tenor.

Three performances each in Munich and Stuttgart followed, and on October 16, he opened his Berlin season with a performance of *Aida*. Though the public was as Caruso-mad as ever throughout the season, the critics had reservations, many expressing the belief that he was not consistently at his best. Quite possibly they were right. There were two plausible explanations. One concerned his health: the painful headaches that had been troubling him in the past had been recurring with alarming frequency and had caused him considerable discomfort while onstage. The other explanation could have been that while in Berlin the tenor frequently, as had happened before, found himself singing with second-rate artists — their low pay would compensate for his own inflated salary — who were not completely familiar with their roles, making it difficult for him to perform at his best.

The last stop on this 1913 tour was Hamburg. There were no complaints of any kind during his three performances there. Neither the singer nor his adoring German public could know that for reasons beyond their control his performance in *La Fanciulla del West* on the night of November 2 was his farewell appearance in Germany.

❋

On November 12, 1913, another shipload of grand opera stars — among them Destinn, Scotti, Jörn, and Didur — arrived in New York. Caruso, apparently free of his headaches, proclaimed that he was the only one among them not to have suffered from seasickness. He attributed this to having kept out of his cabin all day and varying his walks on the wave-swept decks by visits to the smoking room, where he played cards with his fellow artists, easily winning their money since they were too ill to take an interest in the games.

To his relief, the Metropolitan season, which began with a performance of *La Gioconda* on November 17, was once again marked by a high degree of artistry and a notable lack of scandal and controversy. In addition to his already familiar roles in *La Gioconda, Manon Lescaut, Pagliacci, Aida, Tosca, Manon, La Bohème,* and *La Fanciulla del West,* Caruso returned to the role of Riccardo in Verdi's *Un Ballo in Maschera,* which he had sung only a few times before. His only new role of the season was that of the protagonist in Gustave Charpentier's *Julien,* a sequel to the composer's successful *Louise,* which had first been produced in Paris in 1900 but had not yet been given at the Metropolitan. Caruso had studied this new part carefully the previous summer, and Charpentier had enthusiastically approved the tenor's interpretation when he ran through it for him during a meeting in Berlin in October. Unfortunately, the result was not worth all the effort that Caruso had spent in learning a complex role. Geraldine Farrar, his co-star at the première on February 26, 1914, pronounced the work a "wild and confusing hodge podge," and the press and public did not disagree. *Julien* was performed five times that season at the Metropolitan and never again. Farrar noted: "At least there was never talk of revival, thanks be!"

Caruso's year was enlivened by an incident which has become an essential part of the Caruso legend — the first and only time he sang an aria intended for a bass. The occasion was a performance of *La Bohème* in Philadelphia on the night of December 23, 1913. That day, before the performance, the tenor lunched at Del Pezzo, his favorite restaurant in New York, with his good friend Andrés de Segurola, who was scheduled to sing the bass role of Colline in Puccini's opera. During the meal, Caruso noticed that his friend's voice was hoarse and learned that De Segurola feared he might be unable to fulfill his commitment. Later that day, on the train ride from New York to Philadelphia, De Segurola tested his voice and was alarmed to find that it was even worse than it had been at lunch. He turned to the tenor for help, and Caruso suggested that he use his voice sparingly until the last act, at which time he, Caruso, would substitute for him in singing the important aria "*Vecchia zimarra*" if necessary.

De Segurola followed his friend's advice; for three acts, he spoke his part. When he reached the famous coat song in the fourth act, he realized to his horror that his voice was completely gone. Caruso, noting his colleague's panic, whispered, "How do you feel?" and the bass answered, "Terrible!" There was no time to lose, and to the astonishment of the conductor, Giorgio Polacco, Caruso sang the well-known bass aria, pulling De Segurola to his side so that the audience would not realize what had happened. From all accounts, he sang the aria magnificently — though when he finished it he was trembling, and he later confided that he had never been so nervous on the stage. The audience was, indeed, unaware of the ruse. Caruso later recorded the aria, which he presented to the principals; he did not want the recording to be released commercially, however, despite the urgings of some of his friends. "I am not a basso," he said. "Why I should then put my good friend Chaliapin out of business?" (The recording is, however, available today.)

The season ended on a festive note, with a tumultuous farewell to Caruso and Farrar following their closing performance in *Tosca* on April 22, 1914. The hysteria was such that the audience would not go home. After dozens of curtain calls, it became clear that only a speech would send the public out to the streets. Caruso laughingly motioned to his throat, as if to indicate that he was suffering from hoarseness. That wasn't enough. He then removed his wig and waved it at the audience — to no avail. For the next call, he appeared without the Van Dyke which he had worn during the opera, but even that did not convince the audience that he really wanted to go home.

After three more curtain calls, the stars retired to their dressing rooms while the remaining members of the audience pounded heavily on the floor and on the edge of the orchestra pit, demanding their return. After a long wait, Farrar appeared, dragging with her the reluctant tenor, already in his dressing gown. The soprano stepped to the footlights. "When we had to make a speech last year," she said, "Mr. Caruso ran away and left me in the lurch. So now I will just say, 'I thank you.'" Caruso's own speech was equally eloquent: "And I say thank you," he called out slowly and carefully to the public, who finally, after more than forty curtain calls, made its way out of the auditorium.

✳

In 1914, once again, Caruso's first European engagement was at Covent Garden. He opened the season on the night of May 14 with a performance of *Aida*. "There is no dramatic tenor like him," the critic for the *Pall Mall Gazette* wrote. "He is able to accomplish with apparent ease, effects which cost his rivals visible effort. In short, he is still supreme in Italian opera, and, judging by his performance last night, promises to remain so." Victor Gollancz, the noted British publisher and music lover, remembered the Nile Scene of that production, writing in his memoirs, "Who could ever forget Caruso in that act, from the overwhelming exaltation of his *'Pur ti riveggo, mia dolce Aida'* as he burst in on us, to his equally tremendous *'Sacerdote, io resto a te'* as he strode across the stage to surrender? My God, how we leapt to our feet to applaud him as the curtain came down. . . ."

All of London applauded Caruso throughout the entire season in whatever he sang. No performance, however, was greeted more enthusiastically than his final one, on the night of June 29, in *Tosca*. "So packed was Covent Garden last evening, and so eager were all in the crowded audience to make the very most of their opportunities to the way of paying tributes to the 'hero'—in every sense—of the occasion that it might almost have been Caruso's farewell to public life, and not merely his last appearance this season," wrote the critic for the *Daily Telegraph* the following day. "So far as the eye could discover there was no vacant corner in the opera-house, and there must have been any number of the great tenor's admirers who failed to secure admission. Those who thus went away disappointed must derive what comfort they can from the fact . . . that he will be with us once again next summer."

Caruso did not return to Covent Garden the following summer, and, though neither he nor his public could know it at the time, he had made his last appearance in London. Singers and other entertainers are known for their "farewell" performances, yet it was to be Caruso's fate that there would never be any official farewells for him. Without planning it, he had already said goodbye to Vienna and to Germany, just as, at the end of June 1914, he was saying goodbye to his adoring London public, one of the first to champion and cherish him.

*

On June 28, 1914, the day before Caruso's last performance in London, Archduke Francis Joseph Ferdinand of Austria and his wife were assassinated at Sarajevo by a Bosnian revolutionary. There is no indication that Caruso recognized the enormous importance of this event — which triggered the first world war — or the extent to which it would change the course of his own life. He was physically and emotionally exhausted, more so than ever, after many months of singing — he had had little chance to rest between the long Metropolitan season and the Covent Garden season. He looked forward to spending the summer at the Villa Bellosguardo and to visiting the thermal spa at nearby Montecatini, where he hoped he might find relief from the painful headaches which his doctors believed might have been caused by the emotional strains of the past few years. Whatever the cause, he knew that he desperately needed not only a rest, but also, for a short time at least, to stay out of the public eye. The tremendous, never-ending effort to please his public had been one cause of his exhaustion, and he wrote his friend Arachite in Naples that he anxiously looked forward to the day when he could end this hectic existence. "If I had known the high price of celebrity, I would have gladly become a member of the chorus," he confided. "For three years I have suffered from headaches . . . and I don't know what to do, since I no longer belong to myself."

Throughout the summer and early fall, the war spread throughout Europe; most of the continent was involved in a bloody struggle. Ironically, this allowed Caruso to extend his holiday, since his planned tour of Germany, now totally involved in the war, was canceled. However, instead of resting at his villa before returning to New York, the tenor, who had regained his strength, accepted an urgent invitation to sing at Rome's Teatro Costanzi on the night of October 19. He had not sung in his native land for many years; it was announced that his agreement to participate in a special performance of *Pagliacci* in aid of Italian emigrants who had been forced by the war to return to their homes was the result of "a high sense of patriotism." The announcement was not greeted with wholehearted enthusiasm. For many Italians, Caruso had betrayed his country by surrendering to the temptations of the American dollar. The Italian journal *Orfeo* angrily accused him of not being a real Italian, of having become an exile who had forgotten his own country. *Orfeo*, echoing the sentiment of others, advised Caruso to give up his rights as an Italian citizen and face the fact that he had become an American.

These charges were decried by the tenor. He proudly reaffirmed his allegiance to his native land and declared that he would join the Italian army if called upon to do so. (Emma Trentini, when asked to comment, stated that the man she once declared to be her fiancé was too fat to fight, but that he might join the army as a cook.) He assured reporters that only the demands of his career had led him to spend most of his time away from Italy.

In spite of any resentment that might have been harbored toward him, Caruso's first entrance on an Italian stage after so many years was met with thunderous applause. The performance of *Pagliacci* was in every way a gala one; conducted by Toscanini (who himself had spent many years away from Italy), it starred — along with Caruso — De Luca, Bori, and Battistini, at fifty-eight still a matchless performer.

Next day, the press was unanimously enthusiastic; even those critics who were skeptical of his worldwide reputation were convinced by his masterful interpretation of Canio. "Every doubt about his qualities as a singer was dispelled," wrote Edoardo Pompei in Rome's *Il Messaggero*, and the reviewer for *La Tribuna* commented, "He is worthy of the dazzling fame that surrounds him. More than just a singer, he is a stupefying actor who can dominate the stage and seduce the spectator."

Following this unexpectedly gratifying reception in his own country, the tenor embarked from Naples on the *Canopic* for New York — to the delight of his American public, who had feared he might become a victim of the European war.

The late summer and fall of 1914 had presented complicated problems to the management of the Metropolitan, anxious to see to it that their singers, scattered throughout Europe, would somehow be able to fulfill their engagements in America. Gatti-Casazza, Kahn, and other officials of the company had worked tirelessly to arrange this difficult exodus. They not only had to establish the whereabouts of the singers; but they also had to deal with the delicate problem of arranging a complex schedule of sailings, since various nationalities objected to the presence on their ships of singers who had pledged their allegiance to nations hostile to them.

Fortunately, the red tape was kept to a minimum, and the countries involved proved to be cooperative — they all, apparently, were eager to have their culture represented in America. Nonetheless, it was with considerable relief that Gatti-Casazza was able to notify Otto Kahn in New York in late October that the *Canopic* had sailed from Naples, and that Caruso, Farrar, Bori, Hempel, and Destinn were among its passengers, assuring a season of opera at the Metropolitan.

XVI. "Better than Ever"

For many years—certainly since Toscanini's arrival as chief conductor—
the Metropolitan had been one of the world's leading opera houses. Its
resources—its singers, its productions, and its sometimes adventurous pro-
gramming—could be equaled by few other companies. In 1914, as the new
season was about to begin, it was clearly without a serious rival anywhere
in the world—both because of the restrictions brought about by the war in
Europe and because of the ingenuity of the Metropolitan's directors in
gathering together and bringing back to America many of the world's
greatest singers. Nonetheless, what was undeniably a brilliant season was
clouded by two persistent rumors. For one, word spread that it was to be
the last season for Toscanini. Since his arrival in New York in 1908, the
brilliant conductor, the most highly paid and influential in Metropolitan
history, had conducted a total of twenty-nine operas, maintaining an
unprecedented level of excellence. The first three weeks of the 1914–1915
season, the one rumored to be his last in New York, typified his astonish-
ing versatility: he led performances of *Un Ballo in Maschera, Carmen*
(with Farrar in the title role for the first time), *Aida, Boris Godunov, Madama Butterfly, Tristan und Isolde,* and *Tosca.* The loss of Toscanini would
deal a serious blow to the company; and New Yorkers could only hope that
the rumors would be proven untrue.

An equally disturbing rumor was that Caruso—who, along with Toscanini, accounted in large part for the Metropolitan's pre-eminence in the

world of opera — would sing only half his customary number of performances at the New York opera house. It seemed impossible that the company's brightest star would leave the company in midseason, as was unofficially reported. His opening night performance in *Un Ballo in Maschera* with a superb cast (including Destinn, Hempel, Amato, and Rothier) bore out his statements on arrival in New York that his voice was better than ever. Good-naturedly, after the second act, he welcomed to his dressing room a reporter from the New York *Herald*, who asked the tenor to write his own review of the opening. "Last night," Caruso stated, "at six minutes after eight the overture began. The curtain rose at fifteen minutes past eight and stayed up until fifteen minutes past eleven. Then it fell down because it was tired of staying up. Between these three hours everything was just the same as always — music, singing, plot, and all. There you have my criticism. . . ."

When the reporter asked him about his own singing, the tenor answered with a smile, "Better than ever."

Caruso's assessment was not to be taken lightly. He frequently evaluated his own performances, making note of these evaluations in his scrapbooks. For example, following a December 24, 1914, performance of *Manon*, a critic for the New York *Press* had written that "neither Enrico Caruso nor Geraldine Farrar were vocally at their best." The tenor cut out the review, wrote over it "Liar," and pasted it in one of the scrapbooks. Many of the vouchers which accompanied the checks he received for his performances also contain his personal appraisals: they run the gamut from "Fair" to "Good" to "Marvelous."

Those who heard him sing in performances of *Carmen, La Gioconda, Pagliacci, Aida, Manon, Les Huguenots,* and *Manon Lescaut* that followed the opening would undoubtedly have written "Magnificent," or at least "Very good" in their programs. He was singing brilliantly, and when an official announcement was made in late January that he would be sailing for Europe on February 20, two months before the end of the Met season, the New York public was stunned. Again, there was speculation that he was suffering from serious vocal problems that might necessitate another operation, while other reports claimed that he had had serious disagreements with Gatti-Casazza, and would never return to New York. The truth, however, was far simpler. Seven years before, Caruso had promised Raoul Gunsbourg of the Monte Carlo Opéra, one of the first men to help him reach international fame, that he would spend one season there. The commitment had been postponed for a number of years, but the dynamic impresario felt it could be postponed no longer. Because of the war, Monte Carlo — always dependent on tourists — was suffering from the travel restrictions imposed upon those who wanted to visit the French Riviera.

Caruso's presence could provide a sorely needed stimulus, and, upon the urging of the Prince of Monaco, Gunsbourg had finally decided to hold the world's greatest tenor to his word. With Caruso's help, the former gaiety of the well-known resort—now used largely as a recuperation center for wounded soldiers—might be restored.

In spite of the clear-cut explanation of Caruso's reasons for leaving New York before the close of the season, confirmation of his early departure plunged scores of his adoring American fans into mourning. "I desire to make as public a protest as possible against the imminent departure of Mr. Caruso," read a letter to the New York *Times*. "The very thought of the Metropolitan without him is like that of a pudding without sauce . . . when all is said a sauceless pudding is preciously tame, although hunger may compel us to eat it."

The tenor's final performance of the season, in *Pagliacci* on the night of February 17, 1915, was an occasion for both cheers and tears. More than one thousand persons were turned away; there were noisy demonstrations throughout the performance, and at the end the audience, as had happened before, refused to leave, demanding a speech. "It is against the rules to make a speech," he told them when he appeared, already in his street clothes. "Nothing is forbidden to you here," a voice from a box insisted. Visibly moved, Caruso replied: "I am very much touched. There is nothing for me to say. I cannot find words."

On February 20, an enormous crowd came to pay tribute to their hero as he prepared to depart for Europe on the *Duca d'Aosta*. Every room in his suite was filled with flowers, and he was in tears as he told his admirers that he was sorry to go, that he would wait impatiently for the day of his return.

✳

Caruso had not sung in Monte Carlo since 1904, and he worried, as he had on his return to London, that the public might find that his voice had lost some of its remembered freshness and brilliance. His past performances had set a standard he himself believed might be difficult to meet. Camillo Antona-Traversi, a journalist who acted as Gunsbourg's secretary that season, reported in an article published by *Il Progresso Italo-Americano* that the tenor complained to him that audiences would no longer accept anything short of perfection. Expectations had often run so high—as had ticket prices—that he was no longer permitted the occasional, and inevitable, off-night allowed any other singer. He also confided to the journalist his fear of suddenly failing in the middle of an opera, and admitted that to regain his calm he had closed himself in his room two hours before that first performance of the Monte Carlo season.

He need not have worried. The opening night *Aida*—in which he sang with Félia Litvinne, who at fifty-five was nearing the end of her career—was a resounding triumph for the tenor. No one was disappointed, and Caruso cabled Gatti-Casazza in New York that it had been a "magnificent debut." The one negative response came from far away; *Aida* had been performed for the benefit of wounded French soldiers, with Caruso contributing his share by accepting only half the salary stipulated in his contract, and with that gesture he alienated many of his German fans.

Future Monte Carlo appearances in *Pagliacci* and *Lucia di Lammermoor* were equally successful. Caruso had proven to one more skeptical public that he was still the world's greatest tenor; because of him, too, Gunsbourg was able to restore Monte Carlo's opera to at least some of its peacetime splendor.

After Monte Carlo, Caruso was free: he had no fixed engagements until the Metropolitan season in the late fall. The conditions of a new contract with the New York opera company granted him, for the first time, the right to make his own arrangements, apart from his appearances with the Metropolitan; before then the Met had controlled all of his artistic activities. Consequently, the tenor was deluged with offers of work. Among these was one from the impresario Walter Mocchi to join his Italian company on an extended tour of South America. Caruso had not sung there since 1903. He was reluctant to make the long trip and even more reluctant to face again the challenge of singing before audiences that had not heard him since his earlier days and might compare him to his younger self; this unreasonable fear plagued him constantly throughout his later years. He therefore agreed to join Mocchi only on what seemed to him terms the impresario could not possibly meet—a fee three times that paid him by the Metropolitan. To his surprise—and possible chagrin—Mocchi agreed, and on April 21 Caruso found himself on the way to South America.

The lengthy tour, which began in Buenos Aires on May 20, took him throughout Argentina and Brazil, and ended in Montevideo on August 30. Caruso sang fifty-two performances, eighteen more than had originally been scheduled. His success was unprecedented—even greater than that of his early years—and he was overwhelmed by the uninhibited warmth shown him wherever he traveled.

Two occasions were of special interest in the course of the tour. On June 27, he sang for the first time on the operatic stage with the coloratura soprano Amelita Galli-Curci; their interpretation of *Lucia di Lammermoor* (they only sang it twice) made operatic history at Buenos Aires' Teatro Colon. Even more spectacular was Caruso's performance, on August 4, of the first act of *Pagliacci* with Titta Ruffo. Again, the Colon was the setting for an historic evening, one of the very few performances that featured these two great singers.

Following this long tour, Caruso planned to return to Italy for a period of uninterrupted rest at the Villa Bellosguardo. While in Buenos Aires, however, he received a cable from Toscanini, asking him to take part in two special performances of *Pagliacci* he had agreed to conduct at Milano's Teatro Dal Verme. Since these were to be benefit performances in aid of the many musicians who would be out of work because of the war, Caruso was unable to refuse, and agreed to return to the city of some of his earliest triumphs at the end of September, before returning to New York.

Of all of the tenor's unplanned farewell appearances, none would have pained him more than these last performances in his native country. This time his customary nervousness, coupled once more with his fear of being compared to his younger self, almost paralyzed him as he prepared for his first entrance in *Pagliacci* on the night of September 23. Armand Crabbé, who was part of the cast, noted in his memoirs: "When he made his entrance in the circus wagon, he had to be supported as his knees were knocking under him. On seeing this pitiable sight, I thought of the Caruso of yesteryear, so sure of himself, so full of fire and virile youth. . . ."

In spite of this attack of stage fright, Caruso sang with enough "fire and virile youth," according to Crabbé, to delight the large audience which filled the theater. The following day, Carlo d'Ormeville, director of *La Gazzetta dei Teatri*, still under the tenor's magic spell, wrote:

> I am writing immediately after the performance, so as not to delay the publication of the newspaper, and I am writing inspired by the fires of an enthusiasm of which I believed myself no longer capable of feeling. That warm and vibrant voice is still making me tremble, that impulsive and sweeping intonation is still pulsating on my excited nerves, that sculptural and imperious phrasemaking is still dominating my electrified spirit. The part of Canio lives in Caruso, with all the reality and with all the fever of his passion, which makes his veins and his wrists quiver. The great artist is no longer the aria singer, no longer the "furtive tear" which delights those who hear him. It is the bitter weeping, the heartrending sobbing, the sorrowful spasm which springs from his eyes, which chokes his throat and which bursts forth from his chest. His *"Ridi, Pagliaccio"* gives one a sensation that can never be forgotten. People scream, shout, applaud, go

into raptures, and no one regrets having paid so much for that hour of fantastic pleasure of the intellect and of the soul.

I couldn't say whether today Caruso is better as an actor or as a singer. Certainly it is the fusion of these two parts, the lyric and dramatic, that is so well balanced that it makes one feel that virtue which is not believed to be a human quality: that is, perfection.

Caruso's maturity was also noted by Renzo Bianchi, writing in *L'Illustrazione:* "Once he was a refined tenor, a *'tenore di grazia'* a kind of Gayarré; today he has become a dramatic tenor. His voice has lost its former sweetness, but it is now armed with a new, impassioned vigor. . . . Before us was not only a great singer, but also a great actor . . . in Caruso we have seen the rebirth of the glory of the Italian lyric theatre, the sovereign art of song and of the expression of true, human passions."

∗

Once again, during the late summer and fall of 1915, the management of the Metropolitan concerned itself with the intricate arrangements necessary for the exodus from Europe of as many singers as possible to assure an artistically successful opera season for New York. The task had become increasingly difficult as the war spread throughout Europe. "The old Continent," Gatti-Casazza said, "has become a mad-house soaked with blood." The managing director, however, was once again relieved to be able to send a cable to Otto Kahn, on October 6, announcing that he would be sailing from Naples with his star Caruso, who, happily, would sing in New York for the full season this time. Less happy news was the official confirmation that Toscanini would not be among those returning to New York. Italy's entry into the war in May 1915 was given as the reason for his departure, yet it seems the real cause lay in his disagreements with the management and with Gatti-Casazza himself. "I do not even want to criticize any further the absolutely incorrect attitude of my old friend Toscanini," Gatti wrote Kahn on September 6. "One thing is certain, i.e. that the famous conductors of today, although they may talk incessantly of art and its sacred rights, have become worse than the old-time prima donna and they do not even have the excuse of belonging to the weaker sex."

The new season at the Metropolitan opened on November 15 with a lavish production of Saint-Saëns' *Samson et Dalila,* not heard at the opera house since 1895; the new production offered Caruso and the Hungarian soprano Margarethe Matzenauer in the title roles. For those fortunate enough to have been able to follow the tenor's career from the beginning, his assumption for the first time of the heavy, dramatic role of Samson marked a decisive turning point in his career, his emergence as a true dramatic tenor. It was, for Oscar Thompson, the noted critic, the end of his "raw beef period." Reviewing the tenor's career after his death, Thompson wrote,

> The voice in these last years showed wear. Upper tones were not infrequently jagged and had lost something of their vitality. The middle and lower registers . . . were dark and baritonal when power was applied, though still sumptuously beautiful. Increased taste and skill in vocal nuance accompanied the expansion of the great tenor's powers as an actor, and Caruso came to rely for his most appealing effects on his heavenly *mezza voce*, which he had developed and utilized, after having in large measure neglected it during the robust middle period. His style frequently suggested his earlier years in its lyric grace, but there was now greater artistry and far more intellect in the singing. Only in the *mezza voce* was it as entrancing in sheer sound, but his art had gained in restraint and taste what his tone had lost in sensuous appeal.

Caruso's Samson, though on the whole well received, was not one of his most popular roles. The public, and many critics, preferred his performances in those operas which had gained him his early fame. "Why will not Enrico Caruso return again to his first loves and his best — his Dukes in *Rigoletto*, his Alfredos, his Edgardos?" asked the critic for the *Tribune*. "One note of passion as given to him to sing by the early Verdi is worth all the heartbreaks of the modern declamations. . . ."

The tenor did, to the satisfaction of many listeners, sing a number of his most popular roles that season: in *La Bohème, Tosca, Pagliacci, Martha, Manon, Un Ballo in Maschera, Manon Lescaut, Aida,* and *Rigoletto*. His appearance in *Rigoletto*, for the first time since a single performance given in the 1912–1913 season, was the subject of an amusing anecdote recounted by Gatti-Casazza in his memoirs. The role of the Duke of Mantua was one that Caruso no longer wanted to sing; he felt he had outgrown it, and Gatti agreed that the tenor's voice was no longer suited to it. Nonetheless, both men bowed to the wishes of Otto Kahn, and on the night of February 11, 1916, he repeated the role that had introduced him to the American public. "It is impossible to make clear now how bad a performance we gave," Gatti wrote. "Every one, the artists, the orchestra, we were all agreed that it had been pretty bad. . . . And Caruso left the theatre that evening, followed by his usual entourage, which was always at his side. He had his collar up, and his head buried inside his coat. Everyone was in vile humor, and no one spoke a word."

The following morning, the managing director did not even go to the pressroom to look at the reviews, convinced that they would cause him nothing but pain. Instead he went directly to his office, where he was soon interrupted by Caruso joyously singing *"La donna è mobile."* The jubilant tenor had come to show Gatti the critics' response to what both had felt was a disastrous performance; with few reservations, the reviews were excellent. (A year later, Caruso again sang in *Rigoletto;* this time he and Gatti agreed that it had been a marvelous performance, but the critics were almost unanimous in their disapproval.)

Undoubtedly the most colorful performance of the season took place on the night of February 17, 1916, when Caruso sang in *Carmen* opposite Geraldine Farrar. The beautiful Farrar had spent the previous summer in Hollywood, making a film of *Carmen,* and for her first appearance in the role at the Metropolitan that season, she was determined to apply some of the techniques learned while in the film capital. Her performance was, at the very least, a prime example of theatrical hysteria. During the first act, she enthusiastically beat one of the cigarette girls, throwing her to the ground and then pummeling her. In her third-act struggle with Caruso, she slapped and bit the startled tenor — according to Frances Alda, who was singing the role of Micaela, she actually drew blood. Caruso was furious. He admired and respected Farrar as an artist and as a friend, and he certainly had played his share of tricks on his fellow performers while onstage. This uncalled-for display of realism, however, was too much for him. Not the least bit amused, he retaliated by brutally pushing the soprano to the ground; Farrar landed with such a thud that members of the startled audience gasped. At the end of the performance, angry words were exchanged between the two stars. Caruso reportedly told her that she should remember she was not in the movies but on the stage of the Metropolitan, to which Farrar replied that if he didn't like her Carmen, he should get someone else to play the role the next time. No, the tenor retorted; another such scene could be avoided by getting another Don José.

The press had a field day the following morning. Farrar was, according to the *Sun,* "a muscular Carmen." The *Tribune* labeled her a "very rough Carmen." Critics agreed that she had sung poorly, while Caruso was at his best. The opera house's management, instead of capitalizing on all the publicity, did its best to minimize the conflict, and the principals gave out conciliatory statements. Caruso said: "I am a singer, not a fighter. Sometimes families squabble, often somebody says something on the stage which must not be told outside the theater. What occurs behind the stage—that is our business. What occurs on the stage—that is for the public." Farrar noted that the two singers were still good friends, and Gatti insisted that there were no problems at all between them.

Whatever had happened behind the scenes that night, there were no problems when the two again appeared in *Carmen* eight days later, on the night of February 25. The crowd that filled the theater, hoping for another dramatic encounter, was disappointed. There was no slapping and no biting, and the result was a far more convincing performance. The audience burst into laughter when, after the "Flower Song," the couple embraced far more affectionately and for a much longer time than usual—signifying the end to their short-lived conflict.

When the New York season ended, with another performance of *Carmen* on April 1, the company left for a three-week season at the Boston Opera House. Caruso sang in six different operas, and for the first time in many years, he was faced with highly unfavorable criticism in the American press. On April 8, after he had sung in *Aida*, Olin Downes of the Boston *Globe* attacked the tenor (as well as Boston's public), claiming that the house was filled for Caruso while it had been empty for an *Aida* with Zenatello the year before—when the lesser-known tenor had sung a hundred times better than had Caruso. He wrote of "the often atrocious singing of Mr. Caruso," and noted that, "as the evening went on, Mr. Caruso sang more and more badly, and in the Nile scene his singing was positively comical, but the applause was unending."

Caruso was so upset by this adverse criticism—Downes' was not the only negative review—that he granted a special interview to *The Christian Science Monitor* during which he defended his Boston performances. In doing so, he also ably answered both past and future critics who complained of the changes in his voice during his mature years. Joining in the defense, *Musical America* commented on this unusual interview in its issue of May 13, 1916. The article read, in part:

> One of the particular points Mr. Caruso made in his interview and to which I have already called attention is that many people, not only the critics, have a certain mental impression of his singing, from his old records, and so do not understand him as he is to-day, when his art has unquestionably improved, when he phrases better, his enunciation is clearer, when, indeed, he can be said to be just as great and good a singer, but a finer artist than ever before, though he does not sing with the same robust fullness that he used to do in what I have called his "second period."
>
> Those people who have just heard him through one of his old records, hearing him now, would not understand him at all, as he

says himself, unless he had an opportunity of singing to them more than once in his best roles, and then they would discover, as, indeed, I think intelligent New Yorkers did last season, that Caruso is no longer what he was years ago—simply a great voice. Today he has become the greatest master of beautiful singing within the memory of even those who can go back a generation.

At one point during his Boston visit, it was reported that Caruso had decided to cancel any further Boston appearances and return to New York. He was not, he insisted, angry, or even disappointed; he merely believed that if he was not satisfying the press or the public, it would be best for all concerned that he leave. Only the urging of Gatti and others at the Metropolitan—as well as far more favorable reviews, including some from Downes—dissuaded him from doing so.

The short Atlanta season which followed was far more gratifying. The love affair between Caruso and Atlanta continued. During his last visit there, he had sung for a group of prisoners, and during this visit, on April 24, he gave a special performance for Helen Keller at his hotel. The deaf woman placed her fingers on his throat and lips as he sang the opening aria from the third act of *Samson et Dalila*. Both were moved to tears, though unsentimental New York ear specialists asserted afterward that it would have been impossible for Miss Keller to have really "heard" in any way the tenor's golden voice.

XVII. The Patriot

It is entirely possible that Bostonians, accustomed to the rich, ringing tones heard on Caruso's earlier phonograph records, had been disappointed by the inevitable changes in the tenor's voice and had failed to understand the more subtle artistic progress he had made since the time of those recordings. It is also possible that Caruso, again for reasons of health, had not been at his best during that short season. In any case, when he returned to Europe in May 1916, he was once more urgently in need of an extended period of relaxation. The painful headaches from which he had suffered periodically had recurred during the previous season in New York. He had even been forced to cancel one performance because of them — something he was loath to do — and had secretly undergone minor surgery at the hands of Dr. Curtis, who believed that the trouble was caused by nothing more serious than a nasal infection. The surgery, however, had not helped, nor had the intensive massage treatments prescribed by the physician.

※

With European opera houses closed because of the war and no engagements scheduled until his return to New York in the fall, Caruso had ample time in which to rest during the summer of 1916. Nonetheless, as always, he found it impossible to take full advantage of this opportunity to put aside his work in order to regain his health.

He did manage to take the "cures" at a number of Italian spas and he stayed with his sons at the Villa Bellosguardo as much as possible, but he was preoccupied with his work and drove himself with his usual energy and dedication, eager to prove to New York audiences in the fall that his growth as an artist had more than compensated for the loss of the natural qualities of youth.

By this time, of course, New York was his real home and the base of all his artistic activities. The Metropolitan had depended upon him for many years, but with the advent of the war and the consequent problem of getting European artists to America, his presence was absolutely essential to the company's success; Caruso, too, just as badly needed the Metropolitan as the only remaining major showcase for his talents.

Fortunately for both, the relationship between the opera company and its reigning star was an excellent one, based on a rare degree of mutual loyalty and trust. So great was that trust that in his later years with the company, he often performed without a formal contract. On March 27, 1916, Otto Kahn wrote the tenor a letter praising him as an artist, and then adding: "Mr. Gatti-Casazza has informed me that while you prefer not to sign a contract at this time for an extension of your present contract, you have given him your verbal assurance, which, coming from you is just as good as a written contract, that he may depend upon your remaining with the Metropolitan Opera Company. In taking note of this welcome declaration, may I express my sincerest gratification, not only as Chairman of the Metropolitan Opera Company, not only as one of the public, in the affection and admiration of which you have a unique, an unrivalled place, but also as your personal friend and well-wisher who holds you in the highest esteem for the splendid qualities of character which distinguish you as an artist and as a man. . . ."

Kahn's admiration and affection for Caruso knew no bounds. Theirs was a warm friendship but always a formal one — the letters they exchanged always began "Dear Mr. Caruso" or "Dear Mr. Kahn." Caruso never failed to show his respect for Kahn, who in turn never hesitated to remind his star of the great esteem in which he held him.

Kahn and the board of directors of the Metropolitan had every reason to appreciate Caruso not only as an artist but as an extraordinary gentleman in business matters. The tenor often charged unusually high fees away from the Met, but he never took advantage of the New York house's obvious dependence on him. Until the 1914–1915 season, he had been paid two thousand dollars for each performance. When the time came to renew the agreement, it was assumed that he would ask for a huge increase, and he was told that any figure up to four thousand dollars would be acceptable. Instead, Caruso told Kahn he would like to settle for two thousand five hundred dollars, that anything above that would be too great a burden, with which he would not feel comfortable. This most uncommon behavior would have endeared him to any of the world's opera companies.

Even at a figure lower than that which he might have commanded, Caruso was the world's highest paid opera singer. Yet, and it was often repeated, he was always a bargain: a Caruso appearance meant a sold-out house, and he only canceled an engagement if he was forced to by matters beyond his control, such as illness. During the years he sang in New York, the repertory of the Metropolitan was dictated by Caruso's drawing power — he could have asked for anything, and yet he chose only those roles that he felt were suitable for himself and for the company — never making unreasonable demands. Instinctively a serious artist, the tenor pursued his career with extraordinary intelligence, rarely exercising less than well-reasoned judgment based upon the knowledge of what he could and could not do at any point in his career.

✻

Sometimes both the Metropolitan and Caruso did show poor judgment in selecting a vehicle for him. Such was certainly the case with *Les Pêcheurs de Perles*, which was performed on the night of November 13, 1916, shortly upon his return to New York after his quiet summer in Italy. It was the opening night of the season, and Caruso was eager to repeat for a new public one of his early successes — he had last sung it in Genoa in 1898. "I feel as young as I did eighteen years ago," he told a reporter; and the management of the Metropolitan hoped that Bizet's first important opera might achieve the popularity of *Carmen*, his final work. In spite of kind words for the tenor's performance as Nadir the fisherman, neither the critics nor the public found much to praise in what the New York *Evening Journal* called "Caruso's little Ceylon tea party," and the opera was withdrawn after three performances.

For the rest of the season, Caruso satisfied his public with old favorites — again singing, for the first time in twelve years, the role of Nemorino in *L'Elisir d'Amore*, on the night of December 30, 1916. There was such a clamor for an encore of *"Una furtiva lagrima"* that the tenor, stubbornly refusing, finally cleared his throat and sang, in English, "It is not allowed." The audience for the next performance was luckier, he broke the rule and sang an encore of the show-stopping aria, but it was the only time he did so that season.

Caruso was again the object of New York's adulation, both in and out of the opera house. The city's entertainment industry showed its special affection for him on the night of November 26, at a dinner given in his honor by the Friars, a theatrical club. Among the four hundred and fifty guests cheerfully honoring "the champion spaghetti eater of the world" were George M. Cohan and Victor Herbert, along with a contingent from the Metropolitan which included Gatti-Casazza, Scotti, and the conductor Giorgio Polacco. At the end of the evening, all joined in singing a special song to the honored guest, to the tune of "Pretty Baby." "Everybody loves a tenor, that's why I'm in love with you. Oh, Caruso, Oh, Caruso. . . ."

As usual, each Caruso appearance meant a full house for the Metropolitan. For the matinee performance of February 12, his first appearance of the season in *Aida*, an estimated five thousand people were turned away—a record even for a Caruso performance. As had become customary, the tenor's final appearance for the season in New York—in *Rigoletto* on April 20, 1917—was an occasion for near hysteria. At the end of the opera, the crowd simply refused to leave the theater. Caruso bowed, he blew kisses, he waved his handkerchief at the audience. Finally, he found a new way to dismiss his fans, leading them in a rousing "Three cheers for the United States!" followed by "Three cheers for the Allies!" He understood his public, and the year 1917 marked Caruso's emergence as a patriot, and he played the role with boundless energy and dedication, giving his time and talent unselfishly by agreeing to any reasonable request to aid, by his participation in a concert or his presence at a bazaar, the cause of the Allies. His older son, Rodolfo, had entered the Italian army; his younger son, Enrico, Jr., was in Italy with his governess. His two countries, after the entry of the United States into the war on April 6, 1917, were united in a common cause which he enthusiastically supported. He felt it his duty to show his loyalty to both Italy (he was undeniably Italian and never gave up his citizenship) and the United States, a country he had learned to love and in which he had spent much of his life.

✳

Following the long New York season, Caruso again set out on a tour of his "stepmother" country, as he sometimes called it. The first stop was Atlanta, where he performed three times with the Metropolitan. He spent one week there, and his visit was, as always, a cause for celebration. He brought a touch of glamour and excitement to the city; his sartorial elegance never went unnoticed. "The tenor arrived in Atlanta wearing a brown belted suit, light blue shirt and dark blue tie to match, sporty tan shoes and a white cane, with a cigarette holder of sable hue," Atlanta's leading newspaper reported. "He appeared on the streets Monday morning, sporting a creamy white suit with double-breasted coat, fastened with pearl buttons; a pearl-gray fedora, white shoes slashed with tan, a green cane and a cigarette holder of pure white." No detail escaped the admiration of Atlantans.

After his farewell performance, in *Rigoletto* on April 28 — he followed it by singing "The Star-Spangled Banner" to a public almost hysterical with joy — Caruso embarked on a more daring adventure: his first concert tour since 1908. He did so reluctantly. In addition to his fear of singing before an audience alone and without operatic props, he dreaded traveling to new places where he might run the risk of illness. Colds, sore throats, laryngitis — these were his most serious enemies, and he felt immeasurably more secure and protected in New York or a major European capital than he did elsewhere. However, in the early spring of 1917, F. C. Coppicus of the Metropolitan Musical Bureau convinced him to take to the road once again for a limited tour of three cities, hoping that this short tour might persuade the tenor to set out on a more extensive and profitable one in the future. To assuage his fears of appearing on a bare stage with only a pianist, the Cincinnati Symphony Orchestra was engaged to take part in the three concerts.

The tour was arranged by Coppicus with the aid of Edward L. Bernays, who was to serve as Caruso's press agent. Three cities — Cincinnati, Toledo, and Pittsburgh — were carefully selected from among the many who fought for the tenor's services. Once the agreements had been established, Bernays started working over each detail with the star. The press agent — who enjoyed being called both "the Caruso of press agents" and "Caruso's press agent" — never forgot the experience. In his memoirs, *Biography of an Idea*, he wrote of Caruso: "His glamour affected me as it did others. I was talking to the sun god, and the sun god by his light obliterated his surroundings. When we walked down Broadway together people forgot themselves and their interests for the moment and focused their attention on him. And the strange part was that everyone took this attitude for granted; it appeared the natural thing to do. I wondered why I too felt this way. In this case, I recognized I was letting the public's reaction to Caruso affect my own attitudes. This is how people feel toward movie stars. I suppose identifying with someone who has achieved an extraordinary reputation is natural."

No movie star could have been treated more grandly and greeted with more awe than was Caruso during the tour. Accompanying him was his usual large entourage, which this time included the rather somber Coppicus and his wife Maybelle; Bernays; Barthélemy, his accompanist; Richard Herndon, manager of the tour; his valet; and Enrico Scognamillo, his latest secretary and unofficial manager. Caruso demanded a great deal—he maintained a rigid schedule and dreaded neglecting an obligation—but he also gave generously to those who served him, many of whom profited more from their association with the world-renowned star than he did from them.

The Caruso party arrived in Cincinnati by special train from Atlanta early on the morning of April 30. The elegantly dressed tenor—reporters noted that he wore pearl-gray spats, black patent-leather shoes and a green fedora hat and held a gold-topped cane—was not his usual cheerful self as he faced the mobs awaiting his arrival; it was, after all, seven in the morning. Nonetheless, he warmed up when he spotted an American flag outside the station and happily pointed to it, saying with a smile, "Ah, the flag," to the delight of the onlookers.

After that, in Bernays' words, "Cincinnati basked in the radiant presence of Caruso." He quickly entered into the patriotic spirit of the times by becoming the first member to join the Cincinnati chapter of the American Red Cross under its new membership drive. He warmed to the town just as the town came under his spell. He was followed by crowds wherever he went—in and out of stores and up and down the city's main streets. "I felt as though I were walking on the boulevards of Paris with a popular monarch at the height of his glory," Bernays wrote.

Business came to a halt when Caruso entered the city's largest department store, arm in arm with Maybelle Coppicus. The latter wanted to buy a small flacon of perfume, and the tenor startled her, the sales clerk, and the many curious observers by graciously offering to buy her a full gallon of the fragrance.

After a visit to the art gallery of the city's distinguished citizens Mr. and Mrs. Charles P. Taft, Caruso was guest of honor at a dinner given at the Hotel Gibson. Again he impressed those present with his magnetic charm and good humor, disappointing them only by retiring to his suite early, as was his custom the night before a performance.

His charm and good humor temporarily disappeared shortly after dinner, when a wedding party in a nearby room, complete with small orchestra, prevented him from getting the sleep he needed. He was furious and demanded not that he be moved from his quarters but that the wedding party be relocated. An embarrassed hotel manager notified the celebrants of the tenor's complaint, and the group good-naturedly agreed to move elsewhere in the hotel. After a full night's rest, Caruso regained his good humor and sent the newlyweds an autographed photo; on it he wrote, "Thank you for my *not* sleepless night."

The following evening, four thousand people filled Cincinnati's Music Hall to listen to the tenor's first solo concert with orchestra. The audience — which included Governor James M. Cox — greeted him with uninhibited enthusiasm. After the formal portion of the program, the applause was so great that he was forced to sing twelve songs in French, English, and Italian as encores. "Cincinnati surrendered to Enrico Caruso Tuesday night," the *Commercial Tribune* proclaimed the following day. "The beau monde of the city extended a gladsome welcome to the noted singer that was almost regal."

The following day the party, this time including the entire Cincinnati Symphony Orchestra, traveled to Toledo, where another royal welcome awaited the star. The great tenor's appearance in the industrial port city was a major event — Toledo had no rich musical tradition as did Cincinnati, and few artists of comparable fame had ever visited it. As suited the occasion, Caruso and his entourage were met at the station by the Sixteenth Ohio Infantry Band, playing both "The Star-Spangled Banner" and the Italian national anthem. Caruso appeared moved; he responded graciously by proudly saluting the American flag.

The setting for his Toledo concert on the night of May 3 was an unusual one. The Terminal Auditorium — a long, narrow hall with more than one hundred rows of seats on an unraked floor — had formerly been a railroad station, and it still resembled one. The audience, too, was unusual — more than five thousand people, natives of the city as well as many hundreds of Italian-Americans brought there by special train from Detroit and Sandusky, filled the hall. It was an audience as unsophisticated as the setting, and there was loud talking throughout the orchestral selections, which the public considered to be merely background music, preliminary to the concert itself. Caruso fared better: there was rapt silence as he sang, and thunderous applause followed each of his selections.

It was a peculiar experience for the tenor, who was accustomed to the world's most elegant opera houses and audiences, though it was far less disturbing to him than an episode which nearly spoiled his post-concert dinner at the Hotel Secor, when a waiter, unaware of the guest of honor's fear of a draft, opened a window to let some air into the overcrowded dining room. Reacting instinctively to the first trace of a breeze, Caruso, as unobtrusively as possible, placed himself under a table and away from the menacing draft, only returning to his chair when the window had been closed. He was grateful for the enthusiastic reception accorded him by the people of Toledo, but he did not want to catch a cold in their city.

A similar fear almost ruined Caruso's visit to Pittsburgh, the final stop of his tour, where he astonished his hosts by complaining on arrival that the bedroom of his luxurious suite at the Hotel Shenley, the best the city had to offer, was completely unsatisfactory. Everything was wrong with it. He had been given a three-quarters bed, and he wanted a double bed. He had been provided with one mattress and two pillows, while he required no fewer than three mattresses and eighteen pillows. While the hotel staff frantically ransacked the premises in an effort to comply to the celebrity's outrageous demands, Caruso fulminated against the rigors of hotel living in the American provinces, regaining his composure only after the extra pillows and mattresses had been located and put in their proper places, enabling him to sleep high above the floor, in a nest of pillows which would protect him from the perils of a draft. It had been an unusual public display of temperament from a man eager to maintain the image of a good-natured entertainer. Yet in his own eyes, Caruso had not been unduly willful or demanding. His fear of catching a cold was genuine and almost obsessive, and he was merely exercising his right to do everything possible to protect his treasured voice.

The thirty-four hundred people who packed Pittsburgh's new Shriner's Mosque the following evening would have agreed. His concert, similar to those given in Cincinnati and Toledo, was an enormous success, further proof that, though still ill at ease without his costumes and props, he could triumph on the concert stage as he had in the opera house. With all its inconveniences, the tour had been more gratifying than Caruso had anticipated. He took an almost boyish delight in the ingenuous warmth and goodwill with which he found himself surrounded at each stop. He had been accustomed to cheering crowds and thundering ovations, but the noisy bands that met him at railroad stations, the flags waved vigorously in his direction, and the unsophisticated speeches of welcome represented a refreshing change from the more formal and more worldly receptions of the past. Furthermore — and this could not help but please him — the tour was a huge success financially and his fee for each short concert was almost double what he received for singing at the Metropolitan.

XVIII. Wartime in the Stepmother Country

Only five days after his Pittsburgh concert, Caruso set out on another long tour of South America. Having been forced to abandon his annual summer holiday in Italy because of the hazards of travel to and within wartime Europe, he had given up the idea of any vacation and had accepted an unprecedented offer from Mocchi of two hundred thousand dollars for a total of thirty performances in Buenos Aires, Montevideo, Rio de Janeiro, and São Paulo.

It was an offer he had at first declined. Ada Giachetti was living in South America. During his last visit there, their paths had not crossed, but this time the tenor felt certain that they would meet, and he wanted at all costs to avoid an unpleasant encounter; he feared that old wounds, not yet fully healed, would be reopened. Embarrassed to tell Mocchi the real reason for his rejection of the offer, he told the impresario instead that he felt the trip was too dangerous—because of the threat of an attack by German submarines on the way to South America. Mocchi's counteroffer, however, was too good to refuse, and Caruso reluctantly accepted, risking the meeting with Giachetti. (The two did meet on several occasions, and their meetings were very friendly, lending credence to the belief of Caruso's friends that he and Giachetti were in love until the tenor's death.)

The long sea voyage was not a relaxing one, and the singer was nervous from the very beginning—the threat of German submarines was a real one. When he embarked on the *SS Saga* on May 10, 1917, he carried with him a special life-saving suit which would allow him to float in the sea in a sitting position, and once on board, he carefully checked the location of each and every lifeboat. In spite of these precautions he feared the worst.

Fortunately, the crossing was an uneventful one, undisturbed by hostile submarines. Caruso managed to study the role of Flammen in Mascagni's new opera, *Lodoletta,* which he was to sing at its American première in Buenos Aires, but rough seas prevented him from enjoying the pleasures of shipboard life. As a result he was no more rested at the end of the voyage than he had been when he left New York.

From the day of his arrival, even before his first performance, the South American visit was a tiring one. For the three weeks before the official opening of the season in Buenos Aires, Caruso was on display in São Paulo, Rio, and Santos, the center of attention wherever he traveled, greeted with persistent curiosity by the press and lavishly entertained by his Brazilian admirers. He was followed through the streets, feted at official banquets, and the prime attraction at benefits, even when not performing. No effort was spared by the management of the tour in its attempts to stimulate sales in order to recover the huge investment that had been made to bring the world's greatest tenor to South America.

The tour itself was not without its problems. In fact, once he began to sing — on June 17 — the actual performances, overwhelmed by the accompanying publicity, often proved to be anticlimactic, and the reaction to them was frequently disappointing. Journalists had written of the chaos caused by mobs trying to buy tickets for Caruso nights, and newspapers were filled with personal ads offering to buy or sell tickets at even higher prices than those charged at the box office. A Caruso performance was a social event, a pretext for elegance, with merchants advertising expensive dresses, perfumes, or binoculars especially appropriate for such a gala occasion.

Caruso was, as a result, competing again not only with the Caruso of the past but also with a legend overzealously cultivated by the press and the publicity machine that fed into it. The reaction against this ballyhoo was inevitable, and it was frequently reflected in negative reviews by critics who had previously praised the tenor, and by audiences who, wearied by the fanfare and angered by the high prices, did not hesitate, on occasion, to show their disappointment.

Other factors contributed to his mixed reception throughout the summer, among them the complex national rivalries that the war in Europe had intensified among the people of Latin America. It was, almost without exception, the Spanish-language (or Portuguese, in Brazil) press that was most critical of his singing, while the Italian-language press — representing the large Italian communities — indignantly defended him, complaining of the ignorance of the local audiences and press in not recognizing, as had their counterparts elsewhere, that Caruso had gained in musicianship what he had lost in youthful vocal power. These attacks and counterattacks inevitably created a tension which all too often obscured the real merits of his performances.

Other national rivalries, too, manifested themselves on specific occasions during the tour — and Caruso was often the victim of petty jealousies. In July, the management of the Teatro Colon fired a leading French tenor, Fernand Francell, causing a veritable diplomatic storm. A large part of the local press was enraged and blamed the opera house's powerful Italian wing. The Italians responded by asking why the French colony always wanted Caruso and other Italian singers to sing at their benefits, rather than French "stars" like Francell. After having appealed for the intervention of the French authorities, Francell was finally paid off and sent home, but there remained a degree of totally unjustified resentment toward Caruso, who was somehow held responsible for the Frenchman's dismissal.

Another kind of uproar resulted from an incident of a completely different nature, and again Caruso was unfairly blamed, this time by his own people. As part of the tour, over which he had no control, he was to sing five performances in the city of Rosario, six hours from the Argentine capital. The theater in which the operas were to be given was owned by Germans, and the fact that the opera company and Caruso himself would agree to sing there so outraged the Italian residents of the city that they stormed the theater and wrecked it. "War against the management," Caruso wrote above an article describing the furor in his scrapbook of clippings. "These gentlemen won, because the performances were not given," he noted at the bottom of the article.

There was anger, too, on the final night of Caruso's tour, October 10, when the tenor sang the role of Des Grieux in Massenet's *Manon* at São Paulo's Teatro Municipal. The opera was to be sung in its original language — French — but at the last moment the great French soprano, Ninon Vallin-Pardo, became ill, and her substitute, Gilda Dalla Rizza — a young Italian soprano who had recently triumphed at the world première of Puccini's *La Rondine* at Monte Carlo — was able to sing the title role only in Italian translation. The bilingual duets between the two stars were at first met with laughter, but in the middle of the second act members of the audience angrily and unreasonably demanded that Caruso sing in Italian. Only an announcement by a company spokesman that the tenor made a practice of singing his roles in the original tongue managed to quiet the public. Not satisfied with this explanation, however, members of the press the following day insisted on blaming the entirely blameless Caruso for what had happened, in spite of the tenor's own obvious dissatisfaction with the performance.

These were, admittedly, isolated incidents. On balance, the tour was a most successful one, from which both Caruso and the management profited handsomely. Even audiences who had come to express their disapproval found themselves cheering by the end of each performance, and the tenor's popularity was so great that his scheduled thirty appearances became forty. The press and public had registered their complaints, but in the end Caruso triumphed, and when he left for New York he expressed satisfaction that his job had been well done and insisted that he bore no ill will toward the South American public for its erratic behavior during the tour.

✱

Caruso arrived in New York in the fall of 1917 accompanied by cases of gold which he had received in payment for his South American performances. The golden-voiced tenor, one reporter quipped, had appropriately been paid in gold. He was more than happy to be home. Upset during his voyage by the news of the rout of the Italian army at Caporetto—he was concerned not only for the fate of his country but also for that of his two sons—he eagerly looked forward to rejoining his old friends at the New York opera house and to preparing for the new season.

Once again the Metropolitan had managed, in spite of enormous difficulties, to bring an impressive array of singers to New York, among them John McCormack, singing for the first time as a regular member of the company. Though word spread that he and Caruso were rivals, the Irish tenor, more at home on the concert stage than at the opera house, was no threat to his Italian colleague and friend. (It has been said that McCormack once asked Caruso, "How is the world's greatest tenor?" to which Caruso answered, "Since when have you become a baritone?") "Rival or no rival," McCormack said many years later, "there has never been a man whom I loved so much as Caruso. There has never been one like him, and there will never be another."

Both men were an asset to the Metropolitan, but Caruso's presence was more important to the company than ever, since all German operas (with the exception of *Martha*, presumably because it was sung in Italian) had been banned for the duration of the war, and Italian and French operas completely dominated the season's repertory. From his opening night performance of *Aida* on November 12, 1917, to his final performance in *L'Elisir d'Amore* on April 19, 1918, Caruso sang twelve different roles. Some critics complained that his singing showed signs of strain; others noted a deterioration of his breath control; and the distinguished violin teacher Leopold Auer felt that his voice seemed forced in the upper registers. But most observers, critics and public alike, agreed with James Huneker, who, after a performance of *Pagliacci,* wrote that "his voice is now at its richest, his acting is more polished at every performance."

In the course of the season, the tenor sang two roles he had never before sung in any opera house, and one which was new to the Metropolitan. Two of these must be numbered among his few failures. One, which he sang for the first time in New York on January 12, 1918, was that of Flammen in *Lodoletta.* He was held blameless for the opera's failure; he was more highly praised than was the opera. "Obviously the opera was chosen for the sake of Mr. Caruso," the correspondent for *Musical American* wrote, "and just as obviously Mr. Caruso will not be able to save it." After one more season, Mascagni's opera disappeared from the repertory of the Metropolitan. Caruso's second disappointment was the role of Avito in a far more effective work, Italo Montemezzi's *L'Amore dei tre re,* which he sang for the first time on March 14. In this case, the part afforded him little opportunity to display his talent, and he dropped it following that season.

Caruso's performance of his third new role, that of John of Leyden in Meyerbeer's *Le Prophète,* which he sang on February 7, 1918, more than made up for these two failures. Once more, as with Samson a few years before, he was facing the challenge of a role meant for a dramatic tenor — his good friend Chaliapin had even warned him against singing it for fear that it might ruin his voice. Admittedly, it was a courageous act on the part of Caruso, who could easily have satisfied his public in his more familiar roles. Yet he was guided by a sure knowledge of what he could and could not do as well as an awareness of the direction that his artistic career must follow in his mature years — he was about to reach his forty-fifth birthday.

Caruso's first performance in *Le Prophète* confirmed his instinctive judgment; the opera provided him with one of the most solid triumphs of his career. Critics the following day were unanimous in their praise. "Mr. Caruso has never done anything better than this," Sylvester Rawling wrote in the *Evening World.* "No greater tribute to his artistry can be paid than to say that he excelled himself. Some of the multitude of his admirers will acclaim him more in other parts. Not so the thoughtful. In John of Leyden Mr. Caruso reveals himself a thinker, a student, a something more than the possessor of a tenor voice the like of which none of us has heard, or ever will hear." Richard Aldrich of the New York *Times* was equally enthusiastic: "As John of Leyden he sang superbly last night, with an earnestness and dignity, a beauty of voice and restraint of action that made up any lack of inches for the towering figure of the fanatical leader in a historic episode of Holy War."

✻

After his twentieth curtain call, following his final performance at the Metropolitan that season, Caruso dismissed his public, as always reluctant to say goodbye, by shouting, "I want everybody to buy Liberty Bonds!" His words reflected the patriotic spirit of the times, which had dominated the opera house as it had the entire country. Throughout the season, Caruso had given generously to the Allied cause. He had sung at countless benefits, had appeared at charity auctions, had bought Liberty Bonds himself, and had urged others to follow his lead. He had proved to be not merely an opera singer, but a dedicated patriot, a war hero on the home front.

Of all of his acts of patriotism, none solicited more praise and comment than his appearance in February 1918, at the office of "Big Bill" Edwards, collector of internal revenue, at New York's Customs House. The tenor appeared there, four months ahead of the deadline, not only to make out his income tax form, but to pay it on the spot. The astounded tax collector called in members of his staff to assist the singer in preparing the necessary forms, after which Caruso handed him a certified check for fifty-nine thousand dollars. When asked why he had anticipated this payment, Caruso replied in a manner to win the hearts of all patriotic Americans, "I am glad to pay my tax," he said. "It helps my country, Italy, as much as it does the United States in the war. It is legal and right, and the money is due. If I waited, something might happen to me. By paying now I not only perform my own duty, but perhaps I may set an example that others may follow."

It is doubtful that many others followed Caruso's example, but it is certain that his symbolic act brought him even closer to his adoring public.

✻

Because of the war, it was again impossible for Caruso to travel to Europe in the summer of 1918. Instead—and in spite of tempting offers from South America—he decided to spend the summer in the United States, busying himself as best he could.

He continued his efforts in support of the Allied cause, and his frequent appearances as a fund-raiser, marked by his usual energy and charm, were enormously successful. On April 30, he joined in a drive to sell Liberty Bonds, singing his own composition, "Liberty Forever," at Carnegie Hall.

On May 20, he sang for the benefit of Italian War Relief at Poli's Theatre in Washington; in the audience at his first appearance in the capital in ten years was President Woodrow Wilson, who had been the subject of a Caruso caricature in 1915 and again in 1918. Later that month, he sang in two concerts at the Metropolitan — one for the American and one for the Italian Red Cross, and on June 10, he joined four other tenors — McCormack, Hipolito Lazaro, Lucien Muratore, and Giovanni Martinelli — in a benefit for the Department of Navy Recreation. In July, while a guest at the home of Victor Herbert in Willow Grove, Pennsylvania, he traveled to Philadelphia's City Hall Plaza to join in the singing of "The Battle Hymn of the Republic" and "Keep the Home Fires Burning."

In addition to these benefits, the tenor gave two concerts of his own. The first was held on July 27 at the seaside resort of Ocean Grove, New Jersey, where a crowd of twelve thousand people packed into an auditorium with space for ten thousand to cheer their idol, who especially delighted them with his rousing interpretation of George M. Cohan's "Over There." At the second concert, on August 17 at the fashionable spa of Saratoga Springs, New York, he sang three arias and a number of songs as well as "Over There" and "The Star-Spangled Banner" before a cheering audience that included New York's mayor John F. Hylan, Mischa Elman, and Al Jolson.

Caruso combined his Saratoga concert appearance with a short vacation. His friend Scotti was at the spa for the summer, and the two were frequently seen at the city's best-known restaurants and at the races. The tenor stayed at the famed United States Hotel, where his accompanist, the twenty-two-year-old Arthur Fiedler, was also a guest. The future conductor of the Boston Pops remembered Caruso well. "He was always surrounded by eight or ten cronies, plus his own cook, masseur, barber, and other hangers-on," he told his biographer, Robin Moore. "He lived in the grand manner. He had great charm and always seemed full of fun. The night of the concert after innumerable encores, he took his last bow puffing a cigarette through a long ornate holder, as if to disprove the popular conception that tobacco and great voices do not mix. . . ."

Caruso deserved his holiday, for in addition to his benefit appearances and his own concerts, he had spent much of his summer hard at work on his first — and last — movies. The motion picture industry was flourishing, and to one enterprising producer, Jesse L. Lasky, it seemed only logical that movie houses could be filled with audiences who wanted to see the world's favorite tenor — even if they couldn't hear him. It had worked with Geraldine Farrar, who had become a star of the silent screen, so why not Caruso, who was loved not only for his voice but also for his undeniable personal magnetism and common touch? Because of this, the tenor was offered more than two hundred thousand dollars for approximately six weeks' work — the producer decided to make two films rather than one during this period, thereby halving the risk.

From Caruso's point of view, it was a new and potentially profitable challenge, as well as an opportunity to be seen by millions who would never have a chance to watch him in person. It would also stimulate the sales of his records all over the country, to the satisfaction of the Victor Company, which eagerly agreed to help in the promotion of the movies.

He took his work seriously and maintained a grueling pace throughout the production of the films. He arose early — his were no longer the hours of an opera singer — taking his morning coffee at six, and inevitably arriving at the Famous Players Studio, a former riding academy on West 56th Street, ahead of schedule. His director, Edward José, who had directed several early Pearl White serials and as an actor had starred with Theda Bara, was both surprised and impressed by his new star's conscientiousness. Caruso's good humor, too, in spite of the enervating heat, never flagged; there were no displays of temperament at any point, from the first day to the last. As always, in spite of his practical jokes, which he practiced on the set as at the opera house, Caruso was a professional, even in a field completely new to him.

Unfortunately, his seriousness was not rewarded, and for once the Caruso magic failed. The first film, roughly based on a popular Gus Edwards song, "My Cousin Carus," was called *My Cousin*. In it, the star assumed two roles, that of the great tenor Caroli and his cousin, an impoverished artist, whose success as a lover depended on the credibility of his relationship to the tenor. The improbable story was set in New York's Little Italy, and a leading soprano of the Chicago Opera, Carlina White, played opposite Caruso. When the film opened, it was received so poorly that the second film, to be called *The Great Romance* or *The Splendid Romance*, in which Caruso played the role of a pianist-prince named Cosimo, was withdrawn before its first public screening. Lasky had overestimated the public's interest in a voiceless Caruso, and the reviewer for *Photoplay Journal* commented, "Candidly, if you cannot hear his marvelous tenor voice, you cannot possibly enjoy Caruso much. . . . You cannot help but wish the star would step through the silversheet and offer just one tiny song."

XIX. Habits, Hobbies, and a Bride

The summer of 1918 was—with the exception of his brief experience as a movie actor—an unusually inactive one for Caruso, a welcome break from the disciplined life he led during the opera season. Often during his career he was asked how he spent his time away from the stage; his answer was always the same: "I work."

Nearly as rigid in his personal habits as in his dedication to his work, Caruso's life in New York was circumscribed by his celebrity and by his professional activities. His frequent complaints that his fame and his easily recognizable face deprived him of his freedom were justified; he was, uncomfortably, the center of attention wherever he went. He was acutely aware of the importance of his public image and therefore always eager to please his curious public by exchanging friendly words or granting autographs, even when his need for privacy was overwhelming.

The singer's life, however, was above all ruled by the need to preserve and care for his voice, and while working he insisted upon maintaining a rigorous and inflexible schedule that allowed for little variation in his daily routine. A typical Caruso day began at eight in the morning, when he was awakened by his valet. A bath followed, one of at least two that the tenor took each day. Fastidious since childhood, he was inordinately concerned with personal hygiene and grooming. Foul odors distressed him; he used Caron perfume on himself and was often seen walking around his apartment with an atomizer, spraying the room with scent. He once reportedly demanded that a fellow occupant in a box at the opera house leave the auditorium and brush his teeth before returning to take his place in the box. More than a mere aversion to bad smells, this might have been caused by his obsessive fear of germs, whose presence could have been signaled by such odors.

Following his bath, Caruso turned his attention to his throat, treating it with gargles and sprays that were applied regularly throughout the day. A rubdown followed, after which, relaxing in his dressing gown, he would read through the morning newspapers and glance at his mail, often while being visited by a barber whose job it was to see that he looked his best. His external appearance, he felt, reflected his inner well-being.

After dressing — his clothes having been carefully selected and laid out by one of his valets — it was time for a light breakfast of black coffee and dry toast. Then, Caruso was ready to receive an occasional visitor, more often than not someone in need of money. He usually complied with any reasonable request, but at times his response was a firm and occasionally angry no. Even so good-natured a man could sometimes be pushed too far.

By ten o'clock, and this was a firm rule, it was time to begin his work. If no rehearsal was scheduled, this meant a session with his accompanist, vocalizing and preparing roles he would be singing within the next few days. Caruso liked to say that he had three different voices, suitable for different roles, and he would sometimes amuse his accompanists by announcing playfully which voice he would be using, and in which drawer it was kept.

If he was to rehearse at the Metropolitan, he would walk to the theater, inevitably arriving there punctually — punctuality was another obsession. His behavior during rehearsals was exemplary; he seemed to believe that it was his personal responsibility to make the often tiring sessions as pleasant as possible, joking with and encouraging his colleagues, though at all times paying strict and careful attention to the conductor and stage director. There were no unreasonable outbursts of temperament, nor did he ever balk at repetitions — no matter how tedious. Artur Bodansky, who conducted Caruso's performances in *Martha* at the Metropolitan, once told a reporter that "the most conscientious singer in the whole company is Mr. Caruso. He is always willing to go over things, not only for his own benefit but when the general ensemble requires it. He is always cheerful when working."

Following the rehearsals, which usually ended at 1:30, Caruso would go to lunch, generally dining with a few friends or associates at a small neighborhood Italian restaurant. His meal would be a simple one: lamb chops or the white meat of chicken and spinach were his favorites. This was usually accompanied by a bottle of mineral water, though he occasionally indulged in a glass of wine.

Following his spartan lunch — reports of the robust tenor (he weighed 180 pounds and upwards and was slightly more than five feet eight inches tall) hungrily devouring a huge plate of spaghetti might occasionally have been accurate but only during his rare vacation periods and never, during his mature years, in the course of an opera season — he returned to his hotel. There he took care of his correspondence and again met with visitors until it was time for an early dinner; a simple meal, consisting most often of a minute steak, vegetables, and ice cream.

His was the life of an athlete in training — for several months during the year — but his routine was even more inflexible and more severe on those days preceding an evening performance at the opera house. Lunch was then his final meal until after the performance. With the exception of two apples, one preceding the opera and one between the acts, he would eat nothing until a light supper at midnight. After lunch, he would return to his apartment to prepare himself emotionally and physically for his night's work. Late in the afternoon, he would walk to the opera house. Then the ritual began.

That pre-performance ritual, from the time of his arrival at the opera house a few hours before curtain time until his first entrance on the stage, was often described by journalists privileged to watch him, but no account is more amusing than that published in the *Evening Post* of January 31, 1914. It read, in part:

> The opera was *Aida;* Caruso was to sing Radames and he was in his dressing room at five o'clock sharp. The curtain was to rise at eight.
>
> "I like to arrive early and to take my time," he explained. "I am not yet American." In his train came his two valets. Wonderful indeed were they. . . . Of them more later. Caruso took his time in removing his outer clothes; and the valets feverishly unpacked grease paints, atomizers, vaporizers, cigarettes, toilet waters, toothpaste, apples — yes, apples — salt, combs, brushes and heaven only knows what. In long, orderly lines they placed the litter on a shelf, waist high, that ran the entire length of one side of the room. Then, with naught separating him from the world but two woollen garments, Caruso began the homage to the throat. More than passing strange were the rites that were then performed; peculiar, to the eye of the layman, were the preparations; unusual, interesting and illumining were the several operations that nightly, when he sings, Caruso goes through before

he dons his costume for the stage. . . . Two alcohol lamps sputter at the far end of the waist high shelf. One merely heats water — filtered, germless water. The other has a receptacle for a glass, and a long spray. These take the place of the lamps of the ancients in the sacrificial rites.

Caruso sits before a stationary washstand and one of the valets hands him a toothbrush and powder. Then for three solid minutes by his Swiss-movement watch does Caruso cleanse and scrub and polish. The ever alert dressers stand behind him, watchful for a shrug of his shoulders, which they immediately interpret into a command. Caruso takes a long breath — and he needs it. It must be a signal, for one of the valets has a glass of warm water in one hand and in the other a big, round pasteboard box full of little brownish crystals. Caruso takes a handful of the crystals and drops them into the warm water, where they dissolve immediately.

"That's gargling salt," he says. "I use it for my first gargle." The gargle takes four minutes and then comes the vaporizer. A glass of water containing bicarbonate of soda and glycerine is placed in a little stand; a rubber hose connected with the vaporizer is put into the glass, and a thin, forceful sputtering spray shoots out a full foot. Into this tiny Gatling-gun spray Caruso plunges mouth open.

Then the heavy artillery answers the little Gatling gun — for Caruso coughs back at the spray, chokes, bellows and sputters. Into each nostril, then deep into the throat, go the bicarbonate of soda and glycerine over and over and over again, until Caruso coughs no more. "Now it is clear," he says and rises. "You have no idea how much dirt can collect in the throat and nose in one day's time."

The vaporizer bath has taken eight minutes by Caruso's infallible watch; but the end is not yet. There is a cold water gargle — sterilized water, please — minus the salt, to follow; and that in turn by a spray for the nose only, of a very dark color, the name of which Caruso could not recall. Only about six sniffs a piece for each nostril and the spray is put away.

Then menthol and vaseline on absorbent cotton are attached to long sticks and Caruso swabs out his throat with these as a gunner would a cannon. "Dilates the throat," he says between gasps. One more gargle of cold water and the homage to the throat is finished.

It has taken 22 minutes!

On goes his bathrobe and he is in the corridor—smoking a cigarette! Twenty-two minutes of hard work he had given to that throat—and now he is calmly smoking a cigarette and inhaling every blessed puff of it! Shades of bicarbonate of soda, of gargling salt and glycerine and of menthol—and of what avail are you when a nervous man wants a cigarette—and wants it now?

Once the throat treatment had been concluded, makeup was applied, with Caruso carefully keeping his eyes and mouth closed to avoid potentially damaging powder—after which he lit another cigarette. Finally, it was time for the two valets to dress the star. "Not a lost motion is theirs," wrote the reporter. "Not an unnecessary movement; while one is working at Caruso's shoulder, the other is engaged at his knee. Never does the one's busy hands touch the other's busy hands. Everything they need is close to them; there is no running to the end of the room—merely the stretching of a hand for a pin, a piece of cord, a buckle, the Theban earrings, the tunic. They have foreseen what they wanted and put everything within arm's reach."

Outwardly prepared for the performance, Caruso would then begin to vocalize. No matter how perfectly he was dressed and made up—and he was unfailingly meticulous about each detail—it was his voice that mattered most. Full of nervous energy, he paced up and down the corridor, exchanging occasional banter with his fellow performers, retiring to his room to spend some of that energy on his caricatures, emerging again from time to time for another walk in the corridor, another cigarette. . . . No matter how often he had sung a role, each new appearance was preceded by an often terrifying attack of nerves. "Every man who gives of his best must be very watchful that he gives it. That makes him conscious of himself—then he becomes nervous; fearful that he may not give full measure," Caruso commented. "Stage fright is the price one pays for being an artist."

The tension that had been built up and was then released onstage accounted in part for the excitement that was communicated to the audience in the course of a Caruso performance. More than a glorious voice, his was a vibrating presence. This tremendous expenditure of energy inevitably took its toll. It was reported that Caruso lost an average of three pounds each time he sang; he himself admitted that he was exhausted at the end of an evening's work—though the feeling of tiredness did not overcome him until a quarter of an hour after the performance, when he was finally able to relax, greet his admirers who awaited him at the Metropolitan's stage door, and leave for a light midnight supper—usually no more than cold chicken, consommé, and toast.

❊

During the Metropolitan season, Caruso averaged two performances a week. This demanding schedule severely limited his outside activities, but there were apparently few — if any — that he missed. When not singing at the opera house, his evenings were generally quiet. He rarely went to the theater or to concerts, and attended performances of the opera only when especially interested in the work of one of his colleagues. Parties bored him — he was ill at ease and suffered from the strain of forced conversations — and he preferred to remain in his apartment, quietly spending his time organizing his scrapbooks — comprehensive collections of his press clippings — and caring for his stamp collection, a tremendous one which he had accumulated over the years and continued to add to on his travels.

Stamp-collecting was one of his few hobbies. He took no interest in sports, either as an observer or a participant. He never saw a prizefight and baseball was a mystery to him; he played neither tennis nor golf, nor did he enjoy long walks or exercise of any kind — except swimming, which he had learned as a child.

His caricatures were one source of satisfaction to him, and through them he revealed a remarkably sensitive eye and a genuine talent for draftsmanship. He drew everyone he met — opera singers, political figures, composers — and his mocking self-caricatures indicate a keen and gentle sense of humor. He often said that he would rather draw than sing, and after having been told that one of his sketches of Woodrow Wilson was selling for seventy-five dollars, he commented, "Good pay for ten minutes' work. . . . Better stop singing and draw." Though he never drew professionally, he contributed — gratis — a weekly caricature to the Italo-American newspaper *La Follia di New York,* and he further showed his interest in drawing by amassing a huge collection of World War One cartoons which he carefully cut and pasted into scrapbooks.

He was, curiously, a collector of many things. His coin collection included nearly two thousand pieces from the fifth century B.C. to his own time, coins from all over the world, but only gold coins. (King Victor Emmanuel III, also a coin collector, commented, "If I were Caruso, I too would collect only gold coins.") He bought enameled gold boxes and gold watches and gold snuffboxes, rare glass and faience, and in January 1915, he paid $3650 for old French lace from the collection of the Duc D'Avary. He bought bronzes and enamels from the J. P. Morgan collection and accumulated more than three hundred pieces of ancient pottery. He collected paintings, too, but he showed little understanding of them. "Who are your favorite painters?" he was asked by a reporter from *Theatre Magazine* in January 1916. "I don't know," he replied. "I can't remember names. When

I like a painting I buy it." However, he refused to buy one small painting he liked, telling the seller that he could buy a larger painting for the same price.

Caruso enjoyed working on his caricatures, and he took pride in his collection of cartoons and his stamp collection; there is, however, no indication that he found real pleasure in his costly antiquities. He liked to shop for them, he liked to show his wealth by buying them, but for the most part they were stored at the Villa Bellosguardo or kept at a friend's gallery in New York.

Caruso's hobbies were solitary ones, enjoyed for the most part in the privacy of his home. Though surrounded by servants, sycophants, and admirers, he had few intimate friends — Scotti, Calvin Child of the Victor Company, and, later, Bruno Zirato, his first official secretary, among them. There were, apparently, no women in his life, and for several years, the press had been silent about the celebrated tenor's romances, most probably because there had been none — his earlier, unfortunate experiences had made him wary of any involvements and he feared the slightest hint of scandal. Because of this, the announcement on August 21, 1918, that he had the previous day married Miss Dorothy Park Benjamin came as a shock — to his friends, his associates, and to his fans.

Caruso's choice of a bride was even more surprising than the fact of his unexpected marriage. Dorothy Benjamin, twenty years younger than her celebrated husband, was a tall, blond, broad-shouldered young woman with a pleasant face that somehow showed all the unmistakable signs of good breeding. The child of a socially prominent and wealthy New York family, her background was diametrically opposed to that of Caruso. Her father, Park Benjamin, an authority on naval affairs and the author of a celebrated book on electricity, had been the editor of *Scientific American*, and the Benjamin home was frequented by the leading intellectuals of the period. Her mother had taken ill when Dorothy was eleven years old (she spent the rest of her life in a sanatorium) and as a result the young girl was sent to the Convent of the Sacred Heart, and her older brother to boarding school. After four years, she was summoned home to take care of her father. Life in the joyless household was impossible for the young girl. Park Benjamin had become a bitter man — egotistical, domineering, and ill-tempered. He made no effort to conceal his contempt for Dorothy, criticizing her appearance, reminding her of what he considered to be her ignorance, and refusing to allow her friends to enter the house. After a year, bored with his daughter, he convinced Anna Bolchi, a thirty-year-old Italian who had worked as a governess to his cousins, to live with them, act as a companion to Dorothy, and take charge of the household.

Miss Bolchi filled her role admirably, though she proved to be a better companion to Park Benjamin than to his shy and lonely daughter. She shared her love of music with him, accompanied him to the opera, entertained him with her own singing, and interested him in Italy. With her arrival, the house came to life; friends were again invited to dinner, and Miss Bolchi played the role of the charming hostess.

Dorothy was excluded from all these activities, largely ignored by her father and the woman meant to be her companion. Nonetheless, she had reason to be grateful to Miss Bolchi, for it was through her, several years later, that she met Enrico Caruso. According to her memoirs, from the moment she first saw him at a christening party, she knew they would marry.

According to Dorothy, too, their courtship, if it can be called that, was brief. She invited the singer to the Benjamin home for dinner; Park Benjamin found the evening's conversation amusing, as did his guest. Soon Caruso became a frequent visitor, presumably enjoying the company of Mr. Benjamin and Miss Bolchi, and often reciprocating by sending his host three tickets to the opera. Dorothy, apparently ignored during their dinners together, was nonetheless included in these invitations.

Three months after their first evening together, Dorothy had her first meeting alone with Caruso. He was going home after a visit with Park Benjamin and offered to drop the young woman off at the house of a friend with whom she was having dinner. During the drive, he proposed marriage, and she accepted.

A few months after that, the couple were married, despite the objections of Park Benjamin. Dorothy's father had at first consented—she thought he might have been too stunned to say no. In time, however, he withdrew his consent, angrily refusing to allow the tenor to enter their home. A week later, he again changed his mind, agreeing to the marriage on the condition that Caruso give his daughter a half million dollars in cash.

Both Caruso and his fiancée were enraged. Two days later they were married at the Marble Collegiate Church (six months later Dorothy was received into the Roman Catholic Church and they were again married, this time at St. Patrick's Cathedral). Park Benjamin never forgave them and never again saw his daughter.

The day after Dorothy's wedding, the irate father told reporters that he had objected to the marriage because of the couple's differences in age, nationality, and temperament. "I did not want my daughter to marry riches or a voice or an orator, but just a man. However, she is a mature woman and Caruso is forty-five, therefore the match cannot be ascribed to the ardor of youth."

In December 1919, he legally adopted Miss Anna Bolchi as his daughter, disinheriting Dorothy and her brother, who had sided with his sister.

XX. A Summer at Bellosguardo and Other Adventures

There was no honeymoon for the newlyweds — "We intend to make every day a honeymoon," the bride cheerfully informed reporters. Instead, Caruso energetically resumed his round of benefits, this time singing before audiences not only eager to see and hear him, but also curious to get a look at the new Mrs. Caruso. New Yorkers, in search of romance, took the couple to their hearts and cheered their every public appearance, even if some wondered why the world-famous opera singer had chosen a shy, retiring, and unglamorous young American to be his bride.

Dorothy's first official public appearance took place on August 31, when her husband sang at Speedway Park, Sheepshead Bay, Brooklyn. The occasion was the New York City Police Department's Field Day, at which almost three hundred thousand dollars was raised to purchase equipment for the Police Reserves. McCormack and Amato were among the performers, but all eyes were on the newlyweds. Caruso was patriotically dressed in a royal blue coat, with a flaming red tie and white flannel trousers; he was given a police escort for the ride to Brooklyn and loudly cheered as he entered the field, his young bride proudly at his side. A throng of one hundred twenty-five thousand people joined him in singing "Over There" and in the course of the afternoon's festivities he was appointed a captain in the Police Reserves. Four months later, when Caruso was presented with his official badge, he asked if he was then entitled to make arrests.

When informed that he was, he suggested that he might go right to the Metropolitan and make an arrest or two.

Though the war was approaching its end, the mood of the country remained patriotic, and throughout the month of September Caruso continued to perform at benefits to aid the war effort. His presence added prestige to every kind of occasion. His voice rang out in support of the Allied cause as he sang the "Marseillaise" on September 6 at the Waldorf-Astoria before a distinguished gathering that included Nicholas Murray Butler, president of Columbia University, and the Czech patriot Thomas G. Masaryk; and he joined other giants of the entertainment world— among them Ed Wynn, Irving Berlin, Al Jolson, Sophie Tucker, Ted Lewis, George M. Cohan, and Will Rogers—at a benefit for the Tank Corps at the Century Theatre on September 15, where he again sang "Over There" before an audience that included the young Major Dwight David Eisenhower, commanding officer at Camp Colt, Gettysburg, Pennsylvania.

Caruso was especially at ease among these show business personalities. He enjoyed relaxing in their company, and they appreciated his own spontaneous wit and charm. Victor Herbert, the king of operetta, was a good friend, as was George M. Cohan, with whom he often lunched. He was amused by Will Rogers, who, as toastmaster at a dinner honoring Caruso, described the first time he heard him sing at the Metropolitan. "My wife was worried about how we could tell Caruso and I told her he would be the fellow that sing, my lord thats all all of them did. . . . We stuck it out till intermission and then I went up to the Hammersteins to see the three Keatons and a good show. . . . We stayed awake till the early editions of the morning papers come out to see who besides ourselves were there. Well we found out Caruso was the fellow who had played the part of a clown but I could not think of a funny thing that he did." The popular humorist concluded, "I don't think that show Caruso was in was much of a hit; I passed there the next day and they had a different show billed."

The tenor's last appearance before resuming his professional commitments took place on the night of September 30, when he joined McCormack, Galli-Curci, and the seventeen-year-old violin prodigy Jascha Heifetz in a Liberty Loan concert at Carnegie Hall. Following this, he and his wife left for what was to be the start of another extended concert tour. This time, his fears of infection in what he considered the American hinterlands were justified, for they arrived in Buffalo, the first stop of the tour, during an influenza epidemic of such proportions that local authorities forced a cancellation of his concert, closing the concert hall in the belief that a gathering of such size—more than nine thousand people were expected — would constitute a menace to the health of the city. Caruso was grateful to be relieved of his commitment, but before leaving the city he good-naturedly agreed to sing informally at a concert at the Hotel Iroquois. The tenor's patriotism was rewarded — nearly one million dollars' worth of Liberty Bonds was sold at the concert — but his worst fears were nearly realized: while eating at the hotel, a fellow diner sneezed — not once but twice, it was reported — in the direction of the honored guests. Caruso was alarmed; leading his wife by the hand, he immediately returned to his suite, where he vigorously sprayed his nose and throat, inhaled vapors, and did what else he could to disinfect himself. Despite his urging, Dorothy refused to follow suit, arguing that similar precautions were unnecessary for her since she was under no obligation to sing. Shortly afterward, she came down with the Spanish flu and was forced to return to New York and take to her bed; Caruso remained healthy.

As the influenza epidemic spread, the rest of the tour, with one exception, was canceled. That single exception was Detroit, and Caruso, assured that there was no possibility of infection there, agreed to honor a commitment he had made unwillingly in the first place. It was one more example of his insisting upon apparently unreasonable conditions — and learning that even unreasonable conditions were sometimes acceptable. The idea for the Detroit concert had come from a stubborn local manager named Burnett. Caruso did not want to sing in Detroit, so he asked his secretary, Zirato, to demand the exorbitant sum of six thousand dollars for a single appearance. To everyone's surprise, Burnett agreed. Caruso countered by ordering that the money be put in escrow for him, certain that this would put a halt to the negotiations. Once again he failed, and he finally agreed to sing in Detroit, but only in a staged performance of *Pagliacci* and not in a concert. Burnett, undaunted, was delighted. Caruso, singing his most popular role, was more than he had hoped for. He brought together the finest artists available — among them Muzio and Amato — and the performance on October 15 was, according to the Detroit *Times*, "the greatest musical event in Detroit's history."

Untouched by the germs he had so profoundly feared, Caruso returned to New York to prepare for the opening of the Metropolitan. That opening was a triumph in every way; it took place on the night of November 11, 1918, the night all of America was celebrating the armistice that brought an end to the first world war. The opera was *Samson et Dalila* and the performance provided a rousing climax to a riotous day of jubilation. The mood in the opera house was festive. Following the first act, the curtain was raised, revealing the entire company, gathered together to stage an impromptu "victory pageant." Caruso was elated because the end of the war meant he could once again see his sons and return to the land of his birth. Still dressed as Samson, he held a large Italian flag; Louise Homer, the Dalila, waved an American flag; and other members of the company proudly unfurled the flags of the other Allied nations. All joined in the singing of each country's national anthem.

Caruso was at his best throughout the evening, and the audience was appreciative. So were the critics the following day. "There has only been one Samson in the Metropolitan Opera House," Henry E. Krehbiel proclaimed in the *Tribune*, "and it is a woeful reflection of what may befall Saint-Saëns's opera, and even the institution itself, when in the course of time Signor Caruso shall bear away with himself the pillars upon which the house stands. Fortunately, there was nothing in last night's representation to indicate that such a catastrophe is imminently impending."

Caruso proved himself to be unique in another way, as Pierre Monteux, the conductor on that historic evening, pointed out in his memoirs. "I remember Caruso, at our first rehearsal together, arrived ten minutes before the scheduled time," the distinguished French musician recalled. "He was extremely respectful and the opposite of 'temperamental.' I knew he was the highest paid lyric artist in the world, and you can imagine my surprise, in the first hour of rehearsal, to hear him sing every measure of his music absolutely on time. I stopped him and said, 'I beg of you, relax, take your time and interpret the role in comfort. You do not have to be so terribly exact with me on this occasion.' He sighed with relief and answered, 'When I sing with a new maestro, I always sing exactly on measure, until he tells me I may do otherwise.' "

No matter how great his fame or his success, Caruso continued to demonstrate his seriousness as a musician. By the same token, that season he again gave proof of his unfailing generosity toward a new artist when on November 15 he sang the role of Don Alvaro in Verdi's *La Forza del Destino* for the first time (it was also the opera's first performance at the Metropolitan). He was at his best. "There is one word with which to characterize Caruso's singing — glorious," wrote James Huneker in the *Times*. "He interpreted the role as it should be interpreted, robustly. He was the impetuous soldier, the ardent lover. A stirring interpretation."

More surprising on that occasion was the success of a young soprano, Rosa Ponselle, later to become one of the great singers of her time, who might not have been there had it not been for Caruso's help. The daughter of immigrant Neapolitans, Ponselle was born in Meriden, Connecticut, in 1897. She and her sister Carmela had formed a vaudeville act, calling themselves the Ponzillo sisters, and they had achieved moderate success at a number of small theaters and movie houses. Rosa was discovered by a voice teacher named William Thorner, whose connections led to an audition before Caruso, and then, at the latter's enthusiastic recommendation, to Gatti-Casazza, who was looking for a soprano to sing the role of Leonora in Verdi's opera. Six months after the tenor had first heard her, the young, totally inexperienced, and understandably nervous young woman was singing opposite him on the stage of the Metropolitan. Her debut was a memorable one, helped considerably by the sympathetic support she received from her co-star. Ponselle never forgot Caruso's kindness that night and until the end of his life, nor did she ever forget his voice. "The sublime voice," she later told Harold C. Schonberg. "You can't describe it. You die at the first note."

The entire season was a brilliant one; Caruso sang ten different roles, and critics agreed that he had never been better. It was also a season for celebrations, during which he gave himself and his bride a party, and the Metropolitan honored its prize tenor with the most dazzling onstage party in its history.

The first of these celebrations took place on New Year's Day, when the couple gave one of the most lavish receptions of the New York social season. The occasion provided an opportunity for Caruso's friends and associates to meet his new bride, and for the latter's family and friends to make the acquaintance of the tenor. The setting was the entire second floor of the Hotel Knickerbocker, including a ballroom, foyer, and several salons. The New York *Herald* reported on its society page that "palms were grouped in the corners of the rooms, and tall vases filled with flowers added touches of contrasting color. The music of two orchestras filtered through the hum of conversation and was as cosmopolitan as the party itself. For the more serious minded there were melodies from the classics, and for those who wished to dance, all the latest fox trots and one-steps were played by a military orchestra from Governor's Island."

The couple — she wore a gown of light-gray chiffon draped over light-blue satin — stood under a bower of roses in the foyer, greeting the more than one thousand guests. The world of opera was represented by Gatti-Casazza, Kahn, and almost every member of the Metropolitan Opera Company. Among those from the world of theater were David Belasco, John Barrymore, George M. Cohan, and producer Charles Frohman, and diplomatic circles were represented by the consul general of Italy and the consul general of France. The bride's side included, among others, her brother Park Benjamin, Jr., and her uncle, Walter Benjamin.

If the social highlight of Caruso's season was that New Year's Day party, an even more memorable event took place on the night of March 22, 1919, when the Metropolitan Opera paid tribute to the man who had led the company and dominated it for fifteen years. It was billed as Caruso's jubilee: "Twenty-five years ago in his native Italy the wonderful voice of Enrico Caruso first delighted those who listened to his great gift of song," the souvenir program read. If the data was inexact, the sentiment was heartfelt. Caruso had been embarrassed by the elaborate preparations in his honor; he reluctantly agreed to the celebration only on the condition that the proceeds be turned over to the Emergency Fund to benefit the company's musicians. In the end, however, he was unashamedly moved by what John H. Raftery in the *Morning Telegraph* reported to be "the most remarkable, the most spontaneous, and the most genuinely affectionate demonstration of personal and artistic admiration that New York ever bestowed upon any man or woman."

Before one of the most glamorous and festive audiences in the opera house's history, Caruso gave as much as he received, choosing a program meant to show every facet of his genius. First, he delighted his public with one of his earliest successes, singing the third act of *L'Elisir d'Amore* with Maria Barrientos, Scotti, and Didur. This was followed by the first act of *Pagliacci*, the opera he had made his own, in which he was joined by Muzio and De Luca. Finally, he demonstrated the enormous range of the mature artist he had become by joining Matzenauer in the Coronation Scene from *Le Prophète*.

After the dazzling splendor of the Coronation Scene, the curtains parted, revealing Caruso and his colleagues in evening clothes, grouped together behind two tables piled high with gifts of silver, gold, and jewelry—tributes from all over the world which were ceremoniously presented to the beloved tenor. There were speeches by other singers, by Otto Kahn, and by the mayor of New York, who lauded his unique contribution to the city as man and artist, and presented him with the official flag of New York. After the orchestra had played "Pomp and Circumstance" and the audience had joined in the singing of "The Star-Spangled Banner," the guest of honor haltingly pronounced his gratitude. "My heart is beating so hard with the emotion that I feel that I am afraid that I cannot even put a few words together," he said. "I am sure you will forgive me if I do not make a long speech. I can only thank you and beg you to accept my sincerest and most heartfelt gratitude for tonight and for all the many kindnesses which you have showered upon me. I assure you that I will never forget this occasion, and ever cherish in my heart of hearts my affections for my dear American friends. Thank you! Thank you! Thank you!"

Caruso belonged not only to New York but to the entire country. He was, as James Huneker wrote following the jubilee, "a national figure," and he proved it once again by breaking box office records wherever he sang during a tiring month-long tour which followed the regular Metropolitan season. In May, when the tour came to an end, he was eager to return to Italy. He missed his sons, and he had been away from his home for two years. He wanted to show it to Dorothy, and he looked forward to a peaceful summer during which he could introduce his young wife to his children, and to Italian friends and family. He was also proudly bringing with him the news that by the end of the year they would become parents.

*

The summer at the Villa Bellosguardo was not as idyllic as the Carusos had anticipated. Dorothy was enchanted by the breathtakingly beautiful setting of her new home and the splendor of the villa, its gardens and its park, but she was less happy with her introduction to Italian family life and to her husband's enormous entourage, which filled Bellosguardo throughout their stay there. As she wrote in her memoirs, she was often lonely though never alone.

Upon her arrival, the bride had her first meeting with the tenor's two sons. Upon hearing of his father's marriage, the fourteen-year-old Mimmi had wanted to come to America, but Caruso had ruled against it, preferring that he continue his education in Florence. Always desperately eager to have a mother of his own, the overprotected boy—Miss Saer had been reluctant to let him grow up—had anxiously awaited Dorothy's arrival. He was disappointed. His attempts to win his new mother's affection were met with reticence and coolness. The morning after her arrival he placed a vase of freshly picked flowers in her bedroom, but Dorothy's reaction, instead of the hoped-for gratitude, was one of anger at this unasked-for invasion of her living quarters.

Fofò, barely twenty-one years old and not so in need of maternal affection, had learned of his father's marriage while in the trenches. The unexpected news had come via a gift sent by his father—a large photo of the newlyweds, with the message, "This is your new mammina." Communication between this elder son and his "new mammina" was severely limited, since Fofò spoke no English and Dorothy no Italian.

This language barrier existed, too, between Dorothy and the many relatives and friends who populated the villa during the summer—in her memoirs, she admitted that she was never quite sure who most of them were. Prominent among them, and recognizable because of a physical resemblance, was Caruso's brother Giovanni, who tried his best to hide his hostility toward Dorothy when his brother was present but made no attempt to do so when alone with his new sister-in-law. Giovanni had been a zealously loyal and faithful brother, at Enrico's side whenever possible and a grateful recipient of his unfailing generosity. Once asked why he had done little with his own life, he answered: "God gave my brother a magnificent voice and gave me a magnificent brother." The two, linked by affection, were nonetheless separated by wide cultural differences. Enrico, because of his travels and contacts, had become a polished gentleman, while Giovanni remained the provincial Neapolitan.

Also recognizable among the visitors was the white-haired Maria Castaldi, Caruso's beloved stepmother, to whom the tenor was deeply attached. She was a strong and wise woman who rarely spoke; a true Neapolitan who preferred to use her arms and body to express herself. Even these dramatic gestures were foreign to Dorothy, who marveled at the old woman's unlimited devotion to her older stepson and her open hostility toward and contempt for Giovanni, with whom she fought constantly.

Enrico Caruso, Jr., vividly remembers mealtimes at the villa. At the head of the table in the huge banquet hall sat his father, surrounded by the English-speaking members of the group: Dorothy, Miss Saer, and himself. Their dinners, served by one of the tenor's most trusted servants, Mario, were light, usually consisting of boiled chicken or hard-boiled eggs and spinach — the bride insisted that her husband try to keep his weight down. At the other end of the table sat the rest of the party, which included Caruso's nephew Marcello, his niece Anna (known as "*la pelosa*," the hairy one), his old friend Arimondi, and countless others who downed enormous plates of pasta while their host looked on with envy.

Caruso involved himself as little as possible in the problems and conflicts of his household. He had his own routine, which he maintained with his usual sense of discipline. Each morning an accompanist, Bruno Bruni, would arrive from Florence to work with him on the score of Halévy's *La Juive*, which the tenor was to sing at the Metropolitan for the first time the following season. Each afternoon was spent working on the setting for a huge crèche which he was constructing in a room next to the villa's chapel. A few years before, Caruso had bought several hundred antique figurines to inhabit the crèche; his task during the summer was to build an appropriate setting for them out of cork, and he worked seriously, attaching the pieces of cork with fish glue and placing the figures, with the eye of an artist, large ones in front and small ones in back to give a sense of perspective. Because of the strong, offensive odor of the glue, he had few visitors.

Young Mimmi spent his summer quietly, usually under the guidance of Miss Saer. His favorite game was playing soldier, and he paraded around the villa and its grounds, proudly wearing a general's jacket cut down to his size, presented to him by his father's friend Dr. Marifioti, who had been an officer in the Italian Medical Corps.

Fofò, when at the villa, spent his days reading magazines. His brother remembers him approaching their father one day with a request for money so that he could marry. Caruso was so shocked and angered that for the first and only time in his life he struck one of his children, knocking Fofò off his chair in rage. Though embarrassed by this outburst, for which he apologized profusely to his astounded son, he steadfastly refused to aid him in his marriage plans. There was, of course, no marriage.

Dorothy was left on her own. She busied herself by redecorating parts of the villa—which her husband felt needed "a woman's touch"—and working in the flower garden. If not able to establish a rapport with most of the members of the household, she did develop an affection for Mario, who, because he had traveled extensively with Caruso in America, was able to speak English with her. Mario confided to Dorothy that he had had a fiancée, Brunetta, for nine years, but that his employer had refused to let them marry; perhaps now that the tenor had a bride of his own, he might allow Mario to have one for himself. Caruso at first remained adamant when Dorothy approached him on Mario's behalf, contending that no man could serve two masters and that Mario's wife would inevitably become a second master. In the end, however, he gave in, agreeing that Brunetta could accompany them to New York—on the condition that there be no babies and that he would have to have nothing to do with her. (Later, in New York, he relented, and Brunetta became part of the household.)

The summer ended on a bitter note. Postwar Italy was in a state of chaos; it had been a period of strikes, of food riots, and of tremendous social discontent that threatened to lead to open revolution. Living in isolation in their splendid hilltop villa, the Carusos were a natural target for the anger of the poor, and one morning Bellosguardo was invaded by a group of about one hundred and fifty women and children who approached the gatekeeper, complaining that they were hungry, and demanded to see the world-famous tenor. The gatekeeper relayed the message to Caruso, who agreed to see them. After listening sympathetically to their pleas, he ordered an enormous picnic prepared—barrels of wine, loaves of bread, and great quantities of cheese, ham, and salami were offered to the hungry mob. Mimmi noted that the children were throwing much of the food to the many dogs that ran loose around the villa's grounds and pointed it out to his father, who said he knew it but that it didn't matter, that they should pay no attention. He was fulfilling his obligation by giving food to the needy; this was, he believed, the only way to satisfy their demands.

These demands, however, had not yet been satisfied, for within a short time five trucks carrying some one hundred and fifty men waving red flags drove up to the gates of the villa. They angrily announced that they had come to see the filthy bourgeoisie, smashed through the gates and reached Caruso, informing him that they had come to hang his caretaker and confiscate the huge quantities of food stored in the villa. Caruso was livid. If they wanted to hang anyone, he told them, they would have to hang him. When they calmed down, he turned over his supplies of food — wheat, wine, and oil — asking only that they leave him enough to serve his family until they left the villa for America. The revolutionaries agreed, loaded the food in their trucks, and left.

It had been a terrifying experience. Fofò, in the uniform of the Italian army, had wisely remained in hiding during the raid. Dorothy, according to Mimmi, was "scared skinny." Caruso was hurt, stunned that his initial act of kindness had not satisfied the angry mob, and, finally, horrified when he learned that most of the food had been thrown away in the middle of the town square, following the raid.

Not long afterward, the Carusos departed for America. They took with them young Mimmi, whom they felt would benefit from schooling in that country. He was at first entered in the Gunnery School in Connecticut and then was sent to Culver Military Academy in Indiana.

It was with considerable relief that they arrived in New York on September 3. Though the tenor minimized the importance of the incident to members of the American press, he had been deeply upset not only by the sacking of his home but also by the astounding reaction of members of the Italian press. The local Florentine paper, *La Nazione*, had bitterly written, "We wish that they had forced him to leave for the new continent where he can make his fortune — the only place he can find people to take him seriously." And the influential *Corriere della Sera* reacted just as unsympathetically, noting that the singer would have no trouble stocking up on his food again from all the money he would make on his forthcoming tour of Mexico.

✳

The Mexican tour, which had been arranged the previous February, meant a month-long separation for the Carusos, for it was considered best for Dorothy, now six months pregnant, not to accompany her husband on his foreign travels.

Their first year together had not been the endless honeymoon Dorothy had predicted: as a husband, Caruso had proven to be jealous, possessive, and demanding — but he had also been unfailingly generous and affectionate. He had never hidden the fact that his work came first, no matter how it affected his personal life. The Mexican trip, in addition, was a financial necessity. His earnings were tremendous but so were his expenses. He was as generous with others as he was with himself. Enrico Caruso, Jr., estimates that there were as many as two hundred and fifty persons on his father's unofficial payroll, persons to whom he sent money each month.

They included Ada Giachetti, who was living in South America; members of his family in Naples; old friends who had helped him in the past — among them Major Nagliati, Arachite, Arimondi; and countless penniless opera singers all over the world. Because of this, though the money came in regularly, it went out just as regularly, and earnings from a tour in a foreign land — not taxable in the United States — were essential to enable him to pay, however proudly, his American taxes.

When Caruso left New York, only a few weeks after arriving there, he was accompanied by an even larger entourage than usual. It included Zirato; his accompanist, Salvatore Fucito; Mario; and Punzo — another figure from the tenor's past. Caruso had first met Punzo while studying with Vergine. Punzo was the star of the class, the one for whom Vergine predicted a brilliant future and who later married Vergine's daughter. But Punzo, whom Caruso described as "proud and stupid," never amounted to anything, and when he turned up in New York asking for Caruso's help, the latter agreed to take him on as his "valet's valet," so that he might finally learn to do something.

Caruso's Mexican season was not an unqualified success. He was again frequently troubled by poor health and faced with those problems which had plagued him in the past: too much advance publicity and too many comparisons with the Caruso of the past. Furthermore, once again, his high fee — seven thousand dollars a performance — made it impossible for the management to hire artists of major stature to appear with him and thereby ensure effective over-all performances.

Caruso had his first opportunity to assess the local talent, many of whom would be joining him at the opera house, at a special concert given in his honor at Mexico City's Teatro Arbeu on the night of September 26. He was as always a gentleman, and few noticed his displeasure with the concert. Among those who did was the tenor José Mojica, who took part in the program and who later went on to sing at the Chicago Opera. "Caruso occupied a box near one side of the stage, and reviewed the performances, some of which proved to be appallingly amateur," he wrote in his memoirs. "The producers had been quite unselective, and some singers were forced to retire from the stage amid whistles, jeers, and hisses. Others, who had been received well enough on previous occasions, got cold applause and had to leave amid an embarrassing silence. I was one of the last to appear, and I could see that Caruso was growing more weary and bored with every minute." Caruso himself wrote to Dorothy that the concert "was very funny because there was a people who don't know about singing and the public was very severe."

Three nights later, the tenor made his Mexican debut in *L'Elisir d'Amore* at the Teatro Esperanza Iris. Aware that his supporting cast would offer him no support at all, and weakened by head and neck pains which had afflicted him all day—he blamed them on the city's altitude—he feared a hostile reaction from an audience tired of hearing about the great Caruso. In the beginning these fears seemed justified, and the public greeted him with indifference, if not anger. As had happened so often in the past, however, both he and his audience soon warmed up, and at the end of "*Una furtiva lagrima,*" the auditorium resounded with cries of "bravo."

His second appearance, at the same theater on October 2, in *Un Ballo in Maschera*, was a dismal one. The company had rehearsed until past midnight the evening before, but to no avail. The soprano, Clara Elena Sanchez, sang so badly that the conductor, Gennaro Papi, withdrew from his assignment, refusing to take part in what he felt certainly would be an incompetent performance. Caruso stubbornly and courageously insisted upon honoring his commitment, though it was impossible for him to hide his disapproval in the course of the amateurish performance which he was unable to salvage. Sanchez, he wrote Dorothy, was "a very disastre."

On October 5, Caruso sang the first of five times in El Toreo, an enormous bullfight arena which held more than twenty thousand people. The opera was *Carmen,* and though the supporting cast was again poor, the tenor was fortunate enough to sing opposite the Carmen of Gabriella Besanzoni, the only singer in the company worthy of the occasion. This time Caruso, who had been offended by the screeching sounds made by the Micaela and not too pleased with his own singing, felt he had been saved when a heavy rain began to fall during the first act. He misjudged the determination of the Mexican public, which in spite of the downpour refused to leave the arena and insisted the opera proceed. Umbrellas were opened, the orchestra was covered with a huge tarpaulin, and the principals donned their raincoats. Though the music was overpowered by the sound of rain on the sea of umbrellas, Bizet's opera was performed to the very end.

Caruso's bad luck at El Toreo continued a week later, but this time the rain was so hard that the outdoor performance of *Ballo* had to be canceled after the second act. "I think it is the first time in my artistic career that I bring home some money without work," he wrote Dorothy. "What you think if I give half of my check to the poors?" he added with his characteristic sense of justice. Then he reconsidered: "I don't feel to take such money but the impresario don't give back to the public anything. Then I don't see why I must give my money to the poors. I think I will send to my poors relatives."

Caruso's headaches and neck pains were so severe that he literally prayed for bad weather the following Sunday, when he was to sing Samson at the outdoor arena. His prayers were not answered, and for the first time the sun shone throughout the entire opera, which was, surprisingly, a successful one. A subsequent appearance at the arena, in *Aida*, also went well.

In all, Caruso sang twelve times during his month in Mexico. His physical suffering — his entire body was often racked with pain — had been even greater than his discomfort at singing with artists who were at best mediocre. Nonetheless, the season had constituted another personal triumph; against all these obstacles he had managed to win the admiration of the Mexican people. At his last appearance — at the bull ring, on November 2, when he sang one act each from *L'Elisir d'Amore*, *Martha*, and *Pagliacci*—he was thunderously applauded. OVATION AFTER EACH ARIA AND GREAT, VERY GREAT DEMONSTRATION AT THE END, REACHING DELIRIUM, he telegraphed Dorothy. TWENTY-FIVE THOUSAND PEOPLE. AM HAPPY HAVE BEEN HERE AND KNOWING THIS COUNTRY AND ENTHUSIASTIC PEOPLE THAT GAVE ME CONTINUALLY GREAT SENSATIONS.

XXI. Triumph and Decline

Less than two weeks after his troubled visit to Mexico, Caruso was grateful to be back at the Metropolitan, opening the season on the night of November 17 with his familiar colleagues Farrar and Scotti in a performance of *Tosca*. Apart from *Tosca*, which he sang only once, *Manon Lescaut* (also sung only once), *Pagliacci*, *L'Elisir d'Amore*, and *Martha*, the tenor concentrated his efforts during the season on his more dramatic roles in *Samson et Dalila*, *La Forza del Destino*, *Le Prophète*, and undertook one new role, that of Eléazar in *La Juive*.

Caruso's appearance, on the afternoon of November 22, 1919, in *La Juive* was, according to Irving Kolodin, historian of the Metropolitan, "without doubt the most striking artistic triumph of his career." More than ever he revealed himself to be not merely a great singer but a consummate artist, able to bring to life every facet of a complex dramatic figure in a striking portrayal that brought him extraordinary acclaim—even for Caruso.

Halévy's opera, never a very popular work at the Metropolitan (it had last been performed there, in German rather than the original French, in 1889) seemed an unlikely vehicle for Caruso's triumph. Nonetheless, it deserved to be revived. Historically, as an early example of "grand" opera, it was an important work; in addition, it provided opportunities for the kind of dramatic spectacle that could show off to good advantage the New York opera house's vast technical resources. The soprano role of Rachel seemed ideal for the Metropolitan's new diva, Rosa Ponselle; more important, the tenor role of Eléazar, a humble Jewish goldsmith, represented a challenge — dramatically and vocally — for which the mature Caruso was now prepared.

Unconsciously, he seemed to have been preparing for this role — his thirty-sixth at the Metropolitan — for many years. Emil Ledner remembered Caruso's interest, several years before, in attending synagogue services whenever possible — in Hamburg, Vienna, Berlin, Frankfurt, Paris, and Budapest — so that he might study what he felt were the unique vocal methods of cantors in uniting text and music. "Caruso listened with the closest attention to the singers," Ledner wrote, "especially when a soloist performed. Then he went home and worked for half an hour on the precious 'pointers' he had heard demonstrated."

During the previous summer in Italy, when he had learned that he would be singing *La Juive* at the Metropolitan, the tenor had studied the new role with even more than his usual intensity. Back in New York he spent hours in the library, making sure that each detail of his characterization would be accurate, that his makeup and costumes, even the prayer shawl he wore, would be in keeping with the requirements for this difficult challenge. Always meticulous in his preparations for any new role, he sensed that his portrayal of the tragic elderly Jew required a special effort on his part.

His efforts were well rewarded, and critics agreed that the performance marked a milestone in his career. The reviewer for *The Telegraph* called it "a glorious performance," and Henry T. Finck wrote in the *Evening Post*, "Both vocally and in action Caruso interpreted in masterly fashion the fatherly love, the religious zeal and the justified hatred of the persecuted noble man, no nobleman; noble man means so much more." Equally enthusiastic, Henry Krehbiel of the *Tribune* commented: "In Eléazar Mr. Caruso has found a part both dramatically and vocally extraordinarily suited to him. In face, figure and bearing he makes of this operatic Shylock an interpretation which will remain long in the memory of those who saw it. Indeed, it is perhaps the first time in his career when the great tenor has succeeded in giving perfect verisimilitude to a tragic impersonation. By it he raised himself a good notch higher in artistic stature. And he sang the music with a passion, yet with a restraint which revealed only the more exquisitely his golden voice."

Of all the reviewers, it was the critic for the *Sun* who best described the tenor's achievement. "Enrico Caruso, who began life as a lyric tenor, ariel of tone and prone to the youthful passions of operatic heroes, is now a full fledged tenore robusto, battling with the agonies of fatherhood, the subtleties of political plot, and the plangent utterances of French recitative," he began his review. "No one who is familiar with the achievements of the most popular singer of this time would expect to be told that he met all the requirements of such a role as Eléazar. Nor would any of the million devoted admirers of his voice care. Probably no one knows this better than Mr. Caruso himself. All he has to do to evoke thunders of applause is to linger on a high tone and to emit a final phrase at the full power of his voice.

"Therefore he commands the respect and admiration of all who regard operatic creations as of more import in art than their interpreters, for he has again and again shown himself a sincere seeker after genuine dramatic results . . . his Eléazar in 'La Juive' will be remembered as one of his highest flights. . . ."

Unquestionably, *La Juive* was the professional highlight of the season, which marked Caruso's emergence as a full-fledged dramatic tenor. Personally there was cause for another celebration—the birth on December 18, 1919, of his daughter, Gloria. The proud father celebrated his own forty-seventh birthday on February 27, 1920; the event had previously been celebrated on the 25th, but he admitted that in the past he had mistakenly anticipated it by two days. (Enrico Caruso, Jr., believes his father was born on the 25th, and that the birth was not registered until the 27th, but, in his words, "No matter. He was born.") Caruso was in a jovial mood and told reporters that he felt like sixteen, attributing his success to his extraordinarily healthy teeth, and his youthful condition to his young wife.

It was in the role of Eléazar that Caruso concluded his seventeenth season at the Metropolitan on the night of April 23, 1920, before a cheering crowd that was, more than ever, reluctant to let him go. There was no extended tour that year—the tenor had committed himself to only three Atlanta performances—and a return to Europe could have been planned for early May, but memories of the previous summer were still fresh in his mind, and instead he chose to set off on another tour of a Latin American country—Cuba.

Once again his wife had to be left behind, this time because of the difficulties of caring for Gloria while traveling. Dorothy, Gloria, members of Dorothy's family, and a large staff of servants went instead to East Hampton, Long Island, for the summer, where Caruso had rented a huge house belonging to Albert Herter. In many ways, the Herter estate rivaled the splendors of the Villa Bellosguardo; situated among one hundred acres on the shores of Georgica Lake, two miles from the village, it included the main house, a guest house, a gatekeeper's cottage, sumptuous gardens, fountains, and a tennis court. None of the pleasures afforded by such a home could be enjoyed by Caruso, however, until he concluded his professional commitments at the end of June.

*

A Caruso visit to Cuba had long been the dream of Adolfo Bracale, the same man who had first introduced the tenor to Egypt many years before and who had subsequently settled in South America. Caruso's motive for embarking on the arduous tour was again money, for the impresario had agreed to pay him the astounding sum of ten thousand dollars for each of ten evening performances and—as a concession on the part of the artist— half that for each of two matinees. Bracale's opera company was in desperate straits, and he believed that only Caruso could save it.

The celebrated tenor arrived in Havana on May 5, amid the usual fanfare, to begin a visit that was not for the most part any happier than his visit to Mexico had been. Painful headaches again tormented him—they had worried Dorothy even before his departure—and he suffered from the city's stifling heat, which robbed him of his badly needed sleep. Also, for the first time in his life, he had a toothache. In view of his pride in his teeth as a source of his strength, he believed this to be a bad omen.

Though used to the curiosity of crowds wherever he traveled, Caruso was particularly irritated by his total lack of privacy during his stay in the Cuban capital. The public gave him no peace. "I cannot walk any more here," he wrote his wife. "Men, women, boys, girls, everybody knows me and they acting like bad children. They calls me, they follow me, pass before my steps, and lots of annoyance. Sometimes I wish give lots of knock in the face of everybody. I am looking for the end of the season like the people who are near to die and wish to be saved."

Most serious, however, Caruso was again faced with a problem beyond his control—the pre-tour publicity this time was creating a hostility he found almost impossible to combat. Both press and public were outraged by the prices Bracale charged for each performance, and well in advance of his first appearance he was the subject of vicious attacks in the local press, most of which complained of the excessive fees he exacted and what reporters—who had not even heard him—called his waning vocal powers. Though this time he would be singing with casts of a higher caliber than those which had accompanied him in past tours (among his co-stars would be Carmen Melis, Maria Barrientos, Gabriella Besanzoni, and Riccardo Stracciari), he would also be appearing with many lesser known Mexican artists, and reporters predicted a disastrous season.

In the course of the first two performances, in *Martha* on May 12 and 16, the initial coolness of the public was transformed, as usually happened, into warm applause, but the press remained stubbornly hostile. Leading the attack was the Havana daily, *La Nación*. Caruso's first appearance, the newspaper claimed, marked his "artistic Waterloo." On the same day, a piece headlined CARUSO ON THE EDGE OF THE ABYSS compared him unfavorably to Bonci, Lazaro, and Constantino, and went on to say that artistic circles were talking "of the tremendous failure of the ex-divo."

Before his third appearance, the indignant tenor wrote his wife: "Tomorrow we go with 'Elisir,' and if they will not be satisfay, I will go away from this hot place."

Happily, in spite of his depression and his continuing physical discomfort, the performance of Donizetti's opera was well received, as were his later appearances in *Ballo, Tosca, Aida, Carmen,* and *Pagliacci.* After a performance of *Pagliacci* on May 30, he was able to write his wife, "What a 'Pagliacci' I sung! Surprised myself and everybody was crazy. I never see people crying like in such performance."

In spite of such successes, certain members of the press continued to hammer away at both Caruso and Bracale, complaining insistently of the high prices charged for what they termed second-rate performances. An avalanche of articles and letters to the editor contributed to an increasing sense of outrage on the part of the public which, nonetheless, continued to fill the enormous three-thousand-seat Teatro Nacional. The pianist Artur Rubinstein, linked romantically with Besanzoni and in Havana at the time, explained in his memoirs that Caruso's fee for each performance "represented years of work for an average inhabitant. It was no wonder you could feel a certain hostility in the audience."

That simmering hostility finally turned to open violence on the afternoon of June 12. The occasion was Caruso's last appearance in Havana, in the role of Radames. Both he and his impresario had received threatening letters throughout the season, but neither could have expected the explosion of a bomb which shook the theater during the second act while Besanzoni and Maria Escobar, a Mexican mezzo-soprano, were singing their well-known duet. The frightening incident was described by Bracale:

> The bomb exploded with a roar. Instantly total confusion reigned with cries of terror as some of the decorative figures adorning the proscenium arch of the stage began to fall in shattered hunks. It was a miracle that they did not fall on the two singers. One of the balcony columns collapsed, injuring some of the audience, and in the pit the harp and the tympani were totally destroyed. Padovani, the conductor, had run out of the pit like a flash of lightning when the bomb exploded. The supers, one hundred and fifty of them, stationed backstage awaiting the Triumphal Scene, fled into the street in their Egyptian costumes, while the choristers and dancers screamed like the martyrs of Zaragosa. Caruso, attired as Radames, was with me in my office

when the bomb exploded and both of us hurried out onto the stage, dodging bits of scenery, to get the audience to remain calm. The first trumpet of the orchestra, a Spaniard named Rivero, had the good sense to start playing the Cuban national anthem, and the rest of the men who had left the orchestra pit gradually joined in with their instruments. Fortunately, this seemed to hypnotize the audience and avoided any further misfortunes . . . and with incredible self-possession they filed out quietly and in an orderly fashion. . . . This diabolical deed was directed at me and Caruso, inasmuch as the bomb was placed in the area containing my office and the star's dressing room. . . .

The tenor, still in the costume of the Egyptian warrior, was taken at once to his hotel where, thankful for his lucky escape, he quickly recovered his composure. Nonetheless, the incident continued to disturb him, and a degree of bitterness toward a portion of the Cuban press, which he felt responsible for the incident, remained even after his return to the United States, when he wrote an angry letter to the editor of *La Nación*, complaining of his treatment while in Havana.

Problems back home, too, unnerved Caruso during his Cuban visit. For one thing, he had learned while in Atlanta that the Hotel Knickerbocker, his home for many years, had been sold and would be converted into an office building. He felt personally betrayed—he had been given no warning before leaving New York—and unfairly inconvenienced by the need to vacate his apartment by early fall. Dorothy, alone in New York, was by default in charge of finding a new home, and he could participate in any decision only by means of cables and letters between Cuba and New York.

The problem was not, of course, a very serious one. The Carusos wanted and could afford the best, and before too long they arranged to rent a palatial residence on the eighteenth floor of the Hotel Vanderbilt, at 34th Street and Park Avenue. The apartment—with four bedrooms, six baths, a soundproof practice room, and a large roof garden—had been built for Alfred Gwynne Vanderbilt, who had used it as his town house before his death on the *Lusitania*. If anything, it was even more luxurious than the couple's quarters at the Knickerbocker, but the idea of change proved unsettling to Caruso while far from New York.

Far more troubling news from home reached him toward the end of his stay in Havana. It came via a cable, handed him by a representative of the Associated Press, following a performance of *Aida*. It said that Dorothy's jewelry, valued at almost a half million dollars, had been stolen from the couple's summer home on Long Island on June 8. Caruso's immediate reaction to this alarming news stunned Bracale, who was present when he read the cable. At first, the tenor seemed to attach no importance to it, but after a few seconds he turned to the impresario and said, "She deserved it." Neither Bracale nor anyone else has explained Caruso's enigmatic words, though it is known that the tenor had repeatedly cautioned his wife to screen all visitors to the villa and make sure that no strangers entered it. He also feared that one of their eleven servants, dissatisfied for some reason, might seek revenge on the family. In any case, he was soon comforted by a cable from his wife assuring him that she and the baby were well, and that everything possible was being done to apprehend the criminal. He replied with a cable of his own: THANKS GOD YOU AND BABY ARE SAFE. WILL REPLACE JEWELS.

During the next twenty-four hours, further details of the robbery — which had become headline news all over the world — reached Havana. Caruso was deeply upset, not so much about what had happened to the jewelry (which was heavily insured), but about what might have happened to his wife and child if the criminal had been discovered before leaving the house. The story was certainly frightening. Dorothy and her sister-in-law had been in the library, alone, when they heard the alarm in the bedroom safe, which contained all the jewelry, go off. They rushed upstairs, found that the safe had been removed and that the bedroom window had been broken. After a frantic search by a number of servants, the safe — opened and emptied of its contents — was found on the lawn, not far from the house.

A massive manhunt and an intensive investigation led by police and insurance detectives began at once. The entire estate was quickly transformed into an armed camp. Though it soon became clear that the crime had been committed by someone familiar with the house, Dorothy maintained that it had not been an inside job; still, the possibility of the premises having been staked out in advance could not be discarded.

By the time Caruso left Cuba, there were no clues as to the identity of the thief, nor was there any trace of the missing jewelry.

✳

Unnerved by the bomb explosion in Havana and even more by the news which continued to reach him from Long Island, Caruso managed, though exhausted, to finish his Cuban tour. His last two appearances in the country, at Santa Clara and Cienfuegos, were unqualified successes. Upon returning to the United States, however, his stamina was put to a further test: he had two more commitments to fulfill before reaching East Hampton.

The first of these took him directly to New Orleans on June 25, 1920. His reception at the concert the following night was a resounding one, worthy of note. The city's largest available auditorium was the Athenaeum, located on the second floor of the YMCA; because of its relatively small capacity of two thousand, and the tenor's usual high fee, it was necessary to charge ten dollars for each seat and five dollars for standing room. Coppicus, the manager, worried that Caruso would sing before a half-empty house: the weather was hot, even for New Orleans, and the city's rich had fled for the North. Nonetheless, the theater was filled—with five hundred people standing to hear the great tenor—and ten thousand people, who had been turned away, surrounded the building, listening to their idol's voice through the concert hall's open windows.

The second stop before reaching home was Atlantic City, where on June 30 Caruso fulfilled a commitment made months before to his friend Calvin Child to sing before the National Association of Talking Machine Jobbers. Even during the post-concert dinner, where Caruso was seated at a table with Sergei Rachmaninoff, his mind was on his family in Long Island, and he looked forward to going there to resolve, if possible, the problems raised by the spectacular robbery.

When he arrived at the Herter estate, the atmosphere was still tense. Detectives and insurance inspectors swarmed about the house and grounds, hoping to uncover clues that might lead to the identity of the thieves, endlessly interrogating each member of the family and their many servants. Dorothy, Gloria, and Mimmi were under constant surveillance. Even the chauffeur, a former member of the Mounted Police, carried a gun with him at all times. Caruso feared for the lives of his children. A letter had been received from the Black Hand, threatening to kidnap both Gloria and Mimmi.

He was understandably upset by this invasion of his privacy. Upon his return home, he had conducted informal investigations on his own and had become convinced that the robbery had in fact been an inside job. When the insurance company finally gave up its efforts to recover the jewelry and handed Caruso a check to compensate for the loss, he tore it up. He wanted no further interrogations, no intimations that he himself might be covering up for a member of his household.

The matter, as far as he was concerned, was closed, and Caruso turned to the more important task of enjoying himself. He did his best to relax. Photos taken that summer show him on the tennis court, lobbing the ball across the net with an impish smile on his face. Nonetheless, he never learned to play tennis. At Dorothy's urging he had taken lessons, but after one set he was disabled for a week. Similarly, he was photographed painting the bottom of a boat; it was an attractive photo of him holding a paint-brush, but his brush never touched the boat. Instead, Caruso's activities were sedentary. He took time out to sing one more concert at Ocean Grove, and he spent an afternoon at a Southhampton fair, drawing caricatures for the benefit of a local hospital; but he spent most of his time at home, playing with his baby, helping to entertain Dorothy's friends and family, working at his stamp collection (with the help of Mimmi), and readying himself for his fall commitments.

※

In September, the Carusos' Long Island holiday came to an end. On the 14th of the month, he began three days of recording in Camden, New Jersey. These recordings included the great tenor scene from *La Juive* and the *Crucifixus* from Rossini's *Petite Messe Solennelle*. The latter proved to be the last of the great legacy of recordings he left behind him.

Shortly afterward, there was still another extended American concert tour, one Caruso should not have undertaken, as he was still tired. The summer had not afforded him the rest he needed after the heavy schedule which had preceded it, and he was beginning to show symptoms of what was to become a severe cold.

Under the best of circumstances, a concert tour constituted a strain, but a concert tour for Caruso meant not only an exhausting schedule of traveling and singing in unfamiliar places—sometimes under trying conditions—but also being onstage both in the concert hall and away from it. His fame made him an object of curiosity wherever he went, subjected to endless and often nonsensical interviews and required to participate in local events that bore no relationship to his work but were an important element in the public image he felt the need to maintain.

His image was that of the jovial, good-natured entertainer, and throughout the trip he never failed his public. The tour began in Montreal, where the tenor sang at the Mount Royal Arena, commonly used for hockey games and boxing matches. The stage had been improvised for his appearance, the boxing ring moved from the center to one end of the vast arena. More than eight thousand people, packed onto the pine benches generally used as bleacher seats, cheered loudly as he sang his familiar concert program.

The program varied little from city to city—after Montreal he traveled to Toronto, Chicago, St. Paul, Denver, Omaha, Tulsa, Fort Worth, Houston, Charlotte, and Norfolk. The range of his obligatory social appearances, however, was enormous, making almost superhuman demands on a tired man who needed a rest. In St. Paul, he spoke at a meeting of the Community Chest. In Denver, he visited the grave of Buffalo Bill outside the city and was driven to Pikes Peak. In Omaha, he disappointed his fans by his ignorance of American baseball; when asked what he thought of Babe Ruth, he had to admit that he had never heard her sing. In a letter to his wife, he expressed annoyance that he was supposed to be familiar with every facet of American life, but he continued to maintain the image of the jolly Neapolitan. In Tulsa, he unwillingly but good-naturedly visited the oil fields, and in Fort Worth he found time to examine the local stockyards. In Norfolk, the last stop of the tour, he sang in the Billy Sunday Tabernacle.

Wherever Caruso went, he was royally welcomed—presented with gifts, met by prominent city officials, and given the keys to the cities. He was unfailingly gracious—though the strain must have been tremendous—and did his best to hide the fact that he was bored, homesick, and frequently irritated by the attentions of curious journalists with their all too often irrelevant questions. "What devil interest to the public a private life of an artist?" he asked Dorothy in one letter; and finally, in despair, he wrote her, "The day which I will stop to let talking of me will be the most happy one of my life."

Dorothy was upset to find her husband in a state of near exhaustion when he returned to New York at the end of October. The headaches had persisted, he had not yet recovered from the cold that had bothered him throughout the tour, and there were only two weeks before he had to begin another long season at the Metropolitan.

XXII. Finale

Though he himself refused to recognize it, Caruso was a sick man as the beginning of the 1920–1921 Metropolitan season approached. He was exhausted, both physically and emotionally. The cold that had plagued him for so long had reached his chest and his bones, causing him pain he did his best to conceal from those around him, though several of his friends and associates noted his drawn countenance with dismay. Moreover, his nerves were on edge, and he was frequently ill-tempered. He thought increasingly of retiring from the stage and living out the rest of his life away from the spotlight, in peace and privacy, enjoying the fruits of his many years of hard work. Whether a man so absorbed in his art could ever have done so is a moot point, but, tragically, it was too late: he had already driven himself too hard, and the tranquillity he sought could never be his.

Caruso opened the Metropolitan season on the night of November 15 with a performance of *La Juive*; less than six weeks later, on December 24, he again sang the demanding role in what would prove to be the final performance of his brilliant career. The weeks between these two performances were marred by injuries and illness, and distinguished by almost superhuman courage and heroic determination on the part of this singer whom James Huneker described as not only a great artist, but "a genuine man."

The opening performance went well. A month before Caruso had written Gatti, with humor, that he would try his best "to be the greatest of the Jews without losing my little bit of Christianity," and he succeeded once again in bringing to life the tragic figure of Eléazar. Titta Ruffo, who had been moved to tears by the tenor's performance the previous year in the same role, felt that something had gone wrong, but the press and public were for the most part as enthusiastic as ever. If Caruso was not at his very best, all agreed with Richard Aldrich of the *Times* that he showed "perhaps the finest manifestations of his art in certain ways that can be recalled in recent years."

His second performance, a few nights later in *L'Elisir d'Amore*, was not nearly so successful and was severely attacked by three of New York's leading critics. "Here all thoughts of suitability and appropriateness of singing, all feeling for artistic propriety seemed to be simply cast to one side," wrote Aldrich. "Mr. Caruso's treatment of Donizetti's music . . . is exaggerated; an attempt to make portentous and rotund in expression what is really simple, straightforward. . . ."

The tenor was deeply upset. He thought he had sung well and that the attacks on him were unjustified, and he wrote a letter at once to Gatti offering his resignation. If he couldn't please the critics, he would leave. Only forceful persuasion on the part of the tactful managing director could convince him to go ahead with the season.

The response to his next appearance, in *Samson et Dalila* on November 24, was reassuring — even Aldrich agreed that he sang brilliantly — and his performance in *La Juive*, in Philadelphia on November 30, was greeted with unanimous praise. In spite of his fatigue, he was satisfying his public.

Caruso's next performance, at the Metropolitan on the night of December 3 in *Samson et Dalila*, was also acclaimed, but in the course of it he was nearly felled when a piece of a broken pillar hit him forcefully in the chest. The pain was of short duration; the blow was deemed a trivial one by the physician who examined him and found nothing more serious than a slight bruise. Later, physicians theorized that the apparently minor accident might have caused injuries to his pleura and consequently far greater damage than had at first been believed.

Whatever the cause — the blow to his chest or a worsening of his cold — Caruso was seized with a chill the following day while out for a drive with Dorothy. He immediately paid a visit to his personal physician, Philip Horowitz, who ordered him to stay in bed.

During the night, the tenor suffered a dull pain in his side, and his cough worsened. He made light of it, refusing further medical attention the following day and insisting that it would pass. Trying to ignore the obvious deterioration of his condition, he was determined to sing a few nights later, on December 8, in *Pagliacci*. As he left his apartment, however, he ominously asked his wife, who would join him later at the theater, to pray for him.

In spite of what must have been excruciating pain, he began the performance, in which he was joined by his old friends Destinn and De Luca. Toward the end of his great aria, *"Vesti la giubba,"* his voice broke on the high A, and to the horror of the audience, he tripped and stumbled off the stage and into the wings.

The public was alarmed, fearing that he might have seriously injured himself in the fall. The truth, which the tenor had carefully hidden, was far worse. The fall had not been an accident. Caruso, in the midst of his aria, had felt an intense pain in his left side and momentarily blacked out. He had deliberately tripped to deceive the public, to make his listeners believe that a mere accident had been the cause of his broken note. Unknown to the audience, he had fallen unconscious into the arms of Zirato and had to be carried to his dressing room. He was in a state of panic, gasping and sobbing that he felt that his voice had gone forever.

As he lay in his dressing room, Zirato, Dorothy, and his colleagues pleaded that he end the performance. Dr. Horowitz, in attendance, however, minimized the damage. It was, he assured them, an attack of intercostal neuralgia and nothing more. He strapped the tenor to lessen the pain and agreed that he should be allowed to continue the performance. He did so; and the public was assured that it was nothing serious.

At the end of the opera, Caruso was taken home, his fans convinced that the slight delay between acts had been caused by no more than a minor accident. There was nothing to be alarmed about. He had successfully concluded the performance, and his recovery was taken for granted.

The next day, Caruso, still in pain and demonstrably weak, again made light of his problem. There was, he said, no reason for him not to go on with his normal schedule. Though he must have realized that his illness was not the result but the cause of any muscle strain, he preferred to believe the comforting diagnosis of his physician.

Caruso's next performance, in *L'Elisir d'Amore*, was to take place at the Brooklyn Academy of Music on the night of December 11. The optimistic Dr. Horowitz examined him and assured him that there was no reason to cancel, but in spite of this soothing prediction, the evening turned out to be one of the most dramatic and terrifying in the history of opera.

Shortly before the curtain was to rise, the tenor, already in costume, started to cough. Upon entering his dressing room, Dorothy found him by his washstand, rinsing his mouth. The water he spit into the basin was at first pink, which Dorothy believed was the result of a too vigorous brushing of his teeth. It soon turned to red, however, and she realized he was hemorrhaging. She turned to Mario and asked him to summon Dr. Horowitz to the theater, in the meantime pleading with her husband to delay the start of the opera until the doctor's arrival. Caruso stubbornly insisted that the hemorrhage was a minor one and that he would begin to sing as soon as the bleeding stopped.

After applications of ice to the back of his throat, the bleeding did stop, and the performance began. The audience, unaware of the backstage drama, applauded wildly as Caruso, dressed as the innocent, lovesick peasant Nemorino bounded onto the stage. As he began to sing, Dorothy, seated in the first row, noticed that his smock was reddening. She watched in horror as her husband repeatedly turned his back to the audience, coughed, and drew a handkerchief from his pocket. In spite of the incessant bleeding, he continued to sing. From time to time, he went toward the wings, where Zirato and stunned members of the chorus passed him towels and handkerchiefs with which he would wipe off his mouth, then discarding them, bloodstained, into a well which was part of the set. Dr. Horowitz, who had reached the theater and was also standing in the wings, vividly described the tenor's courageous struggle to the New York *Times* a few days later. "I almost died standing there, watching him," he stated. "Of course I did not know what was the matter. I could not tell. I had made no examination. No one could tell. I stood there watching him, fighting to go on. You can imagine how I felt! I beckoned, I tried to make him come off the stage, but he paid no attention to me. All the chorus was standing there watching, aghast. Even the musicians, I am told, looked up, wondering whether to go on. Caruso would not stop, so they did go on."

To the astonishment of all those who witnessed his ordeal, Caruso continued to sing until the close of the act, profusely bleeding yet clear-voiced except for the brief moments when the blood which rushed to his throat threatened to choke him.

When the curtain finally fell, he was led to his dressing room and convinced that he should not go on with the performance — but not before he had official word from Gatti authorizing the suspension. The general manager, at his office in New York, had been notified of the incident by Giuseppe Bamboschek, his musical secretary, and had unequivocally ordered that the opera be terminated. In his memoirs, Gatti noted, "At that very moment I had a fleeting premonition that Caruso was lost."

Caruso did not share that premonition. After an examination by Dr. Horowitz, who stated that the hemorrhage had been caused by the bursting of a blood vessel at the back of the tenor's tongue, and had worsened as he continued to sing, Caruso informed Gatti, who had rushed to the Vanderbilt to be at his side, that there was no cause for concern. The physician informed Caruso, as he would later inform the press, that the accident was a very slight one that would in no way prevent the tenor from going on with the season as scheduled.

As if to confirm the doctor's judgment, Caruso sang again only two nights later in the role of Don Alvaro in *La Forza del Destino*. He sang brilliantly, and his public was delirious with joy over what seemed to be their hero's complete recovery. "Throughout Caruso was as frolicsome as a schoolboy and beaming all over his broad countenance with happiness over his complete recovery and joy at the depth of the welcome sent to him across the footlights," a reporter for the *Times* reported the following day. Other members of the press agreed. NO SIGNS OF WEAKNESS IN CARUSO'S SINGING, ran a headline in *The World*, and *The American* proclaimed, CARUSO SINGS IN SPLENDID VOICE.

Even the tenor himself seemed to believe what the newspapers had reported. He ordered a telegram sent to his son at Culver, assuring him that all was well, and ordered other cables sent to friends around the world, confirming his recovery. To Otto Kahn he wrote, "Thanks God it was nothing to be alarmed."

What Caruso neglected to tell the press or his associates was that the pains in his side had not abated, that his success in *Forza* had constituted a courageous victory in a battle against that pain. The same was true three nights later when he again appeared as Samson. "It was a performance of rare refinement and beauty," according to the *Times*; and "his superb voice was again in good condition," according to the *Herald*. Neither the newspapers nor the public guessed that the tenor's chest had been tightly strapped beforehand by Dr. Horowitz and that he had managed to sing only with the greatest of difficulty one of his most demanding roles.

In spite of the exhaustion that had overcome him and the agonizing pain that he had frequently suffered, Caruso had sung nine times during the first month of the Metropolitan season. None of his appearances had been canceled; only the Brooklyn *L'Elisir* had been suspended—and that under extraordinary conditions. During the night of December 21, however, he again suffered excruciating pains in his side. Assured by his doctor the following morning that all was well, that it was no more than another attack of neuralgia, he was determined to sing again in the Donizetti opera on the night of the 22nd, but by late afternoon the pains had become so acute that he was forced to agree to his first cancellation of the season. It was more important, he reasoned, to rest in order to again sing *La Juive* on Christmas Eve.

✳

The December 24, 1920, performance, his 607th at the Metropolitan, was to be his last. Pale and weak, he arrived at the theater on time, determined to prove, as the doctor had told Dorothy and Gatti, that he was well. Among those present was his son Mimmi, who had come to New York for the Christmas holidays, and was to witness his father's portrayal of Eléazar for the first time.

Before the curtain rose, the sixteen-year-old boy went to his father's dressing room to kiss the tenor's hand, as was his custom before each performance he attended. He knocked at the door and heard a familiar voice say, "*Avanti!*" He opened the door and stepped in. In the corner he saw a stranger — a tall, dignified, bearded old man. Frightened at this unfamiliar sight, he called out, "Where is my father?" The bearded figure turned toward him; it was his father, who had, with enormous effort, literally transformed himself into the character of the tragic old Jew. Young Caruso kissed his father's hand and returned to his seat.

As the opera was about to begin, Caruso was tightly strapped by the now ever present Dr. Horowitz, who assured him that his pain was still the result of the nagging neuralgia. Nonetheless, the weary tenor implored the soprano Florence Easton to tighten her hold on him, to lessen the pain, while he sang his taxing aria "*Rachel! Quand du Seigneur.*" The evening proceeded without incident in spite of Caruso's suffering, though his enormous effort did not go completely unnoticed. Instinctively, he often pressed his hand to his left side in order to relieve the pain, a gesture which troubled one member of the audience, the physician of the eminent critic Hermann Klein, who told Klein that Caruso reacted "as one suffering great pain." Klein noted that the doctor was surprised "that the great tenor should be allowed to sacrifice himself to his sense of duty to the management and the audience." Toscanini, too, in America on tour, witnessed the performance and following it went to see Gatti and expressed his own fears. "The man must be sick," he told the managing director. "He looks very bad. I am very anxious about him."

Removed from his costume, relieved that the performance had come successfully to an end, Caruso returned to his new home at the Vanderbilt, where Dorothy had prepared the traditional Christmas Eve feast for the tenor and his friends. He tried his best to join in the festivities, but his usual enthusiasm was missing. He was weary, and when the company had left and it was finally time to go to bed he admitted to his wife that he still had the pain in his side.

Christmas day began happily. There was a huge, gaily decorated Christmas tree in the Caruso apartment; underneath it lay enormous piles of gifts for the family, the servants, and friends. The tenor had wanted to make this first Christmas for his daughter (she was little more than a year old) an especially joyous one. Under the fireplace was a splendid crèche which Dorothy had prepared for her husband, and on a table was a bag containing the gold pieces he planned to distribute to the employees of the Metropolitan, as was his annual custom.

Shortly after noon, while handing out presents to the servants, Caruso felt a sharp and this time unfamiliar pain. He ran to the bathroom, where he began to wash out his mouth, but the sharp pain persisted and he decided he might alleviate it by taking a hot bath. He drew the water and stepped into the tub; before he could sit down, an even more excruciating pain overwhelmed him. Doubled over in agony, he began to scream, a scream heard throughout the entire apartment. Dorothy, Zirato, and Mario rushed to the bathroom. Mario pulled him from the tub, and, aided by Zirato, carried him to the chaise longue where he sat, bent over and holding his hand to his left side, moaning with pain.

The house doctor was immediately summoned, and after injecting the patient with codeine, the pain eased and Caruso fell asleep. Efforts to reach Dr. Horowitz having failed, Zirato began a frantic search for another physician; before too long, Dr. Evan Evans reached the apartment. He quickly examined Caruso and made his diagnosis. It was pleurisy, and the doctor predicted it would most probably lead to pneumonia.

❊

It was the beginning of the end, though no one involved dared to think about it. The chronicle of the next few months — the agonizing pain, the countless surgical interventions, together with awesome stories of the tenor's courage and will to live — was of such interest that each sign of progress or each setback was front-page news. The doctors' bulletins — and six doctors (Horowitz, having been dismissed by Dorothy, was not among them) signed their names to each one of them — were issued to the public at least once and often twice a day. Caruso was not just an opera singer, he was a personality, and as such he was subjected to what many believed to be an invasion of privacy and which one Italian journal, *Musica d'Oggi*, denounced in a scathing article printed in its January issue:

> For more than a month now, America does nothing but send telegrams, cables, Marconi messages that Caruso's doctors have operated on him, that Caruso has been offered a banquet in hopes of a miraculous recovery, and finally that Caruso has been administered extreme unction because of an unexpected and sudden worsening of his condition. . . . I do not deny that Caruso is a great personality, greater than Wilson. In fact, Wilson has

sung quite out of tune in the European concert while Caruso has never sung out of tune during his many concerts. . . . But that we should every day get sick over Caruso's sickness is too much.

Is it possible that in that great country a poor mortal cannot get into bed, get sick, or even, if he wishes, die without having the Americans poke their noses into his business? Is it really necessary that the people of Old Europe, among whom there are some who do not know who Verdi or Donizetti are, know Italy only through the bronchial catarrh of the celebrated tenor? . . .

Enough, dear Americans. We have enough things to interest us, and we have never enjoyed troubling people who are not well. Do you know what I would do if I were Caruso? I would get well immediately and I would start singing and keep it up for ten solid years. What a terrible revenge! I would like to know if then telegrams would be sent to Europe each day saying: CARUSO FINE, BUT WILL NOT STOP.

The press had certainly offered every detail to a curious — if genuinely concerned — public. The initial diagnosis of pleurisy was confirmed, and a few days later it was announced that the tenor had developed a more serious form of the illness that necessitated a minor surgical intervention. This was successfully carried out at his home. The next day, more radical surgical measures were deemed necessary in order to drain the pus from the pleural cavity. Fortunately, Caruso's ribs were far enough apart so that no parts of them had to be removed — this would most likely have meant permanent damage to his voice. On December 31, Zirato told the press that "we are not alarmed now though we know that he is seriously ill."

Further bulletins were optimistic, and by January 10 the tenor's team of physicians was able to announce that their patient was convalescent and that no further bulletins would be issued. Plans were being made for a visit to Atlantic City, where he planned to complete his recovery.

In early February, Caruso's fever returned. The team of doctors reassembled, and a series of operations was decided upon: the most serious involved the removal of four inches of one of the ribs. Caruso had dreaded this possibility and was not told of it, nor was he told that his left lung had contracted. His suffering was intense, and on the night of February 15 his heart began to fail. Friends, including Scotti, Scognamillo, and the Metropolitan's press representative, William Guard, were summoned to bid their final farewells. Two priests arrived late in the night, and the last rites of the church were completed at 1:30 in the morning. An urgent telegram was sent to Mimmi at Culver — he had returned there when his father was thought to be out of danger—in the hopes that he might be able to see the tenor before what seemed the inevitable end.

Miraculously, Caruso survived the night and by morning even showed some slight signs of improvement. His overpowering will to live had sustained him, and his physicians, though maintaining that his condition remained critical, cautiously predicted that their patient might soon be out of danger. With the arrival of his son on the morning of the 17th, Caruso seemed to take a decided turn for the better. When the boy had received the telegram urging him to rush to New York, he had been working at the stables of the Culver Military Academy; there had been no time to change his clothing before leaving for New York. He was understandably wary as he approached his father's bed, took his hand, and kissed it. Caruso, who had been wavering for hours between consciousness and unconsciousness, opened his eyes and smiled. "You stink, my son," he said. It was a turning point in his valiant struggle to survive.

Another visit, too, cheered him that morning, a call paid by the Italian ambassador, who conveyed the prayers and wishes of the king and the people of Italy. Caruso was moved. "I want to die in Italy," he told his country's representative.

In spite of an apparent improvement, the beloved singer was not yet out of danger. Further surgery—minor but painful—was performed in his hotel suite, which had been transformed into a miniature hospital, and his fever lingered. His moods alternated between optimism and pessimism. On February 26, fearing the end might be near, he asked to see his Metropolitan colleagues once again to say goodbye, and he was visited by Scotti (who had been a daily caller), Bori, Ponselle, Didur, Amato, and the young tenor Beniamino Gigli, who wrote in his memoirs: "We stood round his bed, trying desperately to be cheerful, but most of his old friends . . . were unable to restrain their tears."

Another visitor, Titta Ruffo, who had agreed to sing in *Otello* with Caruso the following season—Caruso's first appearance in the role of the Moor and a performance that surely would have made operatic history— was shocked by Caruso's appearance. "He was totally exhausted," Ruffo noted. "His magnificent torso was nothing but a skeleton."

On February 27, Caruso celebrated his forty-eighth birthday, quietly and without the usual party. He was far too weary for that, and all visitors except his wife and son had been barred by his physicians; the danger of a relapse was serious. He was cheered, nonetheless, by the hundreds of messages of congratulations that reached him. Throughout his illness, there had been a tremendous outpouring of affection from every part of the globe, a steady flow of letters and cards and gifts, as well as suggestions of cures sent by his many friends and admirers throughout the world. Now there were prayers that the adored tenor's recovery might be complete and speedy.

A few days after his birthday, Caruso, still weak, was given a blood transfusion. (The donor was Everett Wilkinson, from Meriden, Connecticut, and the tenor said after the transfusion, "I have no more my pure Italian blood — what now am I?") From then on, he showed slow but steady signs of improvement. Warned that he could not return to his home in Italy until he was fully recovered, he followed doctors' orders and kept his activities to a minimum. By mid-April, he was able to write to Puccini in Milan that he was much better and planned to leave for Naples — where he would fully regain his strength — by the end of May.

Before leaving, Caruso paid one last visit to the Metropolitan to say goodbye to all the employees of the opera house that had been his home for much of his life. The personnel did their best to hide their shock at his appearance — he had lost fifty pounds, his face seemed smaller, his skin was pallid, and he was stooped to one side — and rejoiced with him at his recovery and spoke enthusiastically of his return to the operatic stage the following season.

Caruso, however, was not fooled. He did feel better than he had for months, and he fervently hoped that the Italian sun might restore his strength, but he knew that he was still weak, that his shirt collar had become too large, that there was an unexplained tingling and numbness in one hand, and shortly before sailing he learned to his horror that part of a rib had been removed. This news stunned him; he immediately told Fucito, who had been packing his scores, that he had decided not to take his music with him to Italy.

Caruso, his wife, his daughter, and his brother (who had come to New York to be with Enrico), along with various members of their entourage, sailed for Italy on the *Presidente Wilson* on May 28. He had insisted that Mimmi stay behind and continue his studies, assuring him that they would meet in New York in September. Thousands of fans gathered at Pier 7 in Brooklyn to say goodbye to their beloved hero, who had to be protected by twenty-five private detectives. He was in buoyant spirits, though none could fail to note that he was not the Caruso of old: he was thin and weak, and had to be helped onto the ship.

On June 9, the party reached Naples. Caruso was home. Cheering throngs of his fellow Neapolitans greeted him upon his arrival. Gone were any signs of bitterness which had often characterized the reaction of Italians to the singer who had given so little of his art to his own country. Instead, there was an outpouring of warmth toward a good man and a great artist who had brought so much honor to Naples and to the world of opera.

After a few days in Naples, where Caruso was reunited with his stepmother and with Fofò, who had come from Florence to meet him, they took the short trip to Sorrento, where they planned to spend two quiet months before going on to the Villa Bellosguardo. Settled into a luxurious suite in Sorrento's Hotel Vittoria, Caruso led a quiet, retired life. He swam, he sunbathed by the sea, and he took short walks. On his infrequent visits to the town, he was greeted with affection and awe — for the people he was a king who had returned from voluntary exile to his home. Dorothy, aware that his recovery was far from complete and that his heart was in a weakened condition, did her best to see that he did not exert himself too much. In spite of this, the tenor insisted upon visiting nearby Capri and, later, Pompeii; both short trips exhausted him.

Visitors, except for close friends like Gatti-Casazza, who came to Sorrento in July, were kept away so that Caruso might rest in privacy. Nonetheless, one day he agreed to audition a young Neapolitan singer who had shown the courage to approach him. It proved to be an exhilarating experience. The young man arrived at the hotel with the score of *Martha* in hand. He attempted, pitifully, the popular aria "*M'apparì*" and failed miserably. Caruso stopped him, shouting "No, no!" and began to sing the aria himself. His voice was strong and clear. "Doro," he called ecstatically to his wife. "I can sing! I can sing! I have not lost my voice."

Not since the beginning of his illness had Caruso been so encouraged; if he still had his voice, he was still very much alive. On July 17, he wrote a cheerful note to Fucito, who had stayed behind in New York. "I am in good health, thanks to the sun and sea baths," he wrote. "I have a voice to sell for still a score of years. Whatever I do, I do with great vigor." Two days later he granted an interview to a correspondent of the Chicago *Tribune*. He spoke of his illness in New York and of a vision he believed had been a turning point. "One night I dreamed I was dead. It was when my illness was at its height. I seemed to be buried and, strangely enough, could at the same time see my bas-relief carved on the top of my tombstone. It seemed so calm and peaceful to be dead — no more suffering. A loud automobile horn in the street below brought me back to life, and I woke up to find Mrs. Caruso looking anxiously into my face. I told her one experience beyond the grave would be sufficient for me for some time, and from that moment I have been improving. It's very agreeable to be dead, but it's a great deal nicer to be alive."

He also told the reporter of his recovery. "I am gaining strength and weight every day," he stated. "Those who say that I have sung my last on the operatic stage are wrong, for my voice is unimpaired." When the reporter expressed surprise that he was smoking his customary cigarette, he exclaimed, "Of course I smoke. What do you think? that I am sick?"

Even while issuing his lighthearted public statements, the familiar pains in his side were returning, as was the high fever. For a while, he refused to see any doctor except the old man who had cared for his mother (the same physician who had urged him to spend hours in the polluted waters off Sorrento while one partially open wound remained on his scarred body). But finally, as his condition worsened, other doctors were called in. There were endless consultations, but no decisions were made. No one, it seemed, wanted the responsibility of presiding over what might well be the last days of a world-famous hero. A frantic Dorothy turned for advice to Giuseppe De Luca, who had been visiting his old friend. The baritone, alarmed by Caruso's rapid deterioration, suggested that the Bastianelli brothers, considered among the finest doctors in Italy, be summoned from Rome.

The distinguished physicians arrived on the morning of July 29. After a quick examination they informed Mrs. Caruso that one of her husband's kidneys had to be removed, and set August 3 as the date for the operation, which they insisted be performed in Rome. They assured her that the trip would involve no risk, nor would the wait of several days.

Later that same day, Caruso wrote to the editor of *La Follia di New York*, Marziale Sisca. "Undoubtedly," he reported, "I am passing through an ugly period of convalescence, for I am constantly troubled by acute pains, which worry me." He told Sisca of the forthcoming trip to Rome, and ended with the encouraging news that the Bastianellis had assured him that he would be able to sing again within four or five months.

The resumption of his work had dominated his thoughts for weeks. Just as he had yearned for Italy while ill in America, in Sorrento he had looked forward to his return to New York—that, for him, meant a return to the operatic stage and to his real world. In spite of the doctors' assurances, he had his doubts, which were expressed in a letter written to Gatti-Casazza following his examination. Gatti had written to ask him his ideas concerning the coming opera season, and the tenor had answered with a letter which, Gatti later wrote to Otto Kahn, appeared to be "full of a sad presentiment." He told his friend and *padrone*, as he liked to call him, that he was not yet in good health and could not say anything. He ended the letter with: "The good Lord will do what he wishes."

Caruso wrote no more letters. The following night he became delirious as his temperature rose. Dorothy was desperate; she called Giovanni in Naples and summoned him to Sorrento at once, asking him also to hire a private train to take the sick man from Naples to Rome and to reserve quarters in Naples, where they would stay overnight before going on to Rome.

On July 31, Caruso, Dorothy, and Giovanni arrived at the Hotel Vesuvio in Naples—they were joined there by Fofò, who had been summoned from Florence. The following day, the tenor took a serious turn for the worse. It was a day of suffering and pain so excruciating that none of the many doctors present could alleviate it. Their attempts to do so were clumsy, their diagnoses and treatment inept. The unbearable agony continued throughout the night, and by morning Caruso, short of breath, was only able to moan, *"Calore . . . dolore . . . calore . . . dolore,"* as his helpless family looked on. Shortly after nine o'clock on the morning of August 2, 1921, his suffering ended.

❉

On that same morning, in Culver, Indiana, Enrico Caruso, Jr., awoke early. He was in a cold sweat, having had a vision of his father lying in bed, covered with a white sheet. Young Caruso told his roommate of the premonition, which the latter dismissed as a nightmare. Soon, the two young men and other students at the military academy began a trip to Chicago. They stopped in South Bend to change trains, and Mimmi, leaving his foot locker on the platform, went to the newsstand to buy a magazine. He returned to put the magazine in the locker, but found he couldn't close it. A strange woman came by to help him; her eyes lit upon the name clearly written on the trunk—Enrico Caruso, Jr.—and, suddenly, she hugged the startled young man tightly, saying "Poor boy!" Mimmi was bewildered, even more so when, as he was about to board the train, a loudspeaker announcement called him to the office of the stationmaster. He could only wonder what he had done wrong. When he reached the office, he found one of the officers of the school waiting for him. He was informed that he could not continue his journey, that he was to return to the school with the officer. In the car, he was gently told of his father's death.

❉

In Europe, Gatti-Casazza learned from the newspapers of the death of the great tenor. "We may have now and later tenors possessing some of his qualities, i.e., who may have a beautiful voice, who may be good singers or artists, etc., but I think it will almost be impossible to have the fortune to find again another personality who possesses in himself all the artistic and moral gifts that distinguished our poor and illustrious friend," he wrote to Otto Kahn. The people of New York, where he had most lavishly given of himself, were desolated. Vincent Sheean, whose life had been immeasurably enriched by music, remembered many years later: "The whole city seemed plunged into mourning and actually the words overheard in the streets and in public conveyances were mostly about the departed tenor. Practically every Italian one saw was in tears or dissolved into tears at a word. There were pages about him in the newspapers. It appeared that he was not only a national hero to the Italians but also to the Americans. I was myself sad and personally aggrieved as a child might have been. What it came to was a sense of deprivation. 'Now I'll never hear Caruso!' "

It was the same throughout the world, as tributes poured in from the tenor's friends, his grateful and appreciative colleagues, and countless others who had never seen him, but whose lives had been enriched by his voice and his singular ability to communicate his joy at the simple fact of being alive.

His funeral was that of a monarch. The King of Italy gave orders that Naples's Royal Basilica of San Francesco di Paola, usually reserved for royalty, be used for the services, and the streets of Naples were lined with tearful mobs as the funeral procession moved from the temporary chapel at the Hotel Vesuvio to the church. Caruso, the golden-voiced tenor, was gone. His magnetic presence, the unique charm that enabled him to reach the hearts of the people, had been lost forever. Yet, through the phonograph records he had left behind, his marvelous voice would never be silenced. There have been many pretenders to the throne he relinquished through his untimely death, but none has yet approached his special genius. The legend of Caruso continues to grow, and it is clear to all who listen to the mechanical reproduction of his voice that the reality of this remarkable man's talent was, without question, at least the equal of that legend.

Building a Career: Caruso's Repertory

The following is a chronology of Caruso's first appearances in operas that became part of his standard repertory, as well as in those works which he performed only a few times—either because the operas themselves failed (*L'Amico Francesco, Camoens, Mariedda, A San Francisco*, etc.) or because he felt they were not ideally suited to his voice (*I Puritani, Lohengrin, Don Giovanni, L'Amore dei Tre Re*, etc.). During his early years, for obvious reasons, he sang whatever he was asked to sing; later, he selected his roles with remarkable intelligence and attention to what was most compatible with his capabilities as he grew from a lyric tenor to a dramatic tenor.

1895: *L'Amico Francesco* (Morelli)
   (The date of Caruso's first professional performance, March 15, which contradicts the date given by Pierre Key and followed by the tenor's later biographers, has been established by the Centro Studi Carusiani in Milan.)
   Faust (Gounod)
   Cavalleria Rusticana (Mascagni)
   Camoens (Musone)
   Rigoletto (Verdi)
   La Traviata (Verdi)
   La Gioconda (Ponchielli)

Manon Lescaut (Puccini)
Romeo e Giulietta (Bellini)

1896: Mariedda (Bucceri)
Lucia di Lammermoor (Donizetti)
I Puritani (Bellini)
Carmen (Bizet)
La Favorita (Donizetti)
A San Francisco (Sebastiani)
Pagliacci (Leoncavallo)
Les Huguenots (Meyerbeer)

1897: Un Dramma di Vendemmia (Fornari)
Il Profeta Velato di Korasan (Napolitano)
La Bohème (Puccini)
La Navarraise (Massenet)
Il Voto (Giordano)
L'Arlesiana (Cilea)

1898: La Bohème (Leoncavallo)
Les Pêcheurs de Perles (Bizet)
Hedda (Leborne)
Mefistofele (Boito)
Sapho (Massenet)
Fedora (Giordano)

1899: Maria di Rohan (Donizetti)
Iris (Mascagni)
The Queen of Sheba (Goldmark)
Yupanqui (Berutti)
Aida (Verdi)
Un Ballo in Maschera (Verdi)

1900: Manon (Massenet)
Tosca (Puccini)

1901: Le Maschere (Mascagni)
L'Elisir d'Amore (Donizetti)
Lohengrin (Wagner)

1902: Germania (Franchetti)

Don Giovanni (Mozart)
Adriana Lecouvreur (Cilea)

1903: *Lucrezia Borgia* (Donizetti)

1905: *Madama Butterfly* (Puccini)
La Sonnambula (Bellini)

1906: *Martha* (Flotow)

1907: *L'Africaine* (Meyerbeer)
Andrea Chénier (Giordano)

1908: *Il Trovatore* (Verdi)

1910: *Armide* (Gluck)
La Fanciulla del West (Puccini)

1914: *Julien* (Charpentier)

1915: *Samson et Dalila* (Saint-Saëns)

1917: *Lodoletta* (Mascagni)

1918: *Le Prophète* (Meyerbeer)
L'Amore dei Tre Re (Montemezzi)
La Forza del Destino (Verdi)

1919: *La Juive* (Halévy)

Bibliography

Alda, Frances. *Men, Women, and Tenors*. Boston: Houghton, Mifflin, 1937.

Aldrich, Richard. *Concert Life in New York (1902-1923)*. New York: Putnam, 1941.

Armstrong, William. *The Romantic World of Music*. New York: Dutton, 1922.

Artieti, Giovanni. *Napoli Nobilissima*. Milan: Longanesi, 1959.

Auer, Leopold. *My Long Life in Music*. New York: Frederick A. Stokes, 1923.

Barblan, Guglielmo. *Toscanini e la Scala*. Milan: Edizioni della Scala, 1972.

Barthélemy, Richard. *Memories of Caruso*, trans. Constance Camner. Plainsboro, N.J.: La Scala Autographs, 1979.

Beecham, Sir Thomas. *A Mingled Chime*. London: Hutchinson, 1944.

Bellincioni, Gemma. *Io ed il palcoscenico*. Rome: Quintieri, 1920.

Bello, John. *Enrico Caruso, A Centennial Tribute*. Providence: Universal Associates, 1973.

Bernays, Edward L. *Biography of an Idea*. New York: Simon and Schuster, 1965.

Blaukopf, Kurt, ed. *Mahler: A Documentary Study*. New York: Oxford University Press, 1976.

Bolig, John Richard. *The Recordings of Enrico Caruso*. Dover: The Eldridge Reeves Johnson Memorial, Delaware State Museum, 1973.

Bracale, Adolfo. *Mis Memorias*. Caracas: Editorial Elite, 1931.

Brockway, Wallace, and Weinstock, Herbert. *The World of Opera*. New York: The Modern Library, 1966.

Burke, Billie, and Shipp, Cameron. *With a Feather on My Nose*. New York: Appleton, 1949.

Burke, Thomas. *Nights in London*. London: Allen and Unwin, 1918.

Caamaño, Roberto. *The History of the Colon Theatre*. Buenos Aires: Editorial Cinetea, 1969.

Calvé, Emma. *My Life*. London: Appleton, 1922.

Cambiasi, Pompeo. *La Scala 1778-1906*. Milan: Ricordi, 1908.

Camner, James, ed. *The Great Opera Stars in Historic Photographs*. New York: Dover, 1978.

Carelli, Augusto. *Emma Carelli, Trent'anni di vita del teatro lirico*. Rome: Maglione, 1932.

Caruso, Dorothy. *Enrico Caruso, His Life and Death*. New York: Simon and Schuster, 1945.

——Dorothy Caruso, *A Personal History*. New York: Hermitage House, 1952.

——, and Goddard, Terrance. *Wings of Song, The Story of Caruso*. New York: Minton, Balch, 1928.

Caruso, Enrico. *Caruso's Caricatures*. New York: Dover, 1977.

Cavalieri, Lina. *Le mie verità*. Rome: Poligrafica Italiana, 1936.

Cellamare, Daniele. *Umberto Giordano*. Rome: Fratelli Palombi, 1967.

Celletti, Rodolfo. *Le grandi voci*. Rome: Istituto per la Collaborazione Culturale, 1964.

Ciotti, Ignazio. *La vita artistica del Teatro Massimo di Palermo*. Palermo: Rassegna d'Arte e Teatri, 1938.

Colson, Percy. *Melba: An Unconventional Biography*. London: Grayson and Grayson, 1932.

Cooke, James Francis. *Great Singers on the Art of Singing*. Philadelphia: Theodore Presser Company, 1921.

Crabbé, Armand. *L'Art d'Orphée*. Brussels: Editions Inter-nos, 1946.

D'Amico, Tomasino. *Francesco Cilea*. Milan: Curci, 1960.

Daspuro, Nicola. *Enrico Caruso*. Mexico: Ediciones Coli, 1943.

Davis, Ronald. *Opera in Chicago*. New York: Appleton-Century, 1966.

Dawson, Peter. *Fifty Years of Song*. London: Hutchinson, 1951.

Di Massa, Sebastiano. *Il Café-chantant e la canzone a Napoli*. Naples: Fausto Fiorentino, 1969.

Dressel, Dettmar. *Up and Down the Scale*. London: Selwyn and Blount, 1937.

Eames, Emma. *Some Memories and Reflections*. New York: Arno Press, 1977.

Eaton, Quaintance. *Opera Caravan*. New York: Farrar, Straus and Cudahy, 1957.

Eby, Gordon M. *From the Beauty of Embers*. New York: Robert Speller, 1961.

Farrar, Geraldine. *Geraldine Farrar*. Boston: Houghton Mifflin, 1916.

—— *Such Sweet Compulsion*. New York: Greystone Press, 1938.

Filippis, F. de, and Arnese, R. *Cronache del Teatro di S. Carlo*. Naples: Edizioni Politica Popolare, 1961.

Finck, Henry T. *Musical Progress*. Philadelphia: Theodore Presser, 1923.

—— *My Adventures in the Golden Age of Music*. New York: Funk and Wagnalls, 1926.

Flint, Mary H. *Impressions of Caruso and His Art*. New York, 1917.

Freestone, J., and Drummond , H. J. *Enrico Caruso, His Recorded Legacy*. London: Sidgwick and Jackson, 1960.

Fucito, Salvatore, and Beyer, Barnet J. *Caruso and the Art of Singing*. New York: Frederick A. Stokes, 1922.

Gaisberg, Fred. *The Music Goes Round*. New York: Macmillan, 1942.

Gara, Eugenio. *Caruso, Storia di un emigrante*. Milan: Cisalpino-Goliardica, 1973.

Gatti, Carlo. *Il Teatro alla Scala*. Milan: Ricordi, 1964.

Gatti-Casazza, Giulio. *Memories of the Opera*. New York: Vienna House, 1973.

Gelatt, Roland. *The Fabulous Phonograph*. Philadelphia: J. B. Lippincott, 1955.

Genthe, Arnold. *As I Remember*. New York: Reynal and Hitchcock, 1936.

Gerhardt, Elena. *Recital*. London: Methuen, 1953.

Gigli, Beniamino. *The Memoirs of Beniamino Gigli*. London: Cassell, 1957.

Gollancz, Victor. *Journey Towards Music: A Memoir*. New York: Dutton, 1965.

Haggin, B. H. *Conversations with Toscanini*. New York: Doubleday, 1959.

Harding, James. *Massenet*. London: Dent, 1970.

Hempel, Frieda. *Mein Leben dem Gesang*. Berlin: Argon Verlag, 1955.

Hetherington, John. *Melba*. New York: Farrar, Straus, and Giroux, 1968.

Homer, Anne. *Louise Homer and the Golden Age of Opera*. New York: William Morrow, 1974.

Homer, Sidney. *My Wife and I: The Story of Louise and Sidney Homer*. New York: Macmillan, 1939.

Hughes, Spike. *Great Opera Houses.* London: Weidenfeld and Nicolson, 1956.

Huneker, James. *Bedouins.* New York: Charles Scribner, 1920.

Hurst, P. G. *The Age of Jean de Reszke: 40 Years of Opera 1874-1914.* London: Christopher Johnson, 1958.

Key, Pierre V. R., with Zirato, Bruno. *Enrico Caruso.* Boston: Little, Brown, 1922.

Klein, Hermann. *The Golden Age of Opera.* London: Routledge, 1933.

———— *Thirty Years of Musical Life in London, 1870-1900.* London: William Heinemann, 1903.

Klemperer, Otto. *Minor Recollections.* London: Dennis Dobson, 1964.

Kolodin, Irving. *The Metropolitan Opera, 1883-1939.* New York: Oxford University Press, 1940.

Korolewicz-Waydowa, Janina. *Sztuka I zycie Wydawnietwo.* Warsaw, 1969.

Krehbiel, Henry Edward. *Chapters of Opera.* New York: Holt, 1908.

———— *More Chapters of Opera.* New York: Holt, 1919.

Lancelotti, Arturo. *Le voci d'òro.* Rome: Fratelli Palombi, 1953.

Lasky, Jesse L. *I Blew My Own Horn.* New York: Doubleday, 1957.

Ledner, Emil. *Erinnerungen an Caruso.* Hanover: P. Steegemann, 1922.

Lehmann, Lotte. *Midway in My Song.* Indianapolis: Bobbs-Merrill, 1938.

Lehrmann, Johannes von. *Caruso Singt!* Leipzig: Johannes Lehrmann Verlag, 1940.

Leiser, Clara. *Jean de Reszke and the Great Days of Opera.* New York: Minton, Balch, 1934.

Lochner, Louis P. *Fritz Kreisler.* New York: Macmillan, 1950.

McCormack, John. *John McCormack, His Own Life Story,* transcribed by Pierre V.R. Key, ed. by John Scarry. New York: Vienna House, 1973.

Maria y Campos, Armando de. *El Canto del Cisne (Una temporada de Caruso en Mexico).* Mexico: Editorial El Telón, 1952.

Marx, Arthur. *Goldwyn—A Biography of the Man Behind the Myth.* New York: Norton, 1976.

Matz, Mary Jane. *The Many Lives of Otto Kahn.* New York: Macmillan, 1963.

Melba, Nellie. *Melodies and Memories.* London: Butterworth, 1925.

Mojica, José. *I, a Sinner.* Chicago: Franciscan Herald Press, 1963.

Monteux, Doris. *It's All in the Music.* New York: Farrar, Straus, and Giroux, 1965.

Moore, Edward C. *Forty Years of Opera in Chicago.* New York: Liveright, 1930.

Moore, Robin. *Fiedler: The Colorful Mr. Pops—the Man and His Music.* Boston: Little, Brown, 1969.

Morini, Mario. *Pietro Mascagni*. Milan: Sonzogno, 1964.

———— *Umberto Giordano*. Milan: Sonzogno, 1968.

Moses, Montrose J. *The Life of Heinrich Conried*. New York: Thomas Y. Crowell, 1916.

Mouchon, Jean-Pierre. *Enrico Caruso, His Life and Voice*. Gap: Editions Ophrys, 1974.

Petriccione, Diego. *Caruso nell'arte e nella vita*. Naples: Santojanni, 1939.

Pituello, Luciano. *Caruso a Milano*. Milan: Associazione amici del Museo Teatrale alla Scala, 1971.

Pleasants, Henry. *The Great Singers*. New York: Simon and Schuster, 1966.

Restagno, Enzo, ed. *La Fanciulla del West*. Turin: Utet, 1974.

Robinson, Francis. *Caruso, His Life in Pictures*. New York: Bramwell House, 1957.

Rogers, Will. *The Autobiography of Will Rogers*. Boston: Houghton Mifflin, 1949.

Rosenthal, Harold. *Two Centuries of Opera at Covent Garden*. New York: Putnam, 1958.

Rubinstein, Arthur. *My Many Years*. New York: Alfred A. Knopf, 1980.

———— *My Young Years*. New York: Alfred A. Knopf, 1973.

Ruffo, Titta. *La Mia Parabola*. Rome: Staderini, 1977.

Sachs, Harvey. *Toscanini*. Philadelphia and New York: J. B. Lippincott, 1978.

Schoen-Rene, Anna Eugenie. *America's Musical Inheritance*. New York: Putnam, 1941.

Seligman, Vincent. *Puccini Among Friends*. London: Macmillan, 1938.

Seltsam, William. *Metropolitan Opera Annals*. New York: Wilson, 1947.

Serao, Matilde, and Scarfoglio, Edoardo. *Napoli d'allora*. Milan: Longanesi, 1976.

Sheean, Vincent. *First and Last Love*. New York: Random House, 1956.

———— *Oscar Hammerstein I*. New York: Simon and Schuster, 1956.

Stagno Bellincioni, Bianca. *Roberto Stagno e Gemma Bellincioni intimi*. Florence: Monsalvato, 1943.

Stoullig, Edmond. *Les Annales du théâtre et de la musique*. Paris: Paul Ollendorff, 1906.

Tetrazzini, Luisa, and Caruso, Enrico. *The Art of Singing*. New York: The Metropolitan Company, 1909.

Thomas, Gordon, and Witts, Max Morgan. *The San Francisco Earthquake*. New York: Stein and Day, 1971.

Timberlake, Craig. *The Bishop of Broadway*. New York: Library Publishers, 1954.

Vallebona, G. B. *Il Teatro Carlo Felice*. Genoa: 1928.

Wagner, Charles L. *Seeing Stars*. New York: Putnam, 1940.

Walsh, T. J. *Monte Carlo Opera*, 1879–1909. Dublin: Gill and Macmillan, 1975.

Walter, Bruno. *Theme and Variations*. New York: Alfred A. Knopf, 1946.

Watkins, Mary Fitch. *Behind the Scenes at the Opera*. New York: Frederick A. Stokes, 1925.

Werfel, Alma Mahler. *And the Bridge Is Love*. New York: Harcourt, Brace, 1958.

Ybarra, T. R. *Caruso, the Man of Naples and the Voice of Gold*. New York: Harcourt, Brace, 1953.

Index

Other Da Capo titles of interest